Digital Art, Aesthetic Creation

Is art created with computers really art? This book answers 'yes.' Computers can generate visual art with unique aesthetic effects based on innovations in computer technology and a Postmodern naturalization of technology wherein technology becomes something we live in as well as use. The present study establishes these claims by looking at digital art's historical emergence from the 1960s to the start of the present century. Paul Crowther, using a philosophical approach to art history, considers the first steps towards digital graphics, their development in terms of three-dimensional abstraction and figuration, and then the complexities of their interactive formats.

Paul Crowther is Professor of Philosophy at Alma Mater Europaea – Institutum Studiorum Humanitatis in Slovenia.

Cover image: Gerhard Mantz, *Lokale Revolte (Local Revolt)*, 1998, Cibachrome, Diasec, 120 × 160 cm.

Routledge Advances in Art and Visual Studies

This series is our home for innovative research in the fields of art and visual studies. It includes monographs and targeted edited collections that provide new insights into visual culture and art practice, theory, and research.

The Evolution of the Image
Political Action and the Digital Self
Edited by Marco Bohr and Basia Sliwinska

Artistic Visions of the Anthropocene North
Edited by Gry Hedin and Ann-Sofie N. Gremaud

Contemporary Artists Working Outside the City
Creative Retreat
Sarah Lowndes

Design and Visual Culture from the Bauhaus to Contemporary Art
Optical Deconstructions
Edit Tóth

Changing Representations of Nature and the City
The 1960s–1970s and Their Legacies
Edited by Gabriel Gee and Alison Vogelaar

The Artist-Philosopher and New Philosophy
George Smith

Geneses of Postmodern Art
Technology As Iconology
Paul Crowther

For a full list of titles in this series, please visit www.routledge.com/Routledge-Advances-in-Art-and-Visual-Studies/book-series/RAVS

Digital Art, Aesthetic Creation

The Birth of a Medium

Paul Crowther

Routledge
Taylor & Francis Group
LONDON AND NEW YORK

First published 2019 by Routledge

2 Park Square, Milton Park, Abingdon, Oxon OX14 4RN
605 Third Avenue, New York, NY 10017

Routledge is an imprint of the Taylor & Francis Group, an informa business

First issued in paperback 2022

Publisher's Note

The publisher has gone to great lengths to ensure the quality of this reprint but points out that some imperfections in the original copies may be apparent.

Library of Congress Cataloging-in-Publication Data
Names: Crowther, Paul, author.
Title: Digital art, aesthetic creation : the birth of a medium / Paul Crowther.
Description: New York : Routledge, 2019. | Series: Routledge advances in art and visual studies | Includes bibliographical references and index.
Identifiers: LCCN 2018018278 (print) | LCCN 2018020272 (ebook) |
ISBN 9780429467943 (ebook) | ISBN 9780429886157 (adobe) |
ISBN 9780429886140 (epub) | ISBN 9780429886133 (mobi) |
ISBN 9781138605763 (hardback)
Subjects: LCSH: Computer art.
Classification: LCC N7433.8 (ebook) | LCC N7433.8 .C76 2019 (print) |
DDC 776–dc23
LC record available at https://lccn.loc.gov/2018018278

ISBN: 978-1-138-60576-3 (hbk)
ISBN: 978-1-03-233891-0 (pbk)
DOI: 10.4324/9780429467943

Typeset in Sabon
by Wearset Ltd, Boldon, Tyne and Wear

Contents

Plates

Unless otherwise stated, the plates and figures have been provided by the artists themselves or by their estates. The images are captioned according to the artists' specifications and (unless stated otherwise) are copyrighted to the artists or to their estates.

Figures

Acknowledgments

Thanks are due to Manfred Mohr, A. Michael Noll, Duane Palyka, Edward Zajec, David Em, William Latham, Gerhard Mantz, Chuck Csuri, Harold Cohen, Tom Machnik, Chris Finley, Joseph Nechvatal, Ken Feingold, Frieder Nake, Jean-Pierre Hébert, Vuk Cosič, Victoria Vesna, and Char Davies for their advice to the author during the writing of this book.

A Methodological Prologue

Routledge publish this volume simultaneously with a companion work – *Geneses of Postmodern Art: Technology As Iconology*. In the companion work, it is argued that digital art is a highly distinctive Postmodern art form, and a number of examples of it are discussed. The present book takes this further. It is a dedicated study of the specific historical and philosophical circumstances of digital art's emergence in the Postmodern era. Both books address Postmodern art from a shared methodological position, and thence some of the following introductory material is found in both works.

J.-F. Lyotard famously defined Postmodernism as an 'incredulity towards metanarratives.'[1] He also held that forms of knowledge in the Postmodern era are based on competition between different 'language games' (in the Wittgensteinian sense) where

> each of the various categories of utterance can be defined in terms of rules specifying their properties and the uses to which they can be put – in exactly the same way as the game of chess is defined by a set of rules determining the properties of each of the pieces, in other words, the proper way to move them.[2]

However, Lyotard also suggests that

> The classical dividing lines between the various fields of science are ... called into question – disciplines disappear, overlappings occur at the borders between sciences, and from these new territories are born. The speculative hierarchy of learning gives way to an immanent and, as it were, 'flat' network of areas of inquiry, the respective frontiers of which are in constant flux.[3]

In this passage Lyotard is indicating – without naming it – another key epistemological feature of Postmodernism – deconstruction, where traditional boundaries between forms of knowledge break down and are reconfigured in new hybrid modes. This is why so much 'Theory' in the Postmodern era has emphasized difference, heterogeneity, flux, rhizomatic thinking, territories, nomadism and the like (deriving its inspirations, usually quite dogmatically, from figures such as Derrida, Foucault, and – more emphatically – Deleuze and Guattari). A correlated view is that systematic 'foundational' knowledge is at odds with the intrinsic heterogeneity of discursive practices. It merely reflects the hierarchical interests of white male, middle-class, imperialistic, heterosexist patriarchy.

Now, when 'Theorists' make their claims, we must ask 'and how do you know this?' Such a question arises before consideration of whether their claims are true or not. It concerns how it is even possible to recognize the existence of language games, heterogeneity, or 'difference' of any kind. What enables someone to make cognitive judgments about anything at all?

The answer might seem to be 'language' or 'signification.' But this only pushes the question back one remove. In order to learn language or other signifying practices, the world and our relation to it must be such as to allow such learning to take place. In this respect, Wittgenstein himself qualified the notion of language games in a key way. We are told that 'If language is to be a means of communication there must be agreement not only in definitions but also ... in judgments.'[4] The rules we make may be decided by convention, but our ability to follow rules presupposes that we have criteria for distinguishing between correct and incorrect applications of them. There must be shared criteria which objectively govern such applications – and this is as true for the Neolithic cave dweller, as it is for the Wall Street banker.

The point is put in even starker terms by Donald Davidson. He notes that

> We can make sense of differences all right, but only against a background of shared belief. What is shared does not in general call for comment; it is too dull, trite, or familiar to stand notice. But without a vast common ground, there is no place for disputants to have their quarrel.[5]

And Ernst Cassirer observes that 'All human works arise under particular historical and sociological conditions. But we could never understand these special conditions unless we were able to understand the general structural principles underlying these works.'[6] Wittgenstein, Davidson, and Cassirer occupy different philosophical worlds, so it is surely telling that their positions converge on the same fundamental point. Something cognitively shared – a level of experiential constants – is presupposed in order to recognize anything whatsoever, let alone make judgments that can be tested for truth and falsity. The Heterogenic ideas, in other words, themselves presuppose orientation through experiential constants in order to be formulated in the first place.

But how does this stand vis-à-vis the 'incredulity towards meta-narratives' that Lyotard takes to be definitive of Postmodernism? The answer is that the notion of experiential constants is not a narrative of any kind (indeed, it is presupposed by the very ability to create narratives). A 'meta-narrative' in Lyotard's sense is a way of making sense of temporally unfolding cultures (and the like), by finding an explanatory framework that unifies different areas of the culture in terms of some unifying principle or set of connected principles such as tales of Enlightenment or class struggle. It offers, in effect, a 'story' of this development.

However, the experiential constants at issue in the remarks by Wittgenstein, Davidson, and Cassirer are something more basic – they center on the relation between embodiment and a field of spatio-temporal, material objects enduring in systematic causal interactions with one another. The constant factors are based on the human body's cognitive capacities, and the possibilities of positioning that the aforementioned field allows. Such constants operates throughout Postmodern consciousness, even if its role is concealed or dismissed by Theory.

Of course, there are Theorists who insist that the body and capacities such as vision are themselves 'historically constructed.'[7] Now, if this means that particular cultures at particular times understand the body or the senses in specific terms, then fine – this is simply empirical historical fact. However, even culturally specific understandings of this kind presuppose orientation through experiential constants. Vision, for example, (before any question of its 'historical construction') involves the simultaneous comprehension in singular terms of different heterogeneously constituted phenomena – e.g. '*the* tree,' *this* crowd,' '*that* city,' or whatever. Singular identification is the feature most basic to language, but if the learning of language did not connect with a similar disposition in vision itself, language would not be learnable. Without vision, in other words, humans could not have rational experience of any kind, let alone interpret it in more specific 'historically constructed' ways.[8]

Now, it should be emphasized that, whilst empirical understanding presupposes orientation through experiential constants, these constants are not 'timeless essences.' They are employed only under historically specific conditions, even though this does not reduce them to mere historical realities. *The trick is to see how the experiential constant is at work in the particular historical phenomenon.* And this means investigation of their reciprocal interaction. So far, cultural history in the Postmodern era has been written by Theory mainly on the basis of 'historical construction' as a sufficient method of approach. We have already noted the contradictions of this. So, what if, instead, we allow our historical account to be guided by reference to experiential constants that express embodiment and our finite condition? This can throw an entirely new light on the understanding of empirical circumstances.

Indeed, in the case of art-historical study such an approach should be paramount. This is because (as we shall see) the main aesthetic significance of all the visual arts of representation – analog or digital – centers on transformations of how the world appears. Through art, perceptual constants are imaginatively engaged with on the basis of creative invention and the ontology of the relevant medium. This relation between perception and innovation in the medium provides a conceptual framework wherein what is artistic about art can be done full justice to. This is especially important vis-à-vis digital works because the tendency to date has been simply to describe what they do, or to affirm their broader theoretical significance. It is now time to recognize their meaning, as art.

In the present work considerable importance will be assigned to the aesthetic as a basis of such meaning. The aesthetic is a pleasure grounded in experiential constants, most notably a relation between our capacity to conceptualize in cooperation with the power of imagination – a relation that (as we have shown in detail elsewhere) is the basis of all knowledge.[9] More specifically, aesthetic pleasure arises from the exploration of structure in sensory and/or imaginatively-intended manifolds. There are many varieties of this – extending from simple enjoyment of harmonies of shape and color, to the way an idea is made present, and illuminated through some distinctive sensuous presentation of it.[10]

Of course, it might be objected that the term 'aesthetic' only came into use in late eighteenth-century Europe, and does not have any validity outside that context, let alone in a discussion of digital work. It might even be claimed that, in non-western, and in pre-Enlightenment western contexts, this form of experience did not even exist, and that its invention amounts to nothing more than an institutionalization of the preferences of white, male, middle-class, heterosexist, western patriarchy. The persistence of the aesthetic as a concept, in other words, does nothing more than perpetuate an oppressive value-system. Hence, it follows that the present text's intended use of the aesthetic is disqualified at the outset.

However, it is this 'post-colonial' reduction itself that proves to be the distinctively western power-play. It may be that the aesthetic as a concept was first theorized under the conditions of western Enlightenment culture, but this theorization was itself enabled by the aesthetic's pervasive presence in human experience. Indeed, as we have argued in depth elsewhere, it should even be regarded as a necessary feature of self-consciousness, as such.[11]

To prove this ubiquity, let us consider a set of circumstances that might, at first sight, seem to substantiate the post-colonialist objection. It might be claimed that, in non-western cultures, the making of representations and even decorative practices, are not carried out 'for their own sake' but as elements within broader social institutions. Cave painting and kindred forms of visual representation and decoration, for example, are surely practices whose *raison d'etre* is ritual and/or magical.

However, to refute this objection, we must ask a key question.[12] Why do people believe that making representations by means of the body or through creating images will have magical effects on reality? It may be that the practitioners believe that by representing something, they become joined with that which is represented. But why should people believe this? What *enables* the leap of faith which allows the representation to be taken as capable of acting on reality? The only viable answer is that the making of such representations has a deep *intrinsic* experiential power – it is found pleasurable for its own sake, even if it is not explicitly described in such terms. The resulting representation changes the appearance of that which it represents. The fact that this transformation is taken to give real power can only be explained through the pleasure involved in the very act of and/or beholding it. The representation seems special enough to transcend its created origins. Instead of being refuted by the existence of ritual and magical functions, the aesthetic is actually implied by them.

And this can be explained in deeper terms still. For (as we have argued in many previous works), the aesthetic arises from the stimulated cooperation of experiential constants such as understanding and imagination. This means that, in a sense, it really does bind us to the world in more intense terms – terms, indeed, that are intensified further by the grounds of aesthetic pleasure working intuitively, rather than on the basis of explicit 'theoretical' knowledge. Hence it is hardly surprising that, in many cultures, this cognitive intensification should find expression through ritual, and other important 'applied' contexts.

We are arguing, then, that those ritual practices which might be thought to disqualify the aesthetic actually presuppose it. The things that occasion aesthetic pleasure are culturally and historically variable, but the fact that they can do so at all is down to the aesthetic's grounding in constants in human experience. Given this enduring character, we are more than justified in using it as an explanatory concept in the present work.

Notes

1 J.-F. Lyotard, *The Postmodern Condition: A Report on Knowledge*, trans. Geoff Bennington and Brian Massumi, 1984, p. xxiv.
2 Ibid., p. 10.
3 Ibid., p. 39.

4 Ludwig Wittgenstein, *Philosophical Investigations*, 1975, p. 88.
5 Donald Davidson, 'The Method of Truth in Metaphysics,' included in his *Inquiries into Truth and Meaning*, 1984, pp. 199–214. This reference, pp. 199–200.
6 Ernst Cassirer, *An Essay on Man*, 1944, p. 69.
7 See, for example, Jonathan Crary, *Techniques of the Observer: On Vision and Modernity in the Nineteenth-Century*, 1990, p. 6.
8 It is, of course, possible in principle that non-human rational life-forms could develop with some other sense taking the place of vision.
9 See especially Chapter 3 of the present author's, *Defining Art, Creating the Canon: Artistic Value in an Era of Doubt*, 2006, pp. 67–88. This much revises and extends Kant's approach to the aesthetic.
10 Again, see ibid.
11 See, for example, Chapter 1 of the present author's *What Drawing and Painting Really Mean: The Phenomenology of Image and Gesture*, especially pp. 41–43. A further account is provided in Chapter 5 of his *Philosophy After Postmodernism*, 2003, pp. 78–100.
12 See the present author's *Defining Art, Creating the Canon*, pp. 51–52.

Introduction
The Possibility of Digital Art

This book analyzes the emergence of digital art in the Postmodern era. It considers both historical and aesthetic issues in equal measure (an approach that will be explained in more detail towards the end of this Introduction).

By 'Postmodernism,' we understand cultural practices correlated with post-industrial patterns of production and consumption (beginning in the late 1950s and 1960s). These patterns include an emphasis on service provision over the production of goods, and on knowledge and ideas functioning as a form of capital (especially through cybernetics, information theory, and behavioral economics). Central to all this is computer-based technology. Programmable electronic computers have been in existence since the 1940s and have gradually (especially with the development of silicon chip technology) come to dominate how services and goods are provided. This is what defines – more than anything else – the transition from a Modern industrially based society to an information-based post-industrial one.

Now, the Postmodern cultural practices emergent from this do *not* form a style but, rather, an emphatic plurality of styles – 'deconstructive' varieties of which challenge existing categories and notions of creativity. This pluralism converges on a conceptual shift based on the ramifications of technological creativity and mass production. The shift began in the 1950s and early 1960s when a key insight from Duchamp (made years earlier) was established as a legitimate basis for artistic practice. We call this insight *the contingency thesis*. It holds that artistic creation no longer requires that the artist physically makes his or her artwork. The work can be produced by someone else, or assembled from existing mass-produced artifacts made by other people; it can even be designed as a purely Conceptual work or be created as a concept alone. This sensibility has seeped into consciousness as a legitimate mode of artistic creation. 'Found' materials (in the Duchampian sense) are entirely acceptable artistic means – and are, indeed, more congruent with Postmodern sensibility than those of traditional media such as painting and carving in stone.

The ramifications of this extend far beyond the use of new materials and strategies. As is shown at length in *Geneses of Postmodern Art: Technology As Iconology* (the companion work to this volume, described at the beginning of this book) once art has been extended in these ways, then there is, in principle, no limits to what can count as art. Modernism's constant striving for structural innovation no longer has anything to innovate in relation to. Art becomes locked into a permanent eclectic pluralism. Original works can still be created, but not ones that bring the kind of structural shifts that emerged with Modernist tendencies such as Impressionism, Cubism, and the varieties of abstraction.

Within this, computer-based art has a special significance. The artist in this medium has, by definition, to acquire programming skills, or to cooperate closely with those who have such skills. Computer-based art not only exemplifies the defining technology of the post-industrial era, but also its pluralism – extending certain Modernism tendencies (such as the development of abstraction) and, in many cases, exploring characteristic 'deconstructive' Postmodern questions about how computer-derived strategies both differ from, and overlap with, other modes of art in the post-industrial era. To some degree, indeed, the developing interactive features open up – at least for a limited period – aesthetic possibilities never available from Modernist art. However, all this is the expression of a deeper reality. The pluralism of computer-based art arises (by definition) from use of the main tool in the *infrastructure* of post-industrial society. Given this relation, it has justifiable claim to be regarded as *the* distinctively Postmodern art medium.

To understand the ramifications of this, the technology–Postmodernism relation must now be considered in more detail. Since the 1960s, digital systems have dominated computer technology. Their adoption was stimulated by the development of the FORTRAN and Algol computer 'languages' in the late 1950s. These enabled the easier design of algorithms and the development of applications no longer tied to numerical calculations. For the purposes of the present study, indeed, the correlated development of plotters (i.e. drawing machines) and sophisticated display screens is also of decisive artistic relevance.[1]

All these innovations have changed the conditions of cultural as well as economic and productive life. As far back as the 1930s, Walter Benjamin noted that 'technology has subjected the human sensorium to a complex training.'[2] In the Postmodern world this has been taken much further. *Technology is naturalized.* It is no longer merely a question of training the human sensorium but, rather, augmenting it, directing it, and providing an addictive source of leisure gratifications through mobile phones, gadgets, 'apps' and internet access. *Technology is what we exist in*, as much as something we use – a kind of extended *techno-habitat.*

This naturalization of technology is a key criterion of Postmodern culture. Given this, one might say that art based on digital computing will be the purest expression of post-industrial society – the authentically Postmodern artform. It springs from the organizational technology that is central to both production and to leisure in contemporary society. As we shall see, *digital space – understood as virtuality or, metaphorically, as the zone of possible interactivities – is a key extension of this Postmodern techno-habitat.* Even when computer-generated virtual spaces are pictorial or abstract these still have a techno-look (and related associations) that distinguish them *aesthetically* from what painting and sculpture can achieve.

Before considering the emergence of digital art, it is worth considering something of its meaning and particular aesthetic significance. Computer art, in general, involves works whose creation and/or operation is dependent upon computer technology. One might talk in more specific terms of *digital art* when recognition of the role of the computer as, in some way, a part of the work's meaning. There are four basic idioms to such art: the still-image; the dynamic mode (involving temporally successive sequences of imagery); the digitally assisted (such as robotically executed painting, or installations where computer technology directs how we perceive or are positioned in relation to relevant features); and finally the *interactive* modes – where the spectator has some active involvement in producing or accessing the work's effects. Each of these can, of course, be further subdivided. For example, the still-image can be projected on a monitor or on an external surface. This latter form is itself subdivisible – insofar as it is a printout, or created by an instrument of drawing or painting directed by a program, or an individual image extracted from a temporal sequence of developing imagery.

Andreas Broeckman has observed that

> the notion of the 'image' is not a sufficient category for understanding the current, digitally spurred expansion of the perceptual field. The aesthetics of electronic or digital artwork hinges, to a large extent, on nonvisual aspects such as narrativity, processuality, performativity, generativity, interactivity, or machinic qualities. In order to embrace these practices, we need to develop an aesthetic theory that is able to approach recent works of contemporary art that deploy digital technologies and that expand the categories of art-theoretical reflection.[3]

However, all the supposedly 'nonvisual' aspects that Broeckmann cites can be exemplified through sequences or selections of visual imagery (as we shall see in relation to William Latham's work in Chapter 3). Indeed, if these are to be regarded as visual artworks, then the visual aspect must have some special character – if only because interactive uses depend upon and are often directly structured by the character of the digital images or imagery involved. Such digital visualizations involve configurations composed of individual units of light (pixels) whose positioning is determined by exact numerical values along vertical and horizontal axes. By means of this positioning, gray-scale and color effects can be created, and the illusion of depth. *Digital images are the aesthetic subconscious in which all modes of computer art operate.* Even textual information itself takes on an image-character insofar as it draws attention to the visual style in which it is presented.

Now, in the present study, greater emphasis will be given to still-images than to dynamic modes, or to the digitally assisted, or to interactivity. This should not be interpreted as a hierarchical distinction. Visual narratives based on temporal succession have their own aesthetic distinctiveness in directions that still-images do not. Indeed, we shall consider these in detail in Chapter 6. However, in terms of the historical emergence of digital art in the Postmodern era, the still-image is the focus of artistic innovation.

An emphasis on the still-image has philosophical 'added value.' The experiential and ontological significance of the still-image in general has scarcely been recognized, let alone discussed. The digital artist David Em (whose work we shall consider in Chapter 3) observes that

> I came to understand that even though most of the information our brains process is visual, the vast majority of people simply aren't wired to cope with viewing more than a few minutes of nonlinear moving imagery. I include myself in this group. For whatever reason, the human mind processes moving pictures without a story line in an entirely different manner from music, which can hold audiences rapt for long stretches of time.[4]

However, Em then goes on to emphasize the static image's intrinsic importance

> I was aware that the images we hold in our minds have a rich dynamic life of their own. As I examined my own relationship to, and ever-changing associations with, key paintings and photographs in my life, I came to understand that at a very deep level, those images are always morphing and evolving in my consciousness, but on a very different time scale and in a different way than a film or musical composition that has a beginning, middle, and an end, does. These still images, as manifest in my mind over the course of my life, were in effect profound "one-frame movies" with no limits at either end of the perceptual spectrum.[5]

In these remarks, Em is emphasizing the psychological aspects of an ontological truth about still visual images. They are not inert, but highly active in terms of how they intervene upon the spatio-temporal world. Reality is ever-changing, and never reaches any point of consummation. However, the still image negotiates the elusiveness of the present in interesting ways. Human experience is always-on-the-way-to. As soon as one thing is achieved, we are driven on to a new goal. Moments of understanding and achieved fulfillment are never fixed in place completely. This, indeed, is the very essence of our finitude. However, in the making of pictures or abstract works – in analog and digital media – we preserve a final configuration in an enduring medium.[6]

However, this is not just the freezing of what has been achieved. By being refined through an artistic medium, the visual configuration is taken to a higher stage by refining the experience of our own personal style of being. Indeed, the artist embodies this in a medium whereby others can share his or her sense of what is visually important about the represented state of affairs, or abstract configuration.The artist, as it were, eternalizes a *possibility of experience*. The very fact that the static image does not change when the rest of the world does, allows it to focus feelings and associations that rise above – however slightly – the inexorable flux of all things.

This is why traditional modes of pictorial art have never been rendered obsolete by subsequent visual art inventions such as photography, film, and digital media. Whatever medium it is embodied in, the still-image has a unique aesthetic function that engages with some of the deepest aspects of being finite, and which the different media present in ways that are individually distinctive to them.

But, it might be objected, digital composition surely cannot have this felt significance because it is based mainly on dry algorithmic creation. Of course, the aesthetic worth and artistic status of digital works in general has long been controversial. In 1972, for example, Jonathan Benthall suggested that the developing computer figuration was not experimental in a true sense because it 'merely explores the novel facilities offered by the computer, chiefly its readiness to perform very easily ... a large sequence of repetititive procedures which would be intolerably tedious to do manually.'[7]

Benthall's point is one that many people (even nowadays) would still be sympathetic to. It pinpoints, indeed, the main area of worry in regarding digital works as 'real' art. However, the worry is ill-founded, and Benthall's next point indirectly shows why. He observes that Masau Komura's and Kumio Yamanaka's *Return to a Square* (included in the key 1968 I.C.A. *Cybernetic Serendipity* exhibition) 'has little artistic merit but is ingenious and makes one feel that the computer has earned its keep.'[8]

However, this turns out to be great understatement. The digital images on which Benthall based his initial judgment were (admittedly) relatively simplistic in compositional terms, but *Return to a Square* points ahead – in its presentation of one shape morphing into another – to an aspect of digital art that has since been taken to extraordinary levels of complexity (in terms of both static and dynamic digital imagery). The images created might, in principle, be executable through traditional means, but the key point is that without computer programs, to even conceive final outcomes of this complexity would scarcely be possible. *In both conception and execution, digital images require program designs with corresponding experimental flexibility – a flexibility that goes far beyond the mere elimination of 'intolerably tedious' repetitive procedures.*

Something of what is at issue here is brought out in the following remarks by Duane Palyka (another artist whose work will be addressed in Chapter 3). In 1976, he wrote that

> An emphasis on logically conscious thinking is required with this medium to a certain extent since the computer works this way, but the computer artist's thought processes need not rest solely on this level. Programming is a step-by-step process where the programmer must understand what is happening at every step, but the images one makes using this process need not be totally 'understood.' The images themselves do not have a strict logical tie to the images which follow. The creation of images must have some logical visual flow from one to another to add order to the composition but, unlike the programming which generates it, the system of images will not collapse from the slightest deviation from logical conscious order. In fact, the deviations are what give emotion and tension to the piece. As in painting, with the computer art medium subconscious 'not-understood' constructions can co-exist with conscious 'well-understood' constructions.[9]

Palyka's observations illuminates the creative experimentation and personal expression that program design often involves.[10] This centers on the reciprocity between what the artist suggests and what the developing program *proposes* back. In effect, the work involves compositional strategies. Of course, all artists respond to compositional strategies suggested by their working of the medium, but with the computer, the feedback comes as direct suggestion rather than the artist just following a 'hunch' about where a particular development is pointing. However, the artist can then choose whether or not to follow the suggestion, or perhaps to modify it. The technological basis of digital composition means that the artist/medium relation is a *formalized reciprocity*. This is just as creative as the 'luck and chance' reciprocity of the artist working the traditional medium, but the decisive point is that it *is experimental creativity of a different aesthetic order.*[11]

This subjective dimension of creativity impacts directly on the kind of aesthetic object produced, and response elicited in the spectator. When complete, the digital image exists on the computer screen or is physically externalized in a printout (or whatever). In many of these latter cases, we will recognize that the lines, textures, and coloring is of such precision or complexity (or both) that it can be assumed to have been created on a computer. (In most cases, of course, the work will actually be presented in a broader context announcing it *as* computer-generated.) Now, one might say, 'so what?' Surely, the thing of concern is the visual outcome, and not the fact that it has been designed using a computer program.

However, this knowledge is itself an aesthetic condition. To recognize an image or unique possibility of interactivity as computer-generated is to recognize a distinctive aesthetic effect. In this respect, mention is often made of the digital image's 'immateriality.'[12] But this, in itself, has little explanatory value as a term. With a painting, we know that the work has gone through stages of making by hand and that – no matter what illusionistic properties it has – it has been brought into existence at the level of material things through the artist's bodily gestures. It has an aesthetic character based on work.

The digitally generated image, in contrast, emphasizes finish. This is because the computer's display screen is more physically two-dimensional than autographic picturing – no matter how intensely the latter is finished. In the case of painting and sculpture, the autographic element is a potential distraction from reading the representational content of the work. But digital virtual realization carries no such restrictions. It is possible for the digital medium to project three-dimensional content so comprehensively that it can even exceed the real three-dimensional effects of Super Realist sculpture. Indeed, even if it presents less detailed visual information, the digital work's program-based precision (in terms of outline, texture, light, and coloring in the graphics) tends to conceal any manual artifice. It affirms, rather, the *look* of the technological – a lucidity of appearance that connotes things being under control, and made more efficient. In this sense, it is the perfect expression of that naturalization of technology which is an iconological fundamental of Postmodern art. It symbolizes our belonging to the techno-habitat.

However, there is a deeper and more paradoxical level based on the relation between this look and how we reflect upon it. The digitally generated work can involve an *aesthetics of quasi-magic*. We know it has been planned and designed technologically through information processing. However, the fact that an image of such *sensory* precision or complexity (or combinations thereof) has these abstract informational origins is all the more extraordinary. This connects to something deep. A finite rational being knows its endeavors are limited by bodily constraints. Yet we often yearn to escape those constraints – to find a means to create material things through thought alone. Now, the digital artist designs programs at the level of information but which are realized at the level of sensory presence. He or she, in effect, seeks abstract formulae to *cast the spell* that will conjure up sensible configurations. Of course, this is not literally magic, but the transition from electronic data to final work leaves a gap – it is something that cannot be exactly followed in perceptual terms; we cannot see *how* the information transforms into visual configuration. Indeed, we cannot ever explain why the universe – out of all the forms it might have taken – should allow such generations of sensible structure from mere electronically processed information. The gap between information and digital visual realization is, accordingly, filled with mystery, and it is this which gives the digital *imprimatur* its unique aesthetic fascination. There is a felt harmony between the power of creative thought and the world of the senses through the quasi-magical leap from one to the other – as focussed in the particularity of the work. (This is actually amplified even more in interactive pieces, where the user is linked simultaneously to views of different times and places, or to myriad options in terms of how the interactive 'route' is to be developed.)

It might be asked why similar effects do not arise from photography. The answer is that photography also is technologically based, but in a way that merely preserves a trace of sensory presence. It is causally rigid – dependent on the direct impact of light from its object. Photography has its own unique aesthetic characteristics, but they are different from those of digital works. The computer-generated image is electronically produced. Even if it samples photographic material or, like Patrick Tresset's drawing machines, copies something present before it, this material is converted into a different order of being – electronically and mathematically processed information – before being creatively deployed.[13] *And we know this.*

Sometimes, the quasi-magical experience of digital works has a kind of primal impact akin to a childhood story – known to be no more than a well told 'yarn,' but which is, nevertheless, imaginatively transporting and something we want to be told again and again. Indeed, since in digital art one is transported via a real sensory simulacrum rather than by imagination alone, the effect is all the more aesthetically complete. Of course, generally speaking, the gap between what any artwork is, as a human creation, and the imaginative world it opens up, is always aesthetically significant – in distinctive and positive ways (on the basis of the medium involved). In the case of digital art, the gap between identity and effect is so extreme as to have the quasi-magical aesthetic effect just described.

Let us consider an example, Georg Nees' *Plastik 1* (Figure I.1).[14] The image is of an offset lithograph taken from a photograph of wood sculpture. The image was created in 1970, but the sculpture itself was generated between 1965 and 1968 through a program on a Siemens computer directing a Sinumerik milling machine. The work consists of a field of squares grouped in three columns of six in the upper left quadrant, complex diagonals that join contiguous squares umbilically, and descend into horizontal layers with some slight disordering. This is one aspect of a broader disordering factor spread across much of the field. It arises from variations in the distribution and sizes of the squares, and their having shadowed edging on two sides – which gives them a strong three-dimensional appearance. The digital origins of this work are visually manifest in the precise optical push-pull effects that arise from the features just described. In concert, they do not give the impression of being drawn, or sculpted, or even of being machine-made. Rather they suggest the precision arising from digital composition. They have a 'techno' look – the digital *imprimatur.*

The visual upshot of all this is a configuration that, in visual terms, shifts to and fro – from the appearance of a mere static pattern to that of an insistently *physical* field of units, where the units are striving to change their positions. Although the squares occupy places that we know to have been allocated to them rigidly by a program, at the same time many of them seem visually animated and resistant to such placing. Electronically processed information here issues in forms that *seem* palpable and living. Through this, broader associations with physical changes in nature are suggested – specifically, the decomposition and recomposition of granular bodies at a microscopic level. *And all this from mere equations and formulae...*

Let us also consider a second example – this time from a mode that combines temporal realization and digital mediation of an environment. One of the most important exponents of the latter in the Postmodern era is Erwin Redl.[15] His environmental remodeling is based on visual effects produced by installations of LED lights. Here the viewer's awareness of digital technology acting on physical space involves a deep sense of aesthetic transformation.

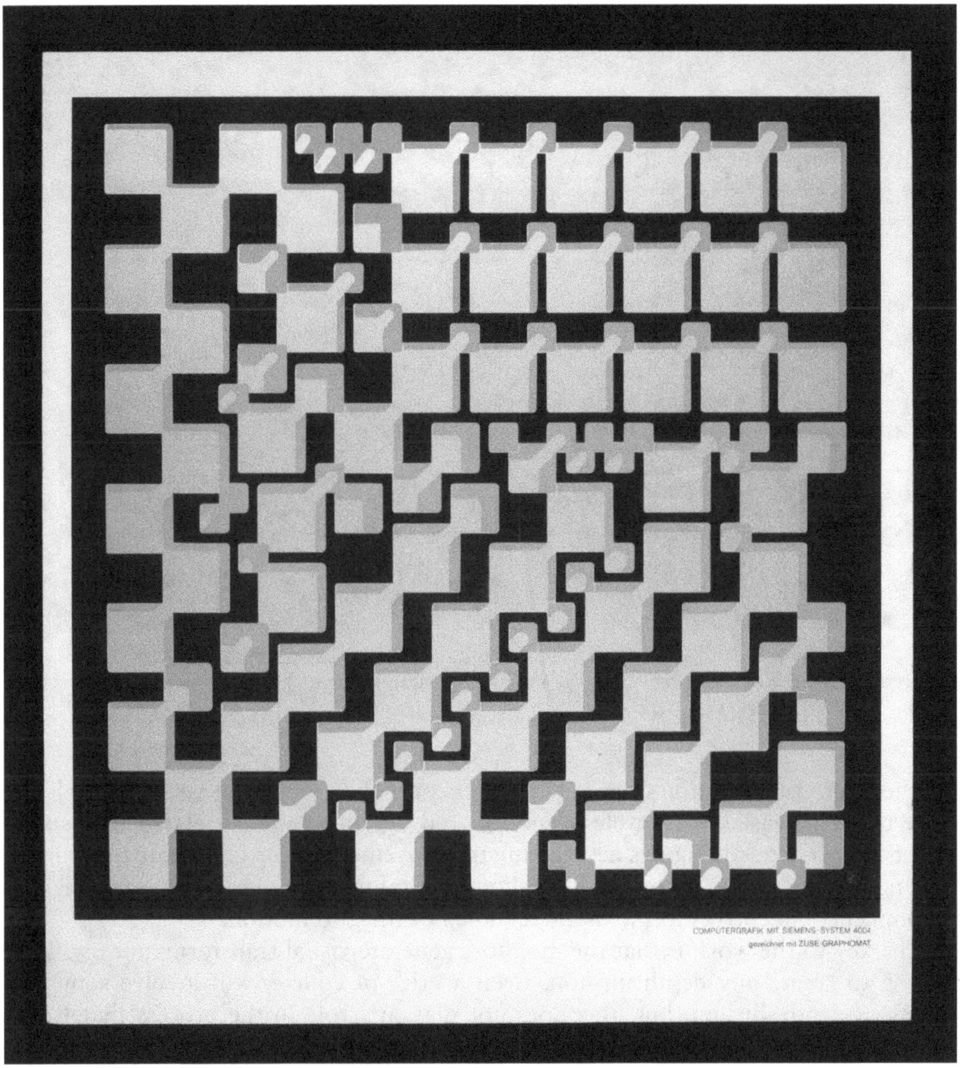

Figure I.1 Georg Nees, *Plastik 1*, 1970 screenprint after a computer-directed milled aluminium plate, 1965–1968, 75.5 × 68.7 cm.

Source: © Victoria and Albert Museum, London.

This is apparent even in an early work such as Erwin Redl's *Corner Study II* (1996–2002) (Figure I.2) an installation comprising a series of monitors arranged next to one another. The visual information on the monitors is simple – gray static grids of vertical lines. These are traversed by a second circular grid that appears to move slowly through each of the monitors from left to right, and a duplicate one that performs a similar movement from right to left. In the course of these motions the contrast between the lighter and darker lines in the grid is gradually diminished, until the monitors become a uniform gray. When this monochrome saturation is

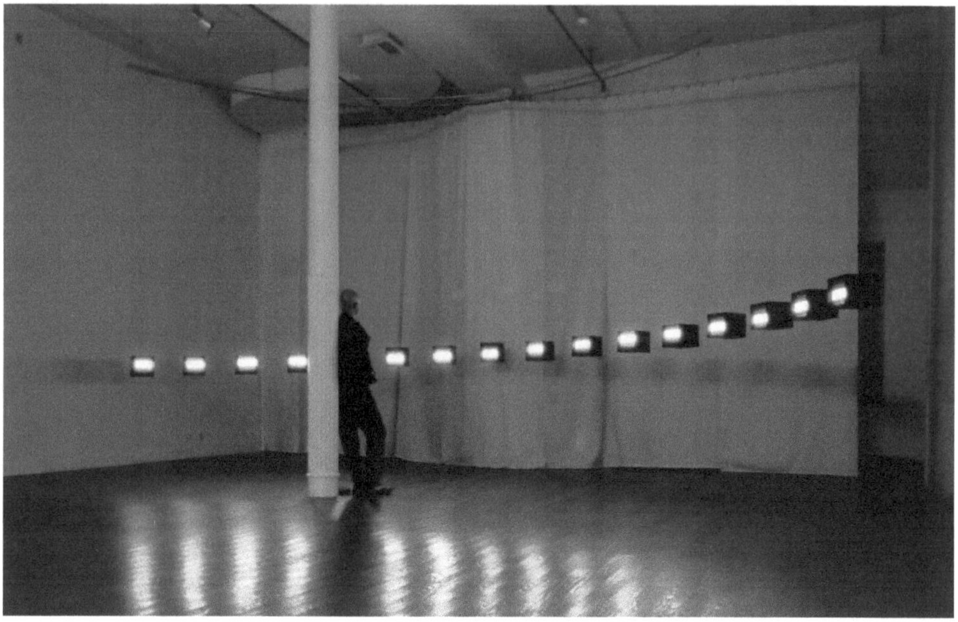

Figure I.2 Erwin Redl, *Corner Study II*, 1996–2002, computer installation with sound, variable sizes, Vienna, Austria.

reached, all visual motion ceases. It recommences only when the contrast levels are once more increased. This cycle of motion and diminution is correlated with sound effects. Short acoustic signals accompany the movement of the grids only to diminish into uniform gray noise with the arrival of the total monochrome. The sound process recommences in correlation with the relaunch of the grid motion.

The key to the work is that the monitors generate visual transformations without having to create any depth illusion. Even a grid, of course, will involve some elements of depth-illusion, but, this does not play any role in the process that Redl's installation presents. *Corner Study II* involves, rather, a visual process with overtones of metaphysical narrative. The narrative consists of transformations of audio-visual phenomena vis-à-vis the extensive and intensive magnitude of sensation. Extensive magnitude is our sensation of how much space a thing occupies in itself or moves through. Intensive magnitude is the sensation of diminution or increase that arises from changes in how perceptual and/or physical stimuli impact upon us.

These sensations are basic to our cognition of the world. They are implicit in almost everything we experience – from things moving close to us, or away from us; to different degrees of emotional feeling and feelings of pleasure or pain. In effect, they are one of those factors in cognition that act as an *horizon* – a cognitive capacity that allows diverse stimuli to be processed in terms of a consistent pattern of intelligibility.

In this respect, we often explicitly remark on how big something is, or on the spatial path it has followed. Even more, we report on how intense or weak the effect of such a stimulus has been upon us. But what we hardly ever remark upon is the horizon of extensive and intensive magnitude that is embodied in such judgments. *Corner Study II*, in effect, presents these *as* an horizon by using an iconic idiom of digitality, namely the monitor. This becomes a vehicle that models the horizon of magnitude. In effect, it is a phenomenological reduction to essence performed by technological means.

The metaphysical importance of this is that the pattern of intelligibility associated with the horizon of magnitude concerns fundamentals of Being in any sense – how things become strong – through occupying space; and how they weaken through dissipation of the form that has allowed them to occupy space in just that way. From a finite embodied perspective, this is – as a phenomenon – cyclical. We may be able to intervene on specific instances of it, but as a metaphysical phenomenon, it happens in general terms whether we will it or not. At the same time, of course, the distinctive thing about humans is that they are self-conscious rational beings who can comprehend such processes and make them into something understood, rather than something one is just the victim of, or deals with as best one can.

Corner Study II engages with all the aforementioned factors. It models an horizon of human cognition with a perspicacity and, indeed, aesthetic presence that is not available through understanding alone; it also models the more metaphysical context which this horizon makes intelligible, namely, growth, movement, and dissolution *as* a cycle of Being. Of course, one might film processes of change with a view to evoking this context. One might even do it through the computer animation of abstract forms. However, the particular idiom employed by Redl in this work has a digital *imprimatur* that is ruthlessly minimal. There are no figurative distractions. The relation between extensive and intensive magnitude is presented *as* process with an extraordinary aesthetic purity.

The main point to gather, then, is surprisingly simple. Digital configurations that visually affirm the *imprimatur* of their digitality have an intrinsic aesthetic fascination. This is because of of the creative disparity between what we know them to be – products of information processing – and what they appear to be, namely realistic and/or visually intense or lucid manifolds imbued with strong avenues of association. The realm of technology here *conjures up* the sensory in terms that sometimes seem more real than reality itself. Paradoxically, to recognize the image's digital origins is to enhance our wonder at its projection of a striking sensible configuration. This creates a unique aesthetic space that intervenes upon both perception and our experience of finite existence.

Of course, digital imagery is ubiquitous in Postmodern life's techno-habitat. Most of the time it is consumed as a source of information and/or entertainment. Generally speaking, this does not require any recognition or wonder at the origins of the image or at how we interact with the computer. For example, in the case of ordinary computer games, the player is immersed psychologically in an interactive process that leads to a successful outcome or defeat. The originator of the game, and the character of the program may sometimes elicit admiration from the players, but this is not the purpose of the game nor is it a requirement in order for it to be played. With other works and programs, in contrast, attention becomes focussed on the particular identity of the visual creation. This means enjoying what it presents in a way that takes account of the creator's ingenuity in devising the quasi-magical visual means and/or outcomes. One could enjoy such a work merely in terms of how it represents or configures the visual, but if the 'how' is impressive enough it will point, also, towards the originating 'who.' In these circumstances, as well as being fascinated by the quasi-aesthetic effect, we can also empathize in aesthetic terms – with this way of presenting visual forms or representations, with the creator's imaginative/technical vision. This is the realm of digital creation regarded *as art*.

Throughout this book we will encounter many different and powerful embodiments of the digital *imprimatur* that embody the aesthetics of quasi-magic in very different ways. As noted earlier, the bulk of our examples will be still-images or stills extracted from image sequences but – as in the case of Redl's *Corner Study II*, we will find it also in many dynamic and interactive works of digital art.

The book's method will be a distinctive one. In emphasizing the aesthetic factors just discussed, we are responding (on the lines set out in our *Methodological Prologue*) to further points raised by Andreas Broeckmann. He suggests that

> There is a notion of the digital that posits a deep break of digital aesthetics away from the aesthetics based on analog techniques ... such an understanding of a digital aesthetics hinges on the technical aspects of artistic production. In contrast, an approach that highlights the experiential qualities of art, and the aspects of reception, is more likely to identify an aesthetic continuum between analog and digital aesthetics. This approach implies that, in this respect, media art should not be discussed in separation from contemporary art practice in general.[16]

In what follows we attempt to bridge the divide that Broeckmann highlights by showing how innovations at the technical level of production are implicated in experiential aesthetic responses via the digital *imprimatur*. This is a new approach. The existing philosophical literature (such as it is), and more technically orientated writing, tend to describe digital works one after another, without offering any detailed phenomenology of the relation between their technical dimension and experiential aesthetics.[17]

Without such investigation, digital innovation becomes no more than gimmicky entertainment or *techno-conceptualism*. The latter involves digital art that mainly draws attention to specific aspects of how the medium presents and/or excludes access to information, or addresses the ethics of its use and misuse, or ways in which electronic media blend with non-electronically originated phenomena to create new behavioral paradigms.

Of course, gimmicky entertainment and techno-conceptualism play their own distinctive roles in the digital world, but there is *so much more* potential to digital art than these levels of engagement alone. It is time to fulfil this potential. The present work offers a way of doing so through its integration of technical innovation and aesthetic response on the basis of the digital *imprimatur*. It also presents detailed ideas supplied by many of the artists themselves in the course of correspondence with the author.

It must be emphasized that the book is *not* intended to be a comprehensive history of digital art that would address world-wide developments down to the present. It seeks, rather, to investigate how such art emerged in the early stages of the Postmodern era – from around 1960 to the first decade of the present century, and on the key structural aesthetic features that this emergence brought with it. (For the most part, these developments centered on Europe and America, initially.)

The organization of the book is as follows. In Chapter 1, Desmond Paul Henry's analog computer drawing machines are discussed. The pioneering works Henry produced in the 1960s are far more sophisticated conceptually than Tinguely's more well-known drawing devices. Tinguely used those mainly in a comical critique of the high-falutin' aspirations of Abstract Expressionism; Henry's machines, in contrast, exemplify a unique way for giving aesthetic expression to the machine's own technological mode of being. His work is an early exemplar of the Postmodern naturalization of technology.

Chapter 2 traces the first historical emergence of digital art in the 1960s and 1970s, paying special attention to the work of A. Michael Noll, Georg Nees, Frieder Nake, and Manfred Mohr. The important influence of Max Bense's 'generative aesthetics' is traced in relation to this work.

These early developments were orientated towards digital abstraction. Remarkably, it was in the context of abstraction, also, that digital art first systematically engaged with three-dimensional illusion. In Chapter 3, this is investigated. We consider how the first strong three-dimensional effects were achieved through buffer-frame technology, and distinctive modes of three-dimensional abstraction (or *digital plasticity* as we shall call it) that were consequent upon this. Special attention is paid to the work of Edward Zajec, Ruth Leavitt, and Duane M. Palyka, in the 1970s; and then to David Em's innovations of the 1970s and 1980s and beyond. William Latham's evolutionary programs and Gerhard Manz's digital objects are also discussed. In this account, sustained emphasis is given to how the creative process, in all cases, incorporates an experimental reciprocity between technological issues, and the artist's creative insights.

This emphasis is maintained in Chapter 4, also. Here the curiously difficult historical development of digital figuration is discussed with reference to the methods and achievements of the most influential artists involved. Specifically, detailed analysis is made of the technical and stylistic development of Nancy Burson, Charles Csuri, Harold Cohen, Gerhard Mantz, and Kenneth Feingold.

In the course of the discussion, it will have become clear that the possibility of many modes of hybridization between different idioms of digital art have emerged in the Postmodern era. Chapter 5 looks at some of these, giving particular attention to Joseph Netchvatal's and Chris Finley's computer-assisted painting, and Robert Mallary's, Robert Mazzarini's, and Jean-Pierre Hébert's computer-assisted sculpture. More Conceptual works by Jenny Holzer and Raphael Lozano-Hemmer are also considered.

Finally, in Chapter 6, we identify varieties of interactive digital art, namely detection interactivity, active interfacing, net access and information environments. These are considered individually and in combination. Amongst the relevant artists discussed are Jim Campbell, David Rokeby, Kenneth Feingold, Maurice Benayoun, Jeffrey Shaw, Char Davies, Olia Lialina, Vuk Cosič, John Klima, and Victoria Vesna.

Notes

1 The best resource for the study of the historical emergence of computer art is Nick Lambert's *A Critical Examination of 'Computer Art.'* There is an online version of this at http://computer-arts-society.com/static/cas/computerartsthesis/index.html. A good introduction to historical material – if, at times, somewhat technical – is Thomas Dreher's online resource 'History of Computer Art,' http://iasl.uni-muenchen.de/links/GCA-III.1e.

html. Christiane Paul's *Digital Art*, 2015, has already established itself as a classic – having now gone into a third edition (from its first publication in 2003). The particular strength of the work is its comprehensiveness – doing justice to many different examples of digital art's varieties. Despite being a survey book, it also has intellectual depth in how it discusses its selected examples. One of the other best survey works is Margot Lovejoy's *digital currents: art in the electronic age*, 2007. This book has the benefit of being a work – like Paul's – that has been republished and reorientated a number of times since its first appearance (under a different title) in 1989. It is, accordingly, a text that has been able to adapt to important changes in its subject-field, as that field has developed and expanded. The book achieves an excellent balance between technical issues, and points concerning the more general significance of the works addressed. Lovejoy's main emphasis is on idioms involving interactivity between work and user, or between work and environment(s) of presentation. An important book that to some degree parallels Lovejoy's interactive emphasis at a similar high level of theoretical sophistication is Frank Popper's *From Technological to Virtual Art*, 2007. Another useful work is Cat Hope's and John Ryan's *Digital Arts: An Introduction to New Media*, 2014. It offers a concise treatment of the different theoretical and historical terms that relate to digital work. In contrast with these four works, the present book focusses specifically on the aesthetics of digital graphics in a Postmodern context. This difference between this and the other works just mentioned is actually complementary – each fills out issues that the other does not address. It is also worth noting *MediaArtHistories*, ed. Oliver Grau, 2007. This is an interesting collection of essays that ranges across a variety of topics relevant to the development of digital art. The essays tend to introduce a theme, and then an extended survey of some of the artists/theorists who have contributed to it. The present study, in contrast, tries to offer a more selective focus on individual figures and steps in the historical development of digital art.

2 'Some Motifs in Baudelaire,' included in Walter Benjamin, *Charles Baudelaire: A Lyric Poet in the Era of High Capitalism*, 1983, pp. 109–154. This reference, section VIII, p. 132.

3 Andreas Broeckmann, 'Image, Process, performance, Machine: Aspects of an Aesthetics of the Machinic,' included in Grau, op. cit., pp. 193–205. This reference p. 196.

4 Em's remarks are contained in an email message to the author of the present work, sent on April 25, 2017.

5 Email message to the author, April 25, 2017.

6 For a discussion of this relation to pictorial art, see Paul Crowther, *How Pictures Complete Us: The Beautiful, the Sublime, and the Divine*, 2016, pp. 49–50.

7 Jonathan Benthall, *Science and Technology in Art Today*, 1972, p. 58.

8 Benthall, op. cit., p. 58. For the catalogue feature on the artists themselves see 'Computer Technique Group from Japan' (no author specified) included in Jasia Reichardt (ed.), *Cybernetic Serendipity: The Computer and the Arts*, September 1968, pp. 75–77.

9 Duane M. Palyka, 'Computer Painting' included in Ruth Leavitt (ed.), *Artist and Computer*, 1976. Online version at www.atariarchives.org. This reference, www.atariarchives.org/artist/sec18.php.

10 We will find some similar points made again by Gerhard Mantz in Chapter 4.

11 This and related issues are discussed in detail in Chapter 7 of my book *What Drawing and Painting Really Mean: The Phenomenology of Image and Gesture*, 2017.

12 See Christiane Paul's discussion 'The Myth of Immateriality,' included in Grau, op. cit., pp. 251–274.

13 The artist's website can be found at http://patricktresset.com/new.

14 See Nees work at www.heikewerner.com/nees_en.html.

15 See www.paramedia.net/installationpage/cornerstudyii.php.

16 Grau, op. cit., p. 194.

17 There are several good treatments of the aesthetic dimension of computer art. Katja Kwastek's *Aesthetics of Interaction in Digital Art*, 2015, is one such work. It is methodologically sophisticated and well-balanced in terms of issues of creation and response. However, in contrast with the present work's emphasis on visual graphics, Kwastek's approach is – as its title suggests – more closely focussed on the ramifications of

interactivity. Another useful contribution is Grant D. Taylor's *When The Machine Made Art: The Troubled History of Computer Art*, 2014. This is an excellent study of the critical reception of computer art, that raises many complex interpretative issues. Taylor has a very different orientation from the one taken in the present work. In particular, he pays much more attention to the aesthetics of the mathematical and scientific aspects than has been possible here. The present author justifies this insofar as the visual/sensory dimension of digital art has been significantly underplayed in the existing literature, and, hence, a sustained emphasis on it is timely. Sean Cubitt's *Digital Aesthetics*, 2009, despite its title, has little to say about the strictly aesthetic dimension, but is concerned, rather, with polemics concerning the socio-political context of digital work. The main philosophical work in the analytic tradition on computer art is Dominic McIver Lopes's *A Philosophy of Computer Art*, 2010. There are many difficulties with Lopes's arguments, not least of which is the lack of any developed criteria for such notions as 'creativity' or 'artistic.' The possibility of aesthetic responses that are unique to digital art is not even addressed. Lopes claims that 'The special feature of computer art is its interactivity, which sets it apart from other art' (p. 7). However, interactive artworks have been a familiar part of the Postmodern art scene since the 1960s – ranging from 'happenings' and Fluxus works such as Yoko Ono's *Cut Piece* of 1964, to many Conceptual and installation works in the 1970s and 1980s. What makes computer interactivity different is the distinctive role played by digital technology in securing unique aesthetic effects, but, as just noted, Lopes does not address this. Mark B.N. Hansen's *New Philosophy for New Media*, 2004, is an interesting attempt to do justice to the role of the body in the experiencing of digital artworks. Unfortunately, the philosophical model it uses – that of Deleuze's obtuse interpretation of Bergson's philosophy – raises as many problems as it does possibilities. Indeed, the relation between image and body that Hansen proposes seems to turn away from Bergson's emphasis on 'intuition' towards an understanding of the image–body relation that is, in its Deleuzian form, quasi-cybernetic. In terms of more technical orientations, a collection of essays on *Aesthetic Computing*, edited by Paul Fishwick, 2006, offers a useful approach, but understands 'aesthetic computing' in a quite technical sense – concerned with the devising of codes that have aesthetic import. None of the contributors to the volume appear to offer clear criteria of the aesthetic, and tend to assume that if theoretical issues about computing are raised, then this is – per se – a problem in aesthetics. Against this, we would argue that 'aesthetic computing' is only an intelligible notion if specific digital innovations are explored in relation to their distinctive experiential effects.

1 Machine-Being

Desmond Paul Henry's Computer Art

On August 8, 1949, *Life* magazine published a four-page feature on Jackson Pollock. This cemented Pollock to the forefront of critical and public attention in American art. In November 1963, *Life*'s successor *Time-Life* Magazine were due to do a similar feature on Desmond Paul Henry's computer-generated art. At that time, Henry was a Lecturer in Philosophy at Manchester University, who had created some highly inventive drawing machines using an analog computer. The resulting abstract works had received widespread attention through publicity in British national newspapers, and developing public and artistic interest in computers. However, the *Time-Life* feature was cancelled to make way for material covering the assassination of President Kennedy. If the feature had appeared, Henry might well have received international recognition at a level that would have enabled his work to be developed much further, and in more influential artistic spheres. As it is, his drawings received significant recognition only by featuring in the famous *Cybernetic Serendipity* exhibition – held in 1968 at the ICA in London, and then in Washington, DC and San Francisco.

Despite this limited recognition, the very fact of *Time-Life*'s interest in artworks by an obscure northern Englishman – not even a professional artist – is highly significant. There is something about his art that is profoundly of its time. The present chapter will, accordingly, consider the significance of Henry's drawings in the origins of Postmodernism. The focus of discussion will be on the visual structures generated by his machines, and their aesthetic and historical significance. It will be argued that his working practice is, in effect, one that makes the machine's own mechanical workings aesthetically accessible to the viewer. He naturalizes technology as something with which we dwell alongside, as well as put to use. In this respect, his work is a significant early expression of the Postmodern sensibility.

One

Even though Desmond Paul Henry's computer-generated art is an exemplar of the digital era, there is, nevertheless, a feature that makes Henry's work unique. His drawing machines were not programmed. Their mechanical workings and settings were the decisive factor. Of course, all computers are machines, but the kind of analog computer that Henry worked with involved visible motions that declared (what I shall call) its *machine-being*. By following this up, the importance of Henry's work as an exemplar of the Postmodern can be clarified.

First, it is worth noting that innovations in the structure and applications of machine technology have an intimate link to Modernity itself. The origins of the Modern world are in large part due to the role of such innovation in revolutionizing productive and transport processes in a way that rendered traditional methods obsolete.

This has an interesting offshoot vis-à-vis *Modernism* – i.e. those cultural practices that aligned themselves positively with the patterns of change that developed in the Modern world. Machines have often been highly regarded by Modernist art. This is not just because they are instruments of new modes of production, but also because they celebrate change by virtue of their efficient physical structure and operational dynamics. Futurism's obsession with the dynamism of technology and the Modern world is an expression of this regard, though it serves more as an inspiration for artistic creation rather than as a technical basis for it. A rather closer engagement between technology and art occurs after World War I, when the Bauhaus in Germany and Vkhutemas in the Soviet Union sought to harmonize craft with technological innovation so as to produce functional artifacts based on artistic design. In such artifacts, functionality was taken to enhance the aesthetic worth of the object rather than inhibit it.

The success of this as a Modernist strategy is shown by the fact that, only ten years or so later in 1934, the Museum of Modern Art in New York staged an exhibition curated by Phillip Johnson on the theme of *Machine Art*. For this, Johnson selected items such as typewriter carriage springs, a self-aligning ball bearing, an outboard propeller, a toaster, a cash register, pots and pans, and other things understood as typifying the aesthetic features of contemporary industrial objects. In his foreword to the exhibition catalogue, Alfred H. Barr explicitly identified kinetic rhythms, beauties of material and surface, visual complexity, and, more generally, the beauties of abstract and geometric form as central to the aesthetic of machine art.[1]

There is also another – more critical – Modernist engagement between technology and artworks that arises as an outcome of Duchamp's ready-mades. These are objects designated to be artworks by the artist but which are actually made by someone other than the artist – often being, indeed, mass-produced items rather than the outcomes of Bauhaus-type high-level design. Duchamp's intent in creating the ready-mades is somewhat opaque – but may be, at least in part – a critique of the unduly high prestige accorded to the process of artistic making. The implication is that it is the idea in art which is decisive, more than the physical accomplishment.

This Modernist use of mechanically produced artifacts as a means of criticizing aspects of art-making was developed in other directions also. In the 1930s the Italian Bruno Munari began building "useless machines" *(macchine inutili)* as a gentle critique of the earlier Futurist generations' obsessive reverence for machine power in all its ramifications. More significant still for the present discussion is the work of the Swiss artist Jean Tinguely.

In the 1959 Paris Bienalle, for example, he exhibited *Meta-Matic no 17*. This (and other drawing machines made by Tinguely) operated through a motor-driven arm using drawing tools that could be chosen by the individual viewer/participant. The means of graphic production in these machines is a surface marked through the superposing of different harmonic oscillations so as to produce a random abstract composition of lines and dots. Its character is determined by the viewer/participant's choice of drawing implements, the physical oscillations of the drawing arm, and by interruptions, deviations, and other irregularities arising from faults in how the machine's motors, belts, cogs, and crank-shafts (etc.) work together.

This dimension of *active contingency* is especially important because it gives the resulting compositions an apparent gestural quality. More specifically (in the Meta-Matic series, at least) it makes the surfaces look like the products of abstract expressionist painting. It is this feature that was especially important to Tinguely, insofar as it showed that the workings of cranky machines could produce works as beautiful as the high-falutin' endeavors of abstract expressionism.

We find, then, that in twentieth-century Modernism there is a celebration of the machine – on the one hand, as something which inspires with its dynamism or whose design can combine functionality with aesthetic worth; on the other hand, there is the idea that the workings of machines can be used to criticize the primacy of processes of making in relation to visual art. However, all this being said, there is one interesting tension between Modernist art and the machine. All the Modernist factors just described, in the final analysis, treat the machine as a means to an end. They furnish ideas (such as the Futurist 'lines of force') which can be incorporated compositionally. And when they are used to make fun of artistic practice, the fact of the matter is that this is a use, rather than a celebration of machine-being. The internal workings and motions of machines can have their own intrinsic aesthetic satisfaction over and above their design appearance and use-value. Once constructed, the machine operated on the basis of natural forces and the interacting momentum of its parts and, in these, finds its own mode of being.

Earlier in this book, it was argued that a central feature of the Postmodern world is the naturalization of technology. Technology is no longer something simply beheld then put to use, it shapes key aspects of the human sensorium itself – determining many of our needs. This naturalization is anticipated when machine-being becomes something found fulfilling in its own right instead of as a means to an end. Henry's work is of decisive significance in this respect. Let us now consider his computer art in detail.

Two

Henry's first drawing machine was made from a World War II Sperry Bombsight analog computer. It was set in motion using a 24-volt D.C. servomotor. For some years Henry would simply enjoy watching the mechanisms of the computer in motion, but then decided to give them an artistic expression. He redistributed some of the structural components to synchronize the relation between a moving pen and a moving table – activated by a wind and air-speed integrator. The pen movement would also move the table supporting the paper. Ball-bearings beneath the table (in conjunction with an oscillating horizontal bar and vertical spring) would facilitate line drawings created – as Henry put it – from 'non-rectilinear wanderings' of the pens ... totally random within the physical limits imposed by the nature of the machine construction.'[2]

The first main body of work from this machine dates from 1961. All Henry's computer-generated works have a threefold basic structure. First, a complex *textural principle* embodied in a linear motion from which the broader shapes and details of the composition are generated; second, *modular* figures comprising the dominant shapes and apparent three-dimensional structures that emerge from the textural principle; and third, the color scheme.

In the works of 1961 (Figure 1.1), the main textural principle is contour lines – like those indicating height in an Ordnance Survey map. However, in this case, the proximity of lines to one another are indicative not of height, but creators, rather, of visual density. In effect, the textures of the 1961 works suggest netting or gauzes of varying degrees of translucency – with the degree of translucency determined by how few or how many contour lines are banded within or around one another, and on how they 'sit' in relation to lines already drawn beneath them or which have been drawn above.

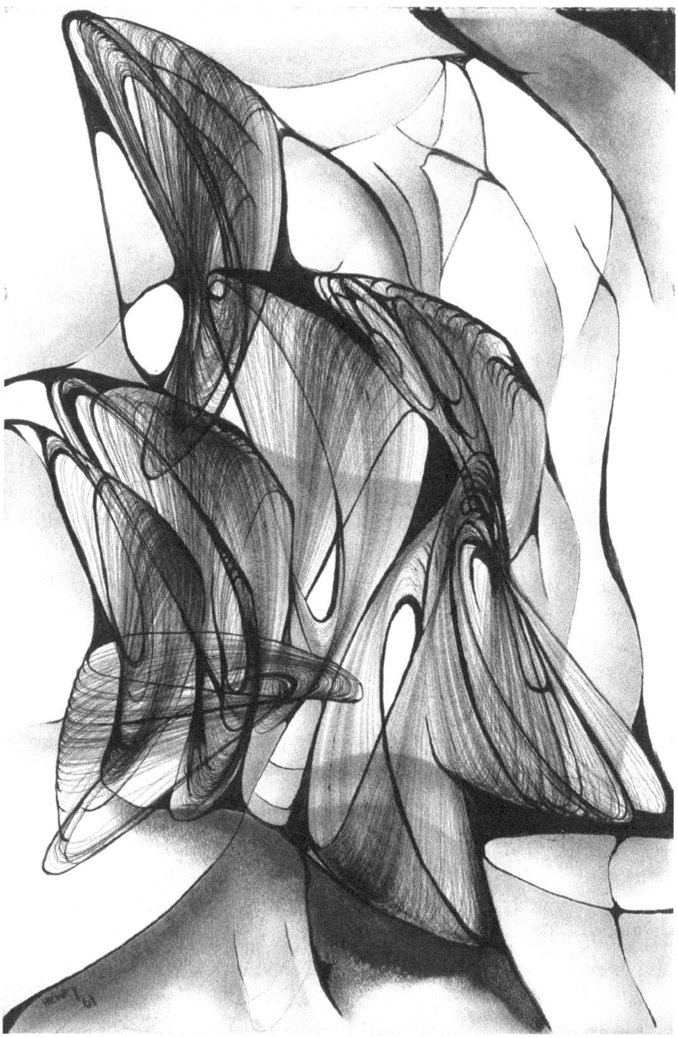

Figure 1.1 Desmond Paul Henry, *1961 no. 600*, 38.5 × 26 cm, biro on paper, background shading, hand embellishments.

Source: Image courtesy of Elaine Ohanrahan.

This texture generates the appearance of modular figures in semi-ellipse – like the outlines of evenly-edged angel wing shells. I shall call these 'angel wings' as a term of convenience, insofar as they are a frequent feature of Henry's compositions over the years. The angel wings tend to have internal contours that are progressively diminishing visual echoes of the outer one. Sometimes the angel wings are rendered from an aerial 'plan' viewpoint as merely shapes within shapes; but on other occasions they presented obliquely giving the impression that the angel wing is actually a three-dimensional figure with netted walls. Some of these – be they two- or apparently three-dimensional – are stiff and relatively autonomous even whilst always being, to some degree, woven into other such modules. Other such angel wings are more flexible or distended – sometimes drooping into one another.

The relation between these autonomous and drooping angel wings gives some of the 1961 works a curiously static animation – suggesting the limbs of a body or bodies made from net, caught in the act of slow movement, or showing a disposition to get up, or otherwise change spatial position vis-à-vis the viewer. These effects are mediated by two interesting compositional principles. In some of the works the modular figures not only emerge from the textural contours, but have distinct additional straight or (sometimes) curved or wavy lines that emerge or intersect with them with varying degrees of complexity. These *tethering lines* are by no means constraints – like being caught in a web; rather they suggest direction through which the figures might move, or which has allowed them to be pulled into shape – like the strings that animate a puppet. Some works have much denser textural contours – at times suggesting extended areas of undifferentiated black. This gives the impression of sinister life-forms or energies constrained – imprisoned even – within the composition's planar emphasis and oblong format.

This sinister feature is augmented by the third main structural principle of the 1961 works – namely the color scheme, with its emphasis on monochrome black. Indeed, even when other colors are used in these works, Henry restricts them mainly to greens, blues, and olive, with only an occasional use of red. In his works of 1962, however, all three structural principles are developed further. I now turn to this.

First, whilst the 1961 works are dominated by contour lines as their textural principle, the 1962 works see an additional factor introduced – one which opens up a more sophisticated way of rendering the three-dimensional allusiveness of the compositions. This involves interwoven oscillating parabolas (similar to the coils of a 'slinky spring'), repeated contiguously with one another. In physical terms the drawings are still produced by the continuous motion of the pen upon the surface, but instead of simply literally drawing lines as lines, linear continuity is here *suggested* by the contiguity of the oscillating parabolas. The lines are rendered, in effect as extended filigrees or broader bands composed of *parabolic ellipses*. This allows a new level of transparency to be introduced into the visual textures of the works.

Given this, it is hardly surprising that many of the works from 1962 also involve a transformation at the level of modular figure. The angel wings always remain a feature of Henry's work, but now a striking new feature emerges – in the form of torus segments (a torus being the shape embodied in such things as doughnuts and life-buoys) and tubular forms. In some of the works, there is also an emphasis on relatively self-contained ovoid, circular, and related concentric figures as a basic compositional principle. All these features are sometimes combined.

Consider, for example, *1962 no 656* (Plate 1). The work is composed of concentric forms that intersect with one another and which seem to destabilize into variously disposed angel wings in the lower part of the work. The circles are composed of parabolic filigrees rendered in layers. Some of the layers are more densely packed with forms than others, and the densities are distributed with increasing magnitude in the transition from the perimeter to the central areas of the concentric figures. This invests the circular forms with the three-dimensional appearance characteristic of tori segments and tubular configurations. Given the transparency effect noted earlier, this brings about an overall appearance suggestive of visually exotic life-form (such as a jellyfish).

Many of the other 1962 works vary this format. In Plate 1, the main body of forms is grounded against areas of pale red with angular definitions. Other works, such as *1962 no. 670* (Plate 2), diminish the role of background areas, sometimes standing completely alone in their pictorial space. These works center on the oblique placing of tori segments and tubes in ways suggestive of different patterns of animation – such as pumping action, or at least the capacity for it. The colors are predominantly green, blue, orange, brown, and black, with the blacks often suggesting invasive forms. Indeed, some of these works have strong areas of black felt-tip edging that is not uniformly distributed and which, in a number of cases, intrudes into the main body of forms, as in *1962 no. 634* (Figure 1.2). This intrusion at once animates and arrests visual 'action' in the composition. These have a more assertive visual presence, often reminding one, peripherally, of the abstract deformations of appearance achieved by Francis Bacon, or surrealist abstraction of the kind done by Mark Rothko in the early and mid-1940s.

Three

In 1963, Henry created a second drawing machine – subsequently described by him as 'The Henry Drawing Computer.'[3] It was built by modifying the original bombsight with two servomotors – one to direct the pens, and the other the drawing paper. By running the rate of relative revolution in these motors out of phase with one another (in regular or random sequences) regular or irregular patterns of great complexity could be produced. The contrasting degrees of pen and table oscillation was varied further by the positioning of clothes pegs that Henry would attach to the paper on the drawing table. In his words 'any number of clothes pegs attaching the paper to the table's circumference or attached solely to the paper itself, could be placed in any number of positions resulting in an infinite number of track variations of the paper.'[4] Once the machine was started, Henry could intervene to alter the developing design.

The compositions of 1963 center on highly self-contained tori of fibrous netting with invasive or augmenting filigree nets of various other dominant modular figures. The notional 'hole' at the center of the torus appears to act as a vortex – drawing modular figures (such as angel wings) into it, or at least holding them in a kind of visual gravitational pull, around it – as in *1963 no. 220* (Figure 1.3).

In other works from 1963, the compositions tend towards multiple modular figures in their construction, with many of them gradually integrating a pale and gentle two-color background – seeming like a deconstructive extract from the Union Jack. These Union Jacks are sometimes just a background, but other times they

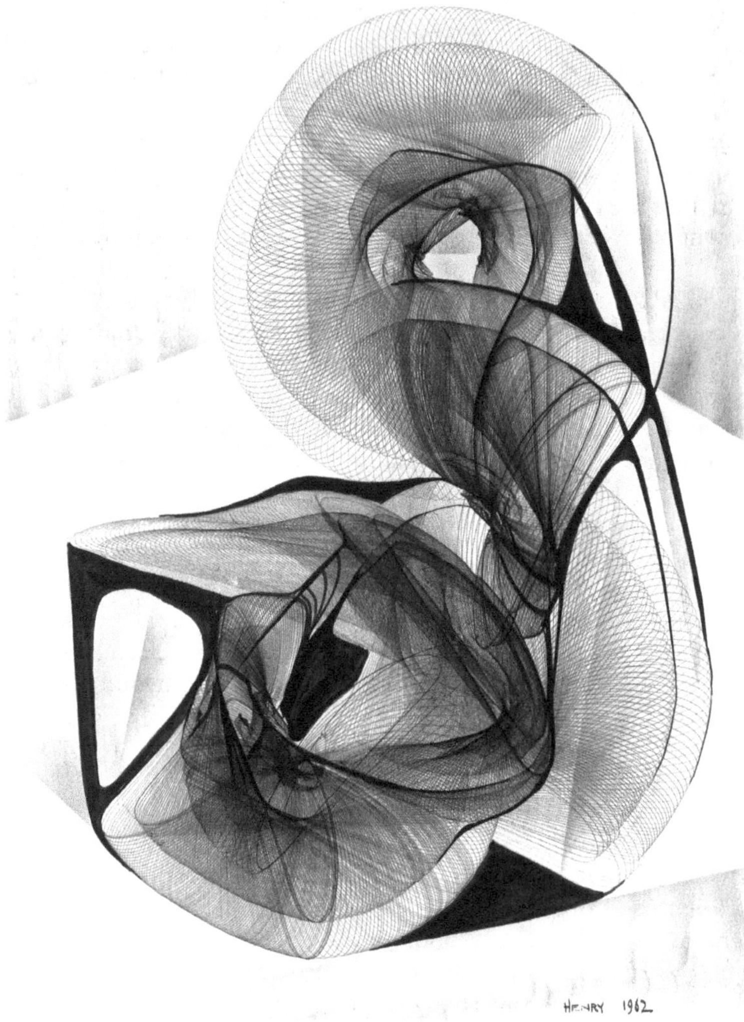

Figure 1.2 Desmond Paul Henry, *1962 no. 634*, 37.5 × 25 cm, biro on paper, hand embellishments black felt tip, background shading.

Source: Image courtesy of Elaine Ohanrahan.

appear to bleed in or out of the dominant compositional structure. This can be seen in *1963 no 258* (Plate 3).

The works of 1964 sometimes use the deconstructed Union Jack background, but now the composition is focussed mainly – sometimes exclusively – on the intertwining of two dominant (vertically orientated) manifolds as in *1964, no. 354* (Figure 1.4). These manifolds are composed of twisting variations on the angel wing, boomerang, or banana shape. They are nearly all monochrome brown; or brown and blue with some limited red elements, and black as an occasional invasive factor.

The exploration of monochrome in many of these works is extended in quite radical ways in some of Henry's works from 1965 onwards. This can be seen in

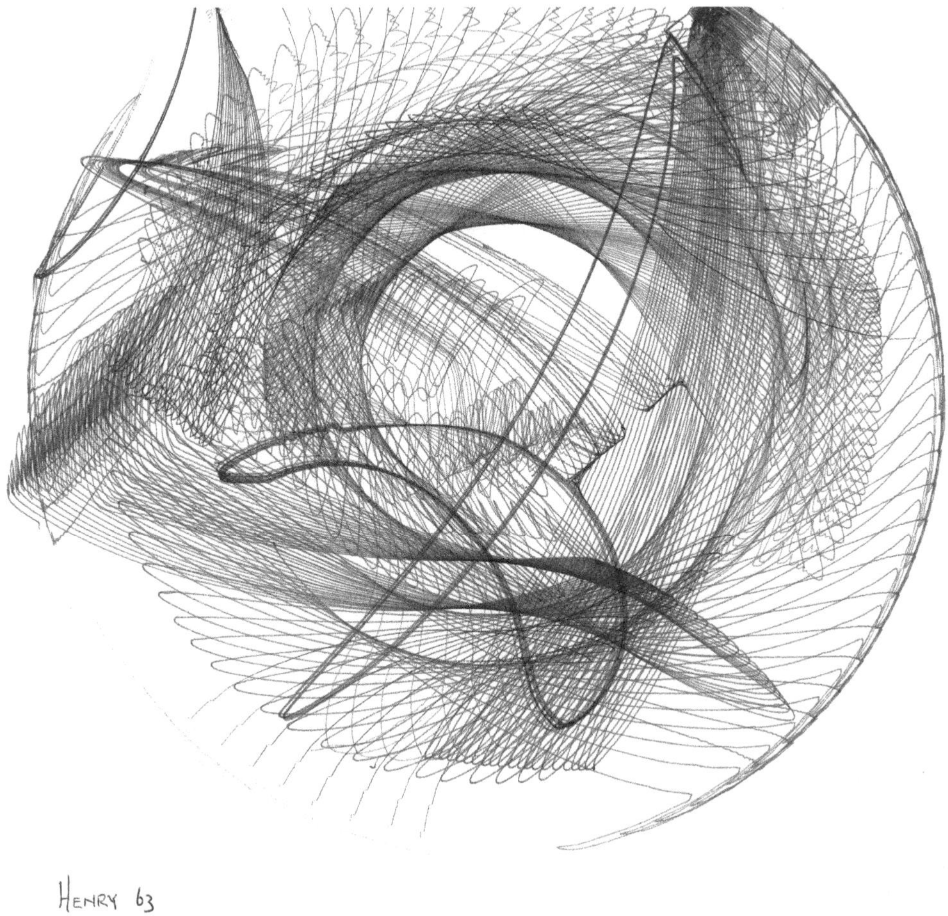

Figure 1.3 Desmond Paul Henry, *1963 no. 220*, 25.5 × 21 cm, biro on paper.
Source: Image courtesy of Elaine Ohanrahan.

1965 no. 096 (Figure 1.5). Here the composition is carried out in indian ink on dark paper. The different layers of parabolic filigree/netting are so dense as to be like organic textured fabric. Alternatively, there is the suggestion of how the microscopic surface of an insect's body or individual organ might be imagined to be. This has the opposite dynamic of most of Henry's work – which usually evokes three-dimensional forms by, at the same time, rendering them as transparent bodies. Here, the impression of substance is through an illusion of layers of extended materials – of different density – stretched on top of another, in different configurations. In this, and similar cases, the composition seems to be closely controlled.

Four

We have now described enough of Henry's work from the 1960s as to draw a first set of important historical conclusions. The real key to Henry's achievement is

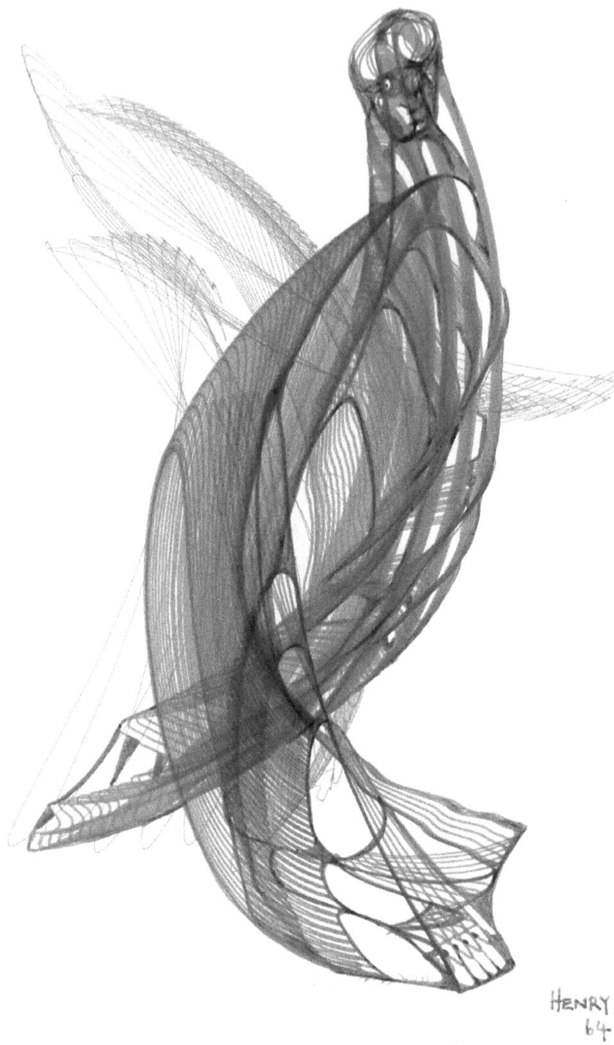

Figure 1.4 Desmond Paul Henry, *1964 no. 354*, 38 × 24.5 cm, indian ink and felt tip on paper, hand embellishments.

Source: Image courtesy of Elaine Ohanrahan.

pointed to by its origins. He would sit for hours watching the motions of the bomb-sight's analog computer – ticking and whirring as it went through the motions of a task whose context of application was no longer present. The machine still worked, but with its purpose removed. Henry created art by assisting the computer to 'do its own thing.'[5] Earlier, we saw that the Postmodern naturalization of technology, involves it setting terms for certain human practices. In Henry's work, this is given an absolutely direct expression – his artwork is produced by following where the computer leads.

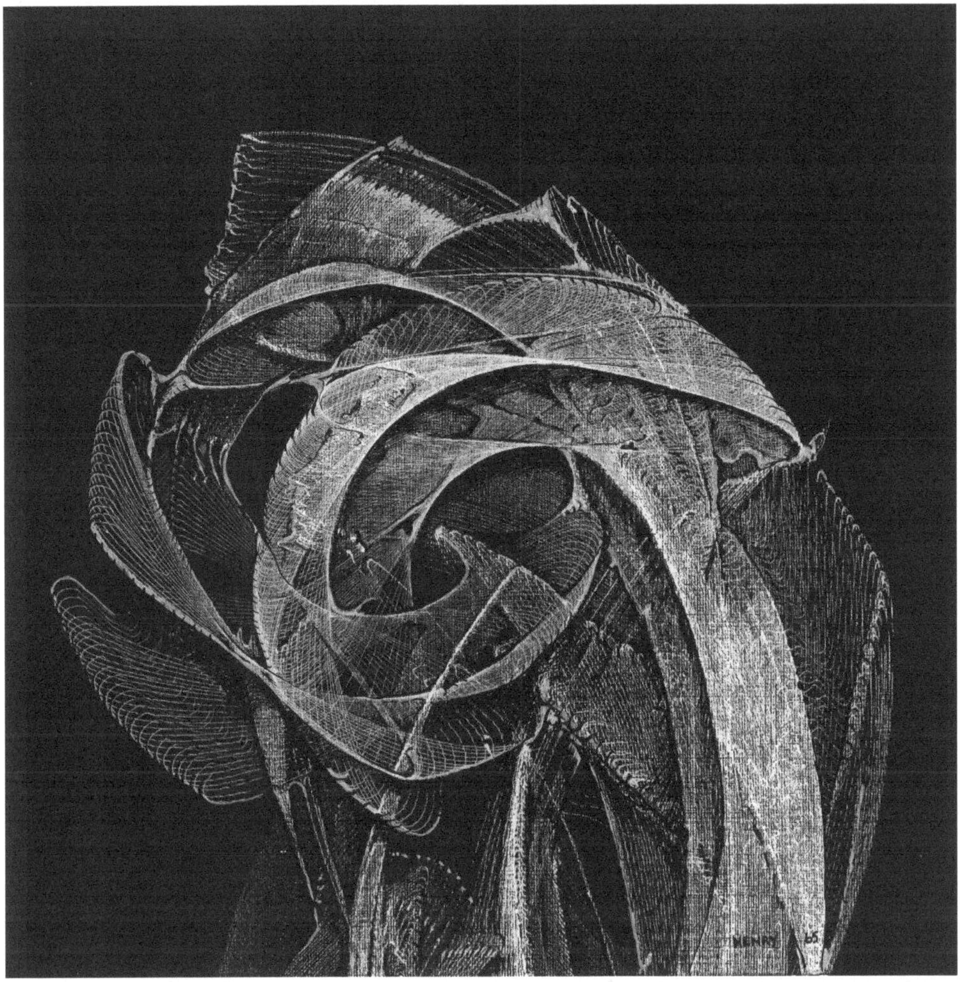

Figure 1.5 Desmond Paul Henry, *1965 no. 096*, 28 × 28 cm, white indian ink on cartridge paper, hand embellishments.

Source: Image courtesy of Elaine Ohanrahan.

This Postmodern step can be thrown in further relief by comparing Henry's specific practice to that of the Modernist artists mentioned in the introduction to this chapter. We will recall that, for them, the machine, as such, was seen very much as emblematic of the Modern world. It served, for example, as an inspiration for Futurism and for applied artistic design intended to harmonize form and function. We will recall also that, in the wake of Duchamp's (as it were) democratization of what can count as art, figures such as Tinguely used drawing machines to produce works poking fun at abstract expressionism.

Henry's approach was rather different. He was inspired by his bombsight computer and the visual elegance of its operations but this did not inspire him to create something representing the wonders of the machine, he created, rather, a way for *machine-being* to find its own mode of expression. By modifying the computer to operate with pens and a drawing table, he allowed the machine's own spatial motions to be expressed. The machine is not used *as* a tool for the artist to draw with, rather, the machine's own being is the ultimate creator of the art.

This also separates Henry's practice from Bauhaus-type productions that integrate form and function. For in these artifacts the aesthetic effect is dependent upon the tool (or whatever) fulfilling its function, and having a physical body that looks good. But with Henry's drawing machines, the machine's original function (in computing spatial distances related to the dropping of bombs) is no longer involved, and the look of the machine – in terms of the physical disposition of its parts – is irrelevant. What counts, rather, is how the machine's own workings are adapted to find expression upon a plane surface.

Henry's work is also radically different from Tinguely's in a very positive way. Tinguely's Meta-Matic machines were designed to do a task. They were to create drawings for a critical purpose. As we saw in the introduction to this chapter, they involve *active contingency* – accidents arising from the specific materials used to draw with and upon, and from awkwardness and technical glitches in how the machines carried out their allotted task. Now the point of this is that it introduces a kind of illusory sense of gesture into the resulting drawing. It suggests that 'even a cranky machine can do what abstract expressionists do – would you believe it?' Tinguely himself supposed that the machines never produced a drawing that was ugly. Perhaps. But it can be said with equal truth that very few of them are strikingly interesting in visual terms. If the machines try to be like abstract expressionists, they quickly come a cropper – the formal range of 'images' produced (despite the active contingencies) seem, for the most part, very limited in terms of compositional scope. Tinguely's machines make a critical point – but, for the most part, that is all they do, and the point made is not especially convincing. The Meta-Matic drawings are very much works tied to the specific conditions of European jealousy of American art in the late 1950s.

The contrast with Henry's work could not be starker. Henry's modifications, and active contingencies (such as the choice of pens, and changing dispositions of the drawing table), are not meant to perform a task. Rather they translate the machine's own operational being into something tangible, into something that endures – in linear and colored traces – after the operation has ceased. And – in contrast to Tinguely's Meta-Matic machine drawings – the active contingencies extend the compositional scope of the machine's own parabolic motions rather than create an illusion of gesture. The upshot is an extraordinarily diverse set of works – even within the compositional parameters that we described in detail in Parts Two and Three. Henry's work, in effect, develops the creative potential of Duchamp's assisted readymades far more than it relates to Tinguely's work. The bombsight analog computer is a found object that Henry helps develop its own aesthetic possibilities.

And it is this that gives Henry's work its particular historical significance. At the end of the Modern era, he goes beyond the Modernist use of machines to focus on the aesthetics of their internal workings. Henry's art springs from a fascination with the machine itself. By adapting it so that the parabolic motions can be traced and made variable, he enables images that manifestly declare themselves as machine-made. But this is not something to be engaged with as a means to the work's compositional unity – *it is actually constitutive of that unity*. The oscillating parabolic ellipses that are the computer's basic motion are the very key to what is distinctive about Henry's work at every level.

A different contrast is relevant here. Some of Naum Gabo's sculptures of the 1930s and 1940s are works that describe space as much by absence as well as presence – through the use of fine netted expanses of wire variously configured between more solid supports. This makes spatial extension into something light and airy – even though the technique of construction makes the work look like a product of machine technology. The look in question here is a neutral feature – neither an advantage nor disadvantage to appreciating the work. But with Henry's compositions – as just noted – the mechanical origins of the work are manifest with unexpected results. The level of complexity they introduce has an extraordinary effect, insofar as it creates images that are often extremely suggestive of organic life-forms and functions.

Indeed, this is the basis of a unique reversal. Machines are produced for the purpose of carrying out tasks. Once made, they operate in the terms that they have come to define – namely, *mechanically*, i.e. with brute efficient causation that sets elements in motion through the operation of force. This is a kind of antithesis to organic nature, where causation is embodied in gradual processes of growth. But it is precisely this antagonism that Henry's works reverse. By assisting the machine to 'do its own thing' the traces of mere efficient causation in all its mechanical complexity comes, in the resulting composition, to suggest the opposite power of organic generation and growth.

In this way, Henry's computer-generated art naturalizes mechanical processes in symbolic terms. This has important ramifications. For example, the formal unity of any aesthetic object involves – in different ways – some harmonious relation between what the object is as a perceptual whole, and the way its parts enable this whole and are modified by it. With things like drawings, however, we are dealing with objects whose meaning extends beyond what is immediately given. The drawing is an artifact that was brought into being through creative strategies that center on gesture. It is not just present visually. Our sense of its presence involves reference to the creator's way of seeing things, and how it is embodied in this particular work. The special features of drawing *qua* spatial dimension, in other words, are dependent on a temporal dimension of human intentionality and activity in how it is brought into being. However, it is not possible – just in looking at a work, to determine how, and in what order the marks were applied. The gestural character of the work, and its temporal genesis – even in Modernist expressionisms – has to be invoked mainly through imagination.

Henry's machine drawings stand in some contrast to this. True, one cannot follow the exact temporal progression of how their compositions were generated, but the overtly machine-generated character of the compositions centers on the *continuously generated* linear structures described earlier. These are made from repeated oscillating parabolic ellipses, and it is this repetitative character that is decisive. *A principle of temporal generation is made spatially present to perception* in a way that it is not in drawing (or, indeed, in other machine art such as Tinguely's).

The point is, then, that Henry's drawings not only bring about a complementarity of machine-being and the Postmodern naturalization of technology, but offer a highly individual 'take' on this. It is possible to investigate this 'take' much further in philosophical terms, by showing the interesting ways that it engages with some constant features in human experience.

Five

First, as we have seen, Henry's work gives expression to *the character of the machine itself*, its workings, and its relation to the energy that drives it. The possibility of taking aesthetic pleasure in this is clearly connected to social development. For the factory worker in the early Modern world, machine-being would clearly have few attractions, but with the growth of better working conditions, and of a broader middle class (including intellectuals and artists) who grew up in an already industrialized society, it is easy to understand how fascination with the machine would develop. But in Modernist art, this becomes a sustained interest rather than just a passing aesthetic pleasure. We must now identify why.

This identification centers on the structure of action. An embodied subject is an agent who performs means-ends orientated actions of great complexity. However, he or she would not be able to perform in such a way without a body configured with the appropriate limbs and internal organs, and the right kinds of supporting physiological processes – such as breathing and nutritional intake, and being subject to the right gravitational pressure.

There is, in other words, an important relation between the *causes* of actions and their *conditions*. In broad terms, an action is caused by an intention to act – an intention that is usually formulated without us having to attend to the details of its formulation in any overtly self-conscious way. We simply do it. However, whilst, in order to carry out such actions, we need the appropriate limbs and organs, and physiological processes (as noted above), this does not mean that these themselves are causes of our actions. Rather, they are the physical conditions or contexts which enable the actions to be carried out. Ontologically speaking, causes and conditions are the joint necessary conditions of action.

However, it is the former that tends to be emphasized. This is because our cognitive orientation towards the world is intentional – it is directed towards salient features that we can comprehend in practical terms. Of necessity, this requires that we select from the stimuli available to us. If we did not, our perceptual orientation would be swamped and paralysed by an excess of stimuli.

But whilst this emphasis on causing actions is practically warranted, it must be carefully qualified. To understand the ontology of being human in the fullest sense requires that we see action-causing as emergent from the conditions of embodiment and other physical contexts and processes. For whilst the distinction between causes and conditions is a cognitive strategy, ontologically they are not so distinguished. They are both aspects of the wholeness of human being.

For this reason, we can describe the cause/condition relation as a constant in human experience. However, the relation is given a different character under the contrasting historical circumstances under which embodied subjects exist socially. In societies dominated by religions (especially the monotheistic ones) the domain of conditions centered on the body and its physicality are seen as sources of sin – as something to be overcome through the right kinds of religiously observant causing-action. This has also had a more general effect in civilized societies. Human agency's emphasis on causing-action has gradually become so dressed up in the attitudes and ideologies of socio-cultural circumstances, that its grounding in the physical conditions of embodiment, and the working of limbs, organs, and physiological processes has been degraded. We are aware of such things when it comes to eating, drinking, sex, and the like, but not in terms of the everyday means-end operations of rational action. Yet this 'cruder' level is just as necessary to them as it is to more overt bodily activity.

This suppression of the conditionality of action is one of the things challenged, in effect, by Modernism. Modernist culture questions the established world of actions and institutions, and seeks a return to something more fundamental – finding inspiration amongst the conditions that enable cultural action rather than the accepted causes and intentions of the status quo. Early twentieth-century Modernism's obsession with more primitive modes of art is an expression of this insofar as such art was thought to tap into more 'primal' layers of feeling, which enabled artistic creativity but which had become suppressed. Even the Impressionism of Monet, Pissarro, and Sisley strives for painting that allows the medium to engage with the conditions of the artist's life – in the form of spontaneous scenes from nature and day-to-day bourgeois urban life, and through a new contact with the light and color that are basic to painting as a medium. All in all, 'finish' and the hierarchy of genres that accomplishes academic art, is abandoned in favor of a practice that returns to the conditions of artistic creativity.

It is in this context that the philosophical significance of machine-being emerges. In the worlds of rational action and, indeed, natural phenomena, we *know* that causing-action and physical change only occur through the appropriate enabling conditions. Sometimes, the events that lead up to an action (human or natural) can be discerned, but the conditions that enable them are rarely revealed, and rarer still in a form suited to attract and sustain attention.

With machines, it is different. When we watch a machine, we usually know what kind it is, and that its actions are intended to produce such and such an outcome. This is the purpose that caused the machine to be made, and which is, in effect, perceived whenever we see the final product emerge from the machine. However, if we attend to the machine's workings, we see a system of parts operating together – calibrated and dynamic in the sense of *multiplicity synchronized*, as well as in terms of physical motion. Whereas human causing-action and natural occurences rarely display their enabling conditions in an accessible way, machines do. They are causes of actions whose conditions of bringing this about – based on repetitative motion – are often manifestly present to perception whenever the machine is used.

If this analysis is correct, machine-being is symbolic of a fuller engagement with reality. It is one that discloses action and the conditions that enable it in a striking and perceptually accessible way that releases the conditions from their normally repressed status. This is why – in the Modern world – we like watching machines. But for the artist it goes deeper still. The machine is itself a created thing. By revealing its enabling conditions in the structure and workings of its machinery, it makes *createdness* itself into a recurrent observable phenomenon. A contrast is apposite here. The gestures involved in creating a painting can be read off imaginatively as an interpretation of the finished work, but when we watch a machine in motion it presents a power to create that is a perceptible reality rather than an imaginary reconstruction. It is an emblem of the power of creation itself.

Now, it might be objected that a machine is *just* a machine. Its creative power is of a different and much cruder order than that of artistic creativity. This is true, but it is not the point. For when we enjoy the workings of the machine for their own sake, the power of creation is made perceptually dramatic – however crude its outcome (in producing a certain product or effect) might be. As a *capturing* of creation-in-the-making it is a starkly inspirational aesthetic phenomenon.

And we are thus, at last, returned to Henry. As we have seen his art involved finding a means whereby a particular analog computer could give aesthetic expression to its own workings. In particular, we noted how the creation of the composition – from lines created by repetitative oscillating parabolic ellipses – allowed a principle of temporal generation to be rendered in spatial terms. This is the key point. For as well as being the causal action that generates the composition, this feature also declares the conditions that enable the action – namely that of machine-being and its motions. Henry's works operate within the field of machine fascination just described. They manifest a 'tight' harmony between the composition as caused action, and as evidence of the conditions that enable this – namely mechanical motion.

The fact that this arises from the machine's product rather than its motion alone, means, of course, that the fascination is taken to further levels. Henry's machine drawings offer things that simply watching machines at work do not. One aspect of this is a special relation to the machine as an emblem of the power to create – in the sense described earlier. We know that machines can do tasks far more efficiently than humans can, and sometimes the thought is troubling, but it is also fascinating insofar as, in effect, it *idealizes* the power to create. Henry's machine-generated drawings are especially significant in this respect. When an artist paints a surface, he or she very often deliberates before placing the mark. Here gesture – the caused-action – is preceded by a myriad of specifically cognitive acts concerned with the placing. In Henry's machine compositions there is no such deliberation. We find a direct transition from the conditions of composition (i.e. the machine in motion) to the caused-action of marking the surface. This is why the composition idealizes the power to create. There is a direct leap from activated conditions to compositional outcome. And this gives the fascinating appearance of paradox, for it makes the mechanical logic of the composition seem almost magical – insofar as the process does not involve the processes of deliberation that human artistic creation must go through.

Another feature of Henry's work must be emphasized again. We will recall that his machines 'do their own thing,' but the assisted features provided by him are of key significance because they introduce conditions of chance into how the pens traverse the paper. This gives the generated outcomes an appearance of great formal freedom even whilst manifestly declaring their machine origins.

This shows another way that the Henry machine drawings engage the caused-action/conditions relation. On the one hand, we are inhabitants of a universe that seems to be driven fundamentally by physical forces and energies; and on the other hand, we are organic beings who are emergent from this in a way that leads to the development of self-consciousness. A sense of both these aspects – and sometimes, of course, the conflict between them – orientates the actions we choose to cause and, very often, how we choose to carry them out.

Why life emerges from mechanistic physical conditions is, of course, a mystery. And even if science explained the processes involved, it would not be able to explain why physical processes of the life-engendering sort, rather than others, exist in the first place. Henry's machine drawings are especially evocative in this context. As we have seen, their visual structure centers on mechanical generation where randomness-enabling conditions enable freedom of appearance. The mechanical seems to create organic effects wherein the lines of oscillating ellipses appear, *simultaneously*, to be mechanically generated and yet organically grown. More specifically, the extraordinary fineness and detail of the work declares machine and deterministic origins, whilst, at the same time, the freedom of appearance and its accidental illusionism (evoking such things as evolving life-forms) point in organic directions.

These drawings, in other words, make deterministic mechanism and the image of life complementary. The aesthetic unity of the completed work is a caused-action that manifests the physicality of mechanism and the suggested genesis of life as its conditions. This is perhaps the deepest source of fascination in Henry's machine drawings.

Conclusion

Our discussion, then, has linked Desmond Paul Henry's work to one of the most interesting features of Postmodernism – the naturalization of technology. Because of the circumstances in which Henry's work developed in the 1960s he was not able to disseminate it so as to become influential upon others – in the way, for example, that Tinguely's drawing machines did. In the absence of such influence, Henry remains a visionary independent who anticipates the ubiquity of technological being in the Postmodernism age.

It should be noted, briefly, that I have said very little about Henry's own physical interventions in the drawing process (such as re-arranging the disposition of table and pens, or adding visual punctuations in the form of shading or specific shapes). These play a significant role in the unity of individual works. But in the final analysis, Henry's own self-expression as an artist is based on what his vision enables – the transformation of machine-being into an enduring aesthetic.

Notes

1 The exhibition is well summarized in an interview with Phillip Johnson, www.moma.org/learn/resources/archives/archives_highlights_10_1991.
2 See Henry, February 1999–April 2000, *Letters to Elaine*, The D.P. Henry Archive, Manchester.
3 Reichardt, *Cybernetic Serendipity*, September 1968, p. 50.
4 Henry, Febraury 1999–April 2000, *Letters to Elaine*.
5 Quoted in Elaine O'Hanrahan, AISB 50 conference proceedings [online]. Available at: http://doc.gold.ac.uk/aisb50/AISB50-S12/AISB50-S12-OHanrahan-paper.pdf (accessed 11/03/2018).

2 The Emergence of Digital Art

In the previous chapter we considered Desmond Paul Henry's analog work. In the early 1960s his drawings – generated by analog computer – were executed for their own aesthetic sake rather than as a means of developing computer graphics. Indeed, his emphasis on machine-being – adapting the computer to produce compositions based on its own physical workings remains a unique achievement.

At the same time that Henry was producing his works, John Whitney was doing interesting work in the United States – like Henry, working with an analog computer constructed from war-surplus optical material. He used this for commercial animated work but, in 1961, used it to create a demo-reel – *Catalog* – of the novel visual effects he had devised.[1] This centers on sequences of visual transformation extending into three-dimensions. It explores a remarkable range of associational material – ranging from two-dimensional kaleidoscopic patterns to mutations of cubes in space. These forms are sometimes crystalline and inorganic in appearance, but are then transformed into apparently organic forms – with the motion of the transformation as important as its content.

The *Catalog* effects arose from the use of the computer to treat film frames. By 1966 – in the sequence *Permutations* – he was able to generate forms on an exclusively digital basis using GRAF and FORTRAN on an IBM 360 mainframe computer, with color added subsequently, by an optical printer.

Henry's and Whitney's explorations connected to the artworld mainly through the *Cybernetic Serendipity* Exhibition of 1968, and other events.[2] However, by the time of *Cybernetic Serendipity*, nearly all the major early breakthroughs in the use of specifically digital computers for artistic purposes had already happened – in the course of broader computer research. In this chapter we will consider some of the most important work in the build-up to *Cybernetic Serendipity*, and some of the key innovations that followed on from it.

One

One of the contributors to *Cybernetic Serendipity* – A. Michael Noll – had already taken the first major steps in creating specifically digital art through his work at the Bell Telephone Laboratories. Indeed, one might even say that digital art receives its formal inauguration in his Memo of August 28, 1962 entitled *Patterns by 7090: Case 38794–23*.[3] The Introduction to this document includes the following.

> The digital computer is presently being used to produce new musical sounds and techniques of composing. The advent of microfilm printing used in conjunction with a digital computer allows similar excursions into the field of visual art. ... This paper describes the results of such an exploratory series of design-producing experiments. Rather than risk an unintentional debate at this time on whether the computer-produced designs are truly art or not, the results of the machine's endeavors will simply be called 'Patterns.'[4]

In this passage Noll clearly sees the artistic possibilities of digital computers, but shrewdly chooses to emphasize their presentation, rather than be drawn into aesthetic speculations about them. The Memo presents detailed analysis of how each of the eight included Patterns was technically generated. Here is a visual analysis of the Patterns themselves.

Pattern 1 (Figure 2.1), is a vertically orientated structure sustained by five tilted but straight vertical lines. These emerge from a bed of horizontal straight tilted lines

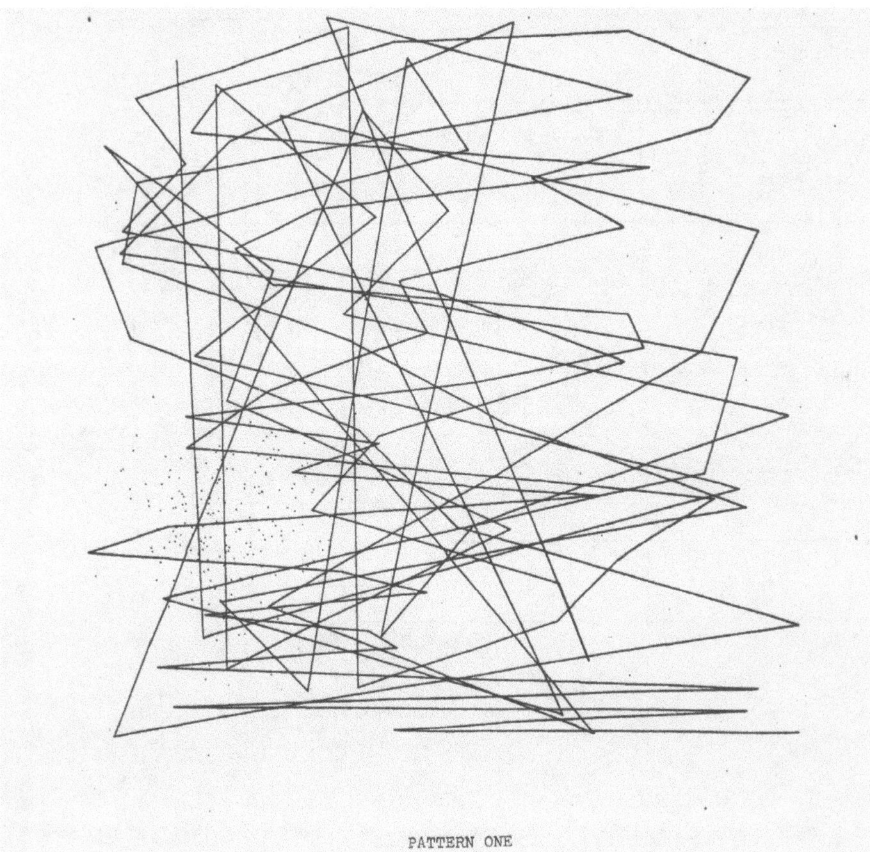

Figure 2.1 A. Michael Noll, *Pattern 1*, from Bell Telephone Laboratories Memo of August 28, 1962, *Patterns by 7090: Case 38794–2.*

Source: Programmed and conceived by A. Michael Noll at Bell Telephone Laboratories, Incorporated in 1962. © copyright A. Michael Noll.

massing to create a formation of zig-zags, and also flattened scalene triangles. Similar horizontal structures intersect the vertical lines higher up also – creating the appearance of tilted planes with irregular boundaries that appear to be either collapsing in on one another or trying to take on regular rectangular form. To the lower left center is a swarm of dots in an open cluster. They appear to be behind the body of the main overall structure, and this accentuates the three-dimensional illusion already suggested by the tilting planes.

Patterns 2 and *3* are variations on what has just been described. *Patterns* 6 and *8* are also akin to it, but they focus and intensify the lines into more compact but massed lines whose sharp intersecting angularities suggest conflicting forces.

Pattern 4 (Figure 2.2), however, is very different. It is composed of straight lines with a regular vertical orientation, intersected by horizontals at ninety-degree angles.

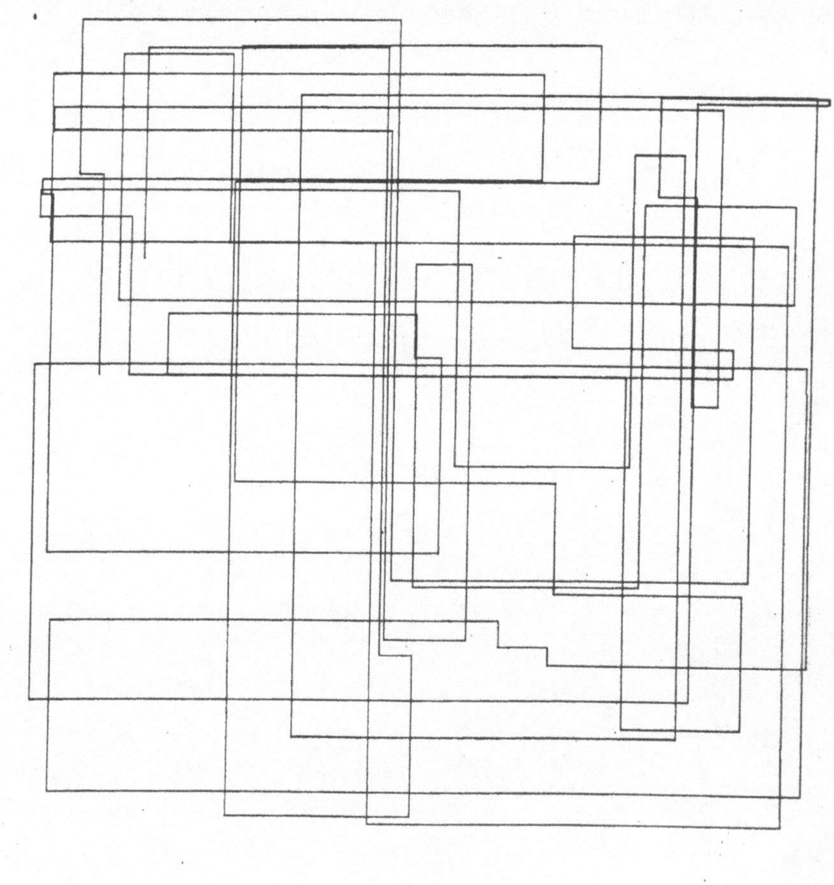

PATTERN FOUR

Figure 2.2 A. Michael Noll, *Pattern 4*, from Bell Telephone Laboratories Memo of August 28, 1962, *Patterns by 7090: Case 38794–2.*

Source: Programmed and conceived by A. Michael Noll at Bell Telephone Laboratories, Incorporated in 1962. © copyright A. Michael Noll.

In some areas (of both the vertical and horizontal axes) these intersections create tightly bunched linear formations. These create the impression of intersecting and/or overlapping square and rectangular planes – pushing and pulling (optically speaking) towards or away from the viewer. This effect is emphasized by some of the lines at various extensions being denser than at others. *Pattern 5* continues this approach by using even heavier lines at various points.

Pattern 7 (Figure 2.3) is the most idiosyncratic of all. It consists of three main vertical sets of straight lines grouped together like musical staves where the internal spacing of lines is not regular. Two further 'staves' (one with many internal lines, the other with just four) intersect the vertical structures horizontally. The most distinctive features of the Pattern are small vertical 'squiggles' which appear to be superimposed upon and thence 'crossing out' areas of the staves.

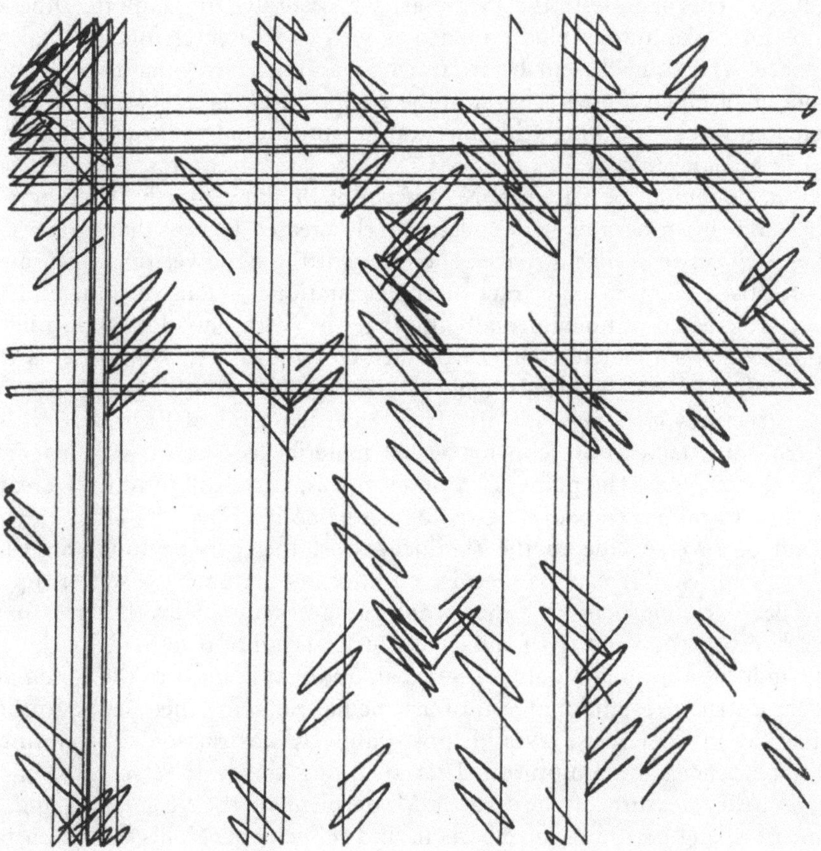

PATTERN SEVEN

Figure 2.3 A. Michael Noll, *Pattern 7*, from Bell Telephone Laboratories Memo of August 28, 1962, *Patterns by 7090: Case 38794–2.*

Source: Programmed and conceived by A. Michael Noll at Bell Telephone Laboratories, Incorporated in 1962. © copyright A. Michael Noll.

We have described Noll's Patterns in some detail because their ways of structuring pictorial space are fundamental – both in terms of the properties of that space, and in terms of the development of digital art. *Patterns 1, 2, 3, 6*, and *8* present spatial forms that create depth by breaking three-dimensional optical space obliquely. This is a kind of depth that tends to be created by representations that depict or evoke actions. The *Pattern 4* and *5* works evoke a three-dimensionality created through the succession of planes before and after one another. This is the most basic way of organizing pictorial space. In order for anything to be *represented* as occupying three-dimensional space it has a point which is nearest to the notional viewer, and a point which is furthest away. These define the basic foreground and background planes between which an object is spatially presented as three-dimensional. In the push-and-pull play of rectangular and square planes, in other words, Noll's patterns declare this fundamentality of 'in front' and 'behind.'

The idiosyncracies of *Pattern 7* introduce an interesting variable in the form of the squiggle. This manifests the fact that, whilst drawn by a plotter, the digital program can evoke autographic presence as well as structures fundamental to pictorial space. The squiggle can be regarded as a simple irregular two-dimensional form, but its placing vis-à-vis the rest of the composition makes it seem like an act of attempted erasure, something with autographic-intentional overtones, and thence a signifier of human presence.

Now, in designing the Patterns, Noll was not thinking overtly in the terms just described. But his programs were imaginatively created in way that intuitively disclose key element of pictorial space. They present the basic vectors which any new idiom of artistic creation – abstract or representational – must negotiate. The fact that they are created in fundamentally linear terms (with only dots and squiggles as additional compositional features) is of further significance. *The Patterns declare their technological origins*. People might doodle in such terms, but the concentration of these structures goes beyond this. They have the kind of form that we would expect from artists who are copying visual material associated with machines or mechanical processes. The point is, in other words, that Noll intuitively creates his Patterns in a form that embodies technology as iconology.

A kind of reverse clue to the significance of this can be found in Clement Greenberg's ideas.[5] He saw Modernist painting as driven by a self-critique that seeks to become congruent with the means and aesthetic effects that are unique to itself. Whatever, the validity of this claim, it is certainly true that, by the 1960s, art was, indeed becoming highly self-critical, addressing itself to the fundamentals of the basic structures and material of art media, reducing their scope to the bare essentials (as in Greenberg-favored 'post-painterly abstraction' in painting, and minimal tendencies in sculpture). This stripping down to essentials, in other words, is a key feature of the end of Modernism in the visual arts and is the outcome of a long period of development and refinement. Noll's first explorations in digital art, however, have a very different significance. He, in effect, treats the bare essentials of digital pictorial space as the starting point for new creation rather than as the outcome of some Modernist process of purification. Unburdened by the baggage of artworld Modernism, he probes the essential pictorial – or, better, *virtual* – structures of the medium with a view to establishing their further potential as a specifically *digital space*. This is a clear step towards what is literally *Postmodern* art.

Noll himself, has never claimed to be an artist in any full sense, but he made some attempts to develop the artistic implications of his Patterns. As early as 1963, he circulated enlarged copies of further Patterns (where the lines were colored-in using felt-tip marking pens) as gifts to his colleagues. In 1964, amongst other works, he designed the *Computer Composition With Lines* – a well-known image that is visually close to Mondrian's abstract *Composition With Lines*. Noll dealt with the relation between these two works (*vis-à-vis* the possibility of discovering empirical intersubjective criteria of aesthetic worth) in a research paper published in 1966.[6]

Of even more importance was Noll's contribution with Bela Julesz to 'Computer-Generated Pictures' – the first exhibition of computer art outside Europe, held between April 6 and 24, 1965 at the Howard Wise Gallery in New York. Julesz was a research scientist at Bell Labs working in the area of visual perception (a fact that will be returned to in the next chapter). His area of specialization involved the digital creation of random-dot images, and these had received considerable publicity – to the degree, indeed, of featuring on the cover of the Februrary 1965 edition of *Scientific American*. Despite these images having been created for purely scientific purposes, and Julesz having no sense of himself as an artist, Howard Wise saw their artistic potential and invited Julesz to exhibit at his gallery. The scientist agreed, and had (his Bell Laboratories colleague) A. Michael Noll's artistically inclined computer graphics included in the exhibition, also. The exhibition was reviewed by Stuart Preston in *The New York Times*, who concluded that 'The wave of the future crashes significantly at the Howard Wise Gallery. ... Freed from the tedium of technique and the mechanics of picture making, the artist will simply "create".'[7]

Interestingly, at the end of his 1962 Memo, Noll observed that

> The programming scheme used to produce the patterns shown in this paper were obviously conceived without forethought for their artistic merit ... some subjective experiments might be attempted to try to determine just what qualities make a picture pleasing or even artistic. With this information at hand, the programmer-artist might be better prepared to produce not just haphazard patterns, but 'true art.'[8]

What Noll is describing here is the possibility of creating aesthetically worthy art using programs based on empirical information about, as it were, the mathematics of taste. This information-based aesthetic was explored subsequently in his Mondrian paper, and is *the single major concept that guides the emergence of digital art in its formative years*. Indeed (and without knowledge of Noll's innovations), it was soon developed in a more extreme way as 'generative aesthetics' (a systematic theory with practical applications) by the 'Stuttgart School' of researchers in Germany. The theory was central to the world's first dedicated exhibition of digital art – *Generative Computergrafik*, held between February 5 and 19, 1965 at the Technische Hochschule in Stuttgart. The exhibition involved works by Georg Nees introduced by the presiding genius of generative aesthetics – philosophy professor Max Bense. It is to the effects of this exhibition we now turn.

Two

Bense is of paramount importance as the first theorist – or, rather, ideologist – of digital art. His work, as described by Christoph Klutsch

> tried to bridge philosophy, psychology, aesthetics,social sciences, and art theory. The goal was to develop a theory that would allow one to measure the amount and quality of information in aesthetic objects, thus enabling an evaluation of art that goes beyond 'art historian chatter.' Information aesthetics investigated the numerical value of 'the aesthetic object' itself. Based on David Birkhoff's experiments on aesthetic measurements around 1928, the theoretical mathematician Norbert Wiener's *Cybernetics: or, Control and Communication in the Animal and the Machine* from 1948, Claude Shannon's information theory from 1948, and Charles Sanders Peirce's semiotic theory, Bense focused on physical concepts such as entropy, process, and co-reality ...[9]

The *Generative Computergrafik* exhibition was accompanied by a manifesto/text of Bense's entitled 'The projects of generative aesthetics.' He sets out its basis as follows.

> Generative aesthetics ... implies a combination of all operations, rules and theorems which can be used deliberately to produce aesthetic states (both distributions and configurations) when applied to a set of material elements. Hence generative aesthetics is analogous to generative grammar, in so far as it helps to formulate the principles of a grammatical schema – realizations of an aesthetic structure. Any generative aesthetics, which leads to an aesthetic synthesis, must be preceded by analytical aesthetics. This process is responsible for the preparation of aesthetic structures based on the aesthetic information found in given works of art. In order to be projected and realized in a concrete number of material elements, the prepared aesthetic information must be described in abstract (mathematical) terms.[10]

The philosophical difficulties of Bense's approach will be considered a little further on. Before that, attention must be focussed upon the important historical catalytic effects of his approach. The basis of Bense's aesthetics had been developed well before the *Generative Computergrafik* exhibition, mainly in relation to literature and music. It was contact with Geog Nees in late 1964 which made him aware of its visual applications. Nees was an industrial mathematician (working for the Siemens company) who had learned to program using Algol. He became familiar with Bense's ideas – a familiarity which happened to coincide with the Siemens' computer center's acquisition of a Zuse Graphomat 64 drawing table. Nees used this to make his first drawings in November 1964. In an interview, he describes what he felt as the second drawing was created.

> It ran cold along my spine and I thought 'Here is something that will not vanish again. Look artists, one can make abstract art in mass! Why should an artist not let himself be helped by the computer? The artist could use computer graphics as primary designs and work them out by hand.'[11]

In December 1964, Nees acted on this enthusiasm and wrote to Bense including a number of his computer drawings with the message. In response, Bense published six drawings by Nees in the journal *rot* (edition 19, February 1965) together with his generative aesthetics manifesto.[12] Bense also organized the aforementioned *Generative Computergrafik* exhibition to present Nees' drawings publically. A colloquium with artists from the Stuttgart area held on February 5 aroused considerable controversy and, on April 28, 1965, *Der Spiegel* reported the colloquium and reproduced the upper part of one of Nees's works *23 Ecken* (Figure 2.4) – together with its design program.[13] This work centers on two compositional strategies, one of which,

Figure 2.4 Georg Nees, *23-Ecke (Polygon of 23 vertices)*, computer-generated ink on paper. From *Zeitschrift Grundlagenstudien aus Kybernetik und Geisteswissenschaft*, 1964.

again, negotiates a feature that is fundamental to pictorial media, and the other of which is an iconological aspect that proves generally important for early digital art in the Stuttgart school and beyond. The foundational feature is its exemplification of the strategy of creating pictorial space by distributing forms across the surface in harmony with the picture plane instead of penetrating or layering it recessionally to produce a manifest illusion of depth. This approach is basic to much medieval art as well as to some aspects of 'all-over' painting in late Modernism. There is also an affinity with the so-called cubist grid which has been seen by some to be fundamental to different modes of twentieth-century Modernist art. In this context, the grid provides a basic orientation wherein different key structures of pictorial space can be explored but without disrupting the two-dimensionality of the picture plane.

What is interesting is the way that Nees reinvents the strategy without significant reference to visual art. Rather, his inspiration is a semiotic one. The compositional units viewed in conjunction form a *field* composed from columns of quasi-hieroglyphs, or elements in some strange extended alphabet. This latter impression is emphasized when the units are considered individually. Each involves some square or rectangular or irregular planar form intersected by horizontal or vertical straight lines, or, occasionally, diagonal ones. The visual effect of each is to suggest some kind of machine – which makes the whole field seem emblematic of a pictographic language based on machine elements – each different from the other, but with cognate formal features.

This semiotic field is decisive for much of Nees's other work in the formative years of digital art.[14] However, he introduces quite significant variations on the structure. In *Schotter* (made between 1965 and 1968) (Figure 2.5) there is a field of equally sized squares, with the twelve in the top row in exact conjunction with one another. However, the rows of squares beneath gradually become unstable – through being tilted, and then jumbled, and, eventually overlapped with one another. With each successive row, the instability of the arrangement is amplified. Even before the bottom of the image is reached, the lower field has broken up into a manifold that seems to be composed of squares in motion, or even in agitated conversation with one another.

Nees's early work also makes interesting moves towards the third dimension. Consider, for example, the drawing *Corridor* (*c.*1965–1968) (Figure 2.6). Here, a notional planar field is broken up into obliquely presented three-dimensional units, redistributed – unevenly, and in different concentrations – in the form of two opposite planes, both receding towards a vanishing point suggested by orthogonals projecting from the image's lower floor. Some of the units have come loose from these planes and hover in bunched formations between them. The overall impression is of a field of signs being transformed into representations of physical realities, in this case through the suggestion of architectural fragments.

Another pioneer of computer art inspired by Bense is Frieder Nake. Nake worked as an assistant at the Technical University of Stuttgart, and in the early 1960s did work on machine code programming – developing computer graphics software. He began producing designs using the Zuse plotter in 1963. He is featured in the *Der Spiegel* article on Nees's exhibition and, from November 5 to 26, 1965, exhibited his own works alongside Nees at the Galerie Wendelin Niedlich in Stuttgart.

Nake's works have both kinship and important differences from Noll's and Nees's works from the early 1960s. Two early drawings – *Polygonzug 6/7/64 No. 2* and

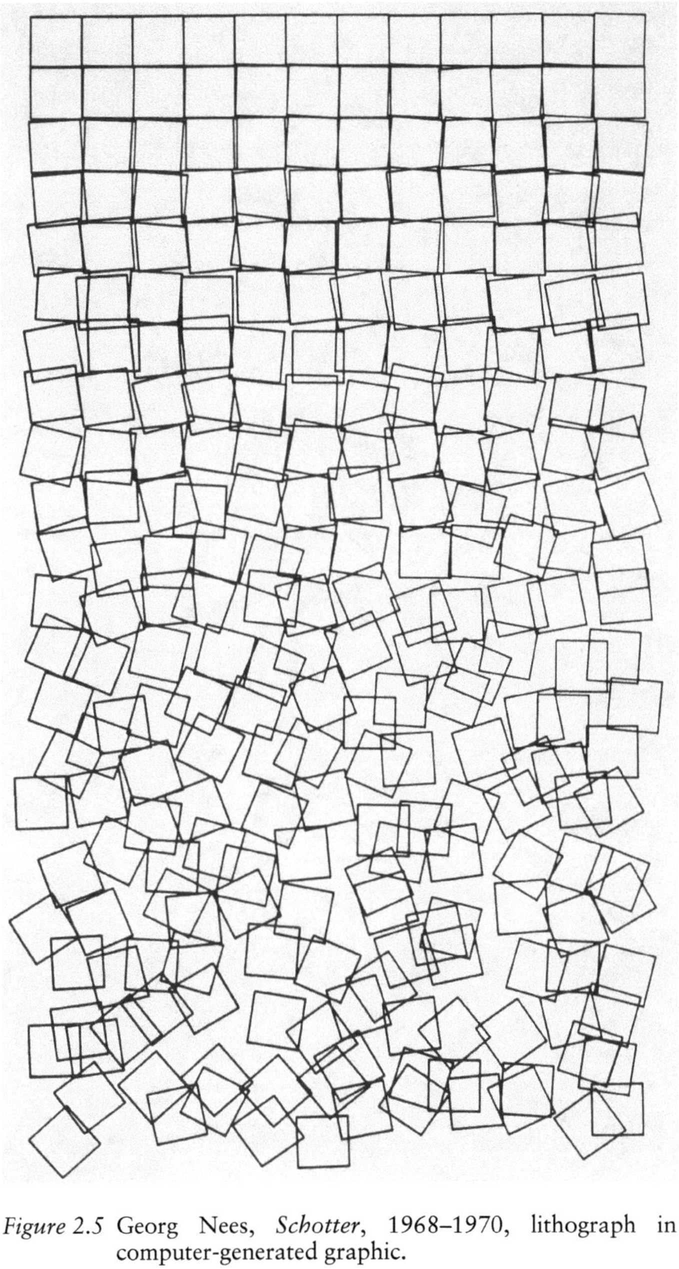

Figure 2.5 Georg Nees, *Schotter*, 1968–1970, lithograph in black ink from a computer-generated graphic.

Source: © Victoria and Albert Museum, London.

Achsenparalleler Polygonzug (25/02/65 Nr. 13) – are interesting in the way that the former explores the same strategy of creating pictorial space as Noll's *Pattern 2* (through angular lines breaking obliquely through the plane) whilst the latter creates space in the manner of Noll's *Patterns 4* and *5* – through horizontal and vertical lines setting forth recessional layered planes.

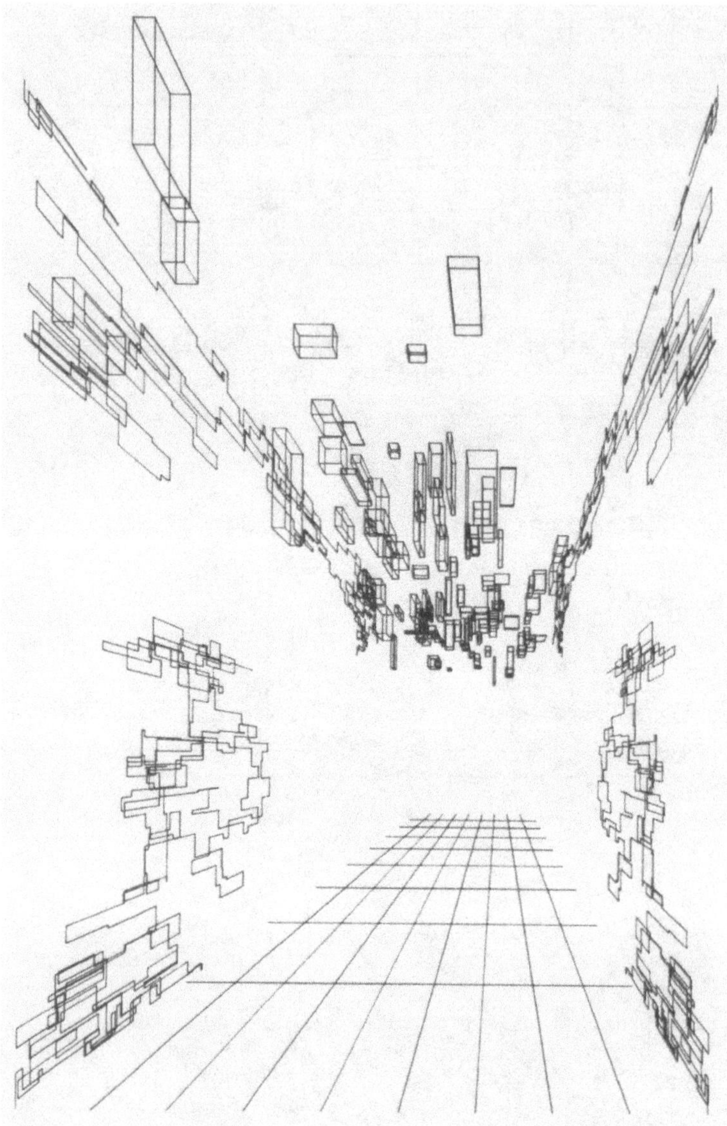

Figure 2.6 Georg Nees, *Corridor*, *c.*1965–1968. Computer-generated plotter drawing, 87.9×58.7cm.

In *13/9/65, Nr. 5, Distribution of Elementary Signs* (Figure 2.7) Nake offers a sophisticated composition of the pictorial plane from a field of signs. Here, in contrast to Nees's approach, the field is composed from tiny squares and dot-marks where the key feature is the density with which these are distributed, and the visual gravitational force of underlying (but only suggested) square and triangular structures. In effect the configuration of present elements is given vibrancy by their relation to unpopulated and/or sparsely populated areas in the field. The individual

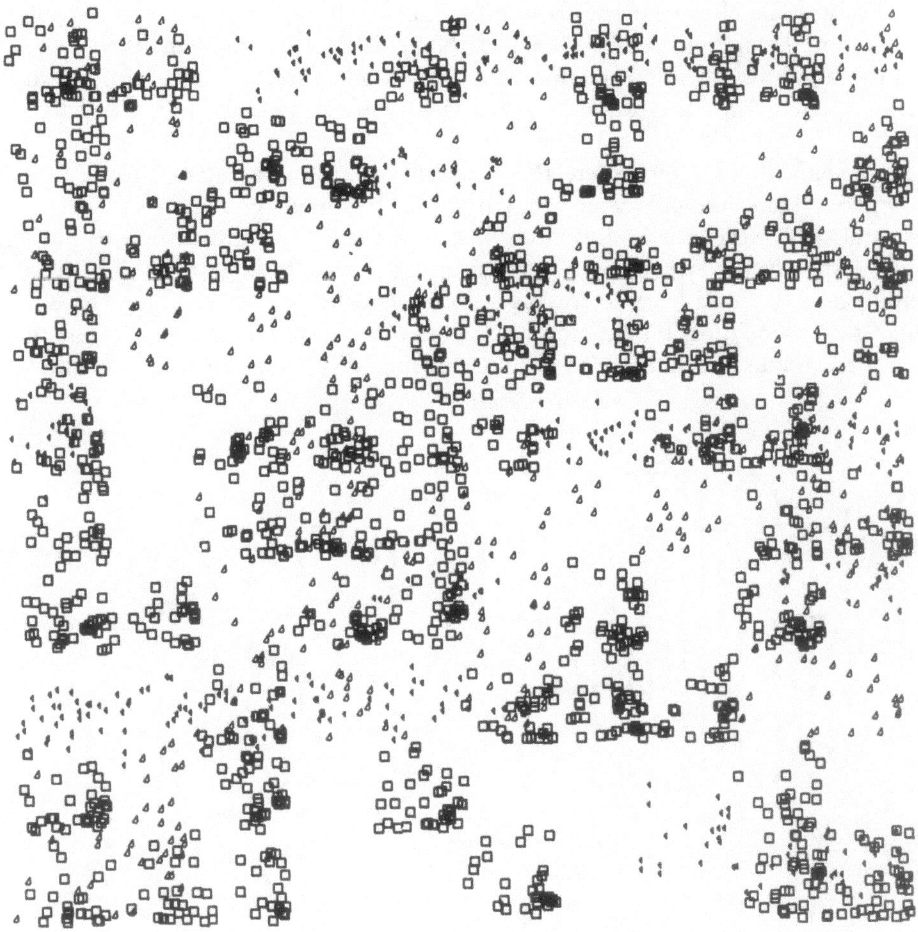

Figure 2.7 Frieder Nake, *13/9/65 Nr. 5*, 1965, 'Distribution of Elementary Signs.'

identity of signs is not only a function of physical difference and difference of position, but of the contextualizing effects of the space in which these features are located.

This approach is an important feature of other works by Nake from 1965 and 1966, notably several series entitled *Walk-Through-Raster*. Of these works, Nake says

> The long vertical lines that we see are not constructed as such. They are, as the entire image, constructed from a repertoire of the short horizontal, the equally short vertical line and the empty elementary cell. A Markov chain is determined according to non-stationary (i.e. depending on location) transition probabilities. This mathematical feature gives me a certain measure of non-deterministic macro-structure.[15]

The creative promise of this strategy is expressed in the character of the individual works. They contrast on the basis of different ways of using the available repertoire of graphic elements, and from differences in how the transition probabilities are set in the individual case. Hence, Nake employs a mathematical structure whose digital realization enables broader associations. *Walk-Through-Raster 2.1–4* (Figure 2.8), for example, consists of long straight vertical lines some of which intersect with one another at right angles, and which, in toto, suggest a square-shaped field. However, the distribution of these intersections, and the absence or truncated character of the lines (in the upper right and lower left quadrants of two of the works, and in the border areas, and central region of the other two, respectively) introduce a surprising range of optical effects. There is the appearance of quasi-organic fraying – like a textile that is becoming threadbare. But, at the same time, this fraying has a kind of induced quality – where the inducing force seems mechanical in origin. Indeed, this technological play allows a

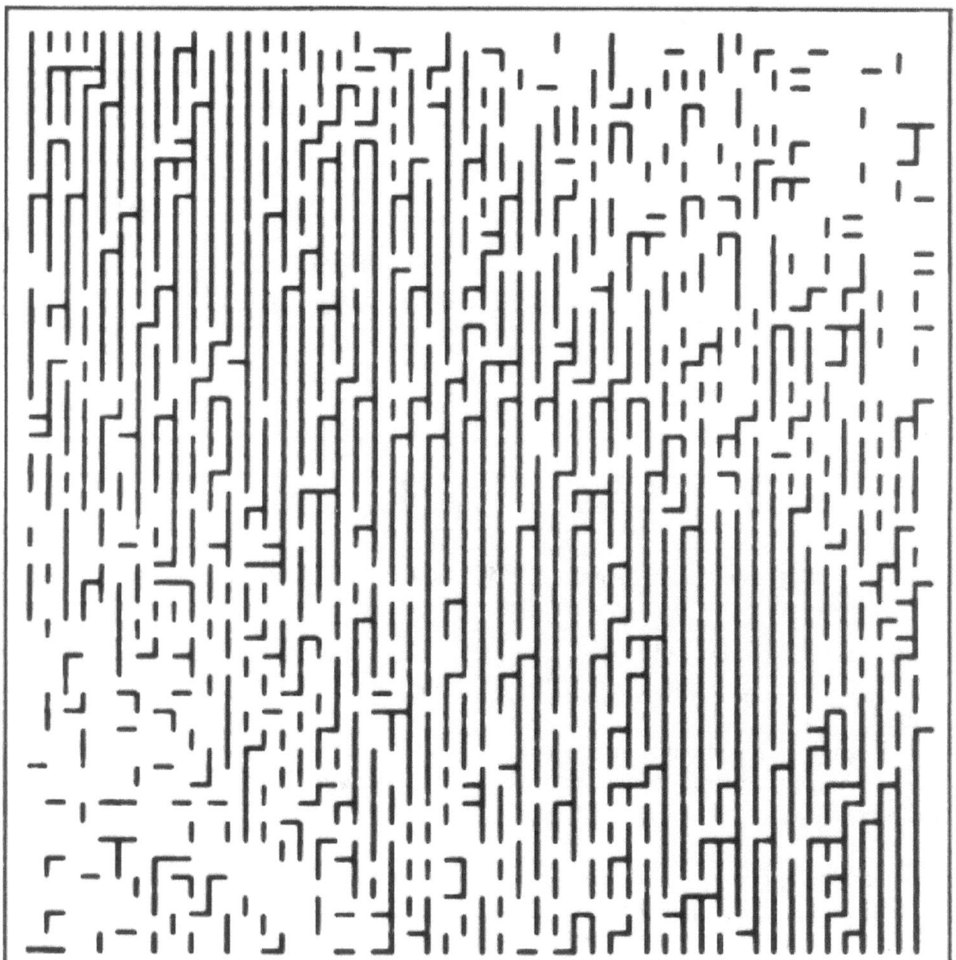

Figure 2.8 Frieder Nake, *Walk-Through-Raster series 2.1–4*, 1966.

further direction of association where the strict vertical structures may seem like curiously rigid organic capillary forms being engendered artificially in a laboratory process. Yet another associational avenue is created by a sense of the more densely massed areas as having shallow three-dimensional form – like shallow plates being overlaid on one another in a process of chemical formation, or separated in a process of gradual disintegration.

One of the key features of Nake's achievement in this and other works is the element of formalised reciprocity – of the artist programming different possible visual outcomes which are then realized by the program and fed back to the artist for a decision. The truly experimental dimension of this can be illustrated by reference to what is possibly Nake's most important early work – *Hommage à Paul Klee 13/9/65 Nr.2*, 1965 (Figure 2.9). This important drawing was inspired and guided by Paul Klee's oil painting *Highroads and Byroads* of 1929 (presently in the collection of the Ludwig Museum, Cologne). Of Nake's work Honor Beddard observes as follows.

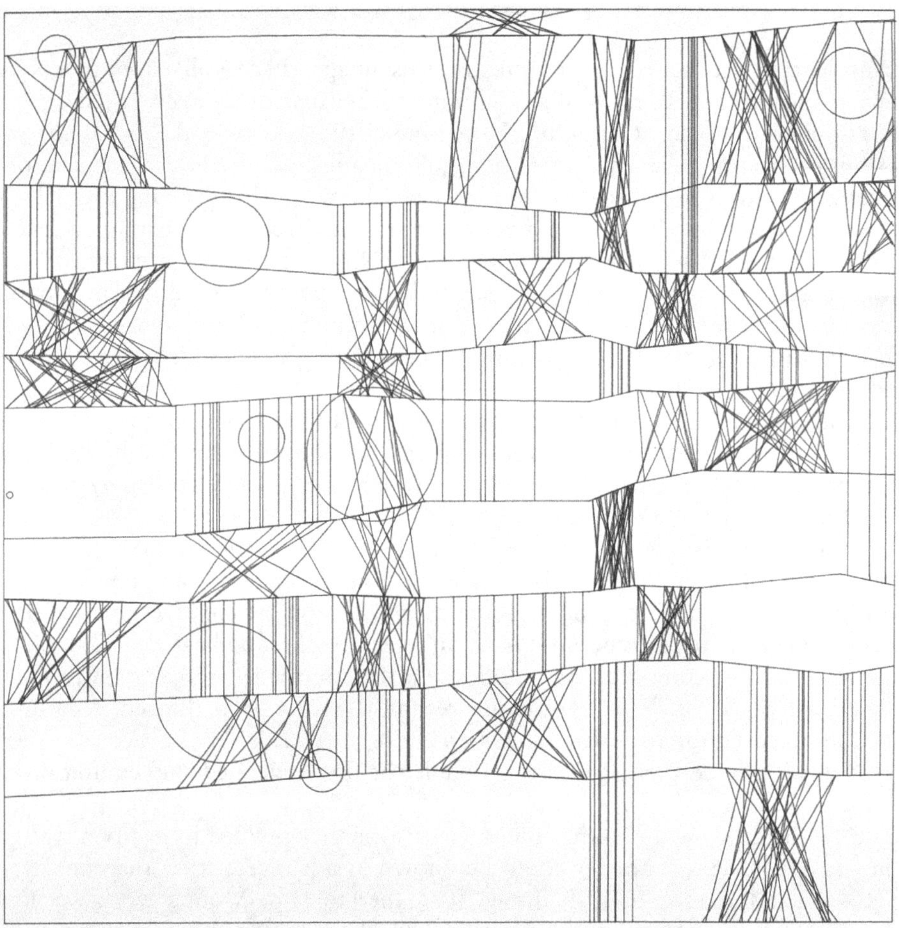

Figure 2.9 Frieder Nake, *13/9/65 Nr. 2*, 1965, 'Hommage à Paul Klee.'

> Klee's painting consists predominantly of a series of horizontal and vertical lines which Nake used as the basis for writing a computer program, or algorithm. Creating set parameters for the drawing, such as the square frame, Nake deliberately wrote random variables into the program to explore different visual effects, based on Klee's 'repertoire' of imagery. Nake allowed the computer to make choices from a limited bank of options based on the outcome of the previous decision, thus introducing an element of chance, albeit a controlled one. The program itself was written in machine code and input directly into the computer, which would have had no interface or operating system at this time. The process of creating the drawing involved a series of formulae developed away from the computer. Nake has written that, 'I was thinking the drawing. But thinking the drawing never meant to think one particular drawing. It meant a class of drawings, an infinite set, described by many parameters that would usually be selected at runtime by series of random numbers.' There was no screen or monitor available on which to preview the drawing, and the final result would only have been apparent when the machine had finished. The final image we see here was just one of many possible variations from a wider series, the most successful of which was determined by the artist.[16]

In terms of the 'art' aspect of digital art, this image (like Noll's treatments of Mondrian and Bridget Riley) is of special interest because of its overt reaching out to the established world of painting. However, in the case of Nake's drawing, at least, this has mainly the character of a guiding idea or, better, an inspiration. Interestingly, there is a major structural contrast between this drawing and Klee's painting. The latter involves a patchwork of variegated rectangles arranged recessionally – like a path set out before the viewer. Nake's drawing, in contrast consists of irregular, loosely horizontal lines linked by verticals of different length, with some abbreviated diagonals (occasionally bunching), and curious ovoids which seem to pull parts of the structure towards the viewer, and leave other parts behind. The configured lines also have this push-pull effect – like uneven facets indented across a crudely banded three-dimensional form, containing visual impurities. The upshot is a structure whose digital origins appear mainly undeclared. (In this, it is unusual vis-à-vis digital art, and is dependent upon its display context for the affirmation of this status.)

Noll, Nees, and Nake were primarily mathematicians and applied scientists. However, through the influence of Bense's work, Manfred Mohr – an already established artist – came to learn programming as a basis for his creative practice. His work is of signal importance because he is, in effect, the first dedicated digital artist, i.e. one who uses the computer for specifically artistic purposes, rather than producing digital art as an offshoot of broader technical exploration. Indeed, 'Manfred Mohr Computer Graphics – *Une Esthétique Programmée*' (ARC – Musée d'Art Moderne de la Ville de Paris, 1971) is probably the first dedicated solo exhibition of a digital artist *qua* artist.

Bense's ideas drew Mohr to the computer because they seemed to justify a way of creating art whose end-character could be known in advance, rather than achieved through luck and chance, as in painting. It is, therefore, to Mohr's work we now turn. (Given his importance, the discussion will also consider important work by him extending beyond the original era of digital art.)

Three

In the catalogue to his 1971 Paris exhibition, Mohr pinpoints the origins of his turn towards the digital medium in more exact terms.

> Accepting that creative work is an algorithm which represents a human behavior in a given situation, it is natural to ask: how is such an algorithm built up, and which precise mathematical laws could be extracted for later use in different circumstances? If one is now curious enough to look for his own aesthetical parameters, he is ready to engage in an interesting line of research. ... These considerations led me to use the computer as a PARTNER in my work. The first step in that direction was an extended analysis of my own paintings and drawings from the last ten years. It resulted in a surprisingly large amount of regularities, determined of course by my particular aesthetical sense, through which I was able to establish a number of basic elements that amounted to a rudimentary syntax. After representing these basic constructions through a mathematical formalism, and setting them up in an abstract combinatorial framework. I was in a position to realise all possible representations of my algorithms.[17]

The influence of Bense on these observations is unmistakable – from the willingness to interpret creativity as a form of algorithm, to the mathematical formalization of factors involved in the artist's previous aesthetic choices. On his website, Mohr describes how, between 1969 and 1972,

> For the first time algorithms (rules with a beginning and an ending) are used to calculate the images. My consequent thinking is rendered visible through computer programs I wrote. The resulting drawings were realized by a computer controlled drawing machine (plotter). With a choice of different line characteristics, an alphabet of arbitrary generated elements is created. Individual algorithms are invented for each work from which all forms and structures are solely generated. The algorithms are built from imposed as well as from random selection principles which I called 'aesthetical-filters.'[18]

As an example of this strategy, consider a work from Mohr's 1971 Paris exhibition, *P-049/R, 'a formal language'* (Figure 2.10).[19] Here, we find the – by now – familiar semiotic field structure. In this case the individual units appear as elements of a pictographic language distributed as a field (in strict harmony with the picture plane) in such a formalized way that even the gaps between units appear as strikingly precise as the units themselves. The visual character of these elements means that whilst they are set out in horizontal rows, rhythms are also created through contact and contiguity in the vertical and diagonal dimensions. In this way, the field is *animated* by the individual characters and their spacing. The pictography suggests a sense of operational life over and above the juxtaposed alphabetic units.

The field structure is basic to much of Mohr's early work with occasional instances of it which – like Nake's *Hommage to Klee* – conceal their digital origins, at least partially (a work in point being the pseudo-quilted effect found in another work from the Paris show – the horizontally banded *P-71, 'serielle zeichenreihung'* (1970) (Figure 2.11). However, Mohr's early innovations are by no means confined

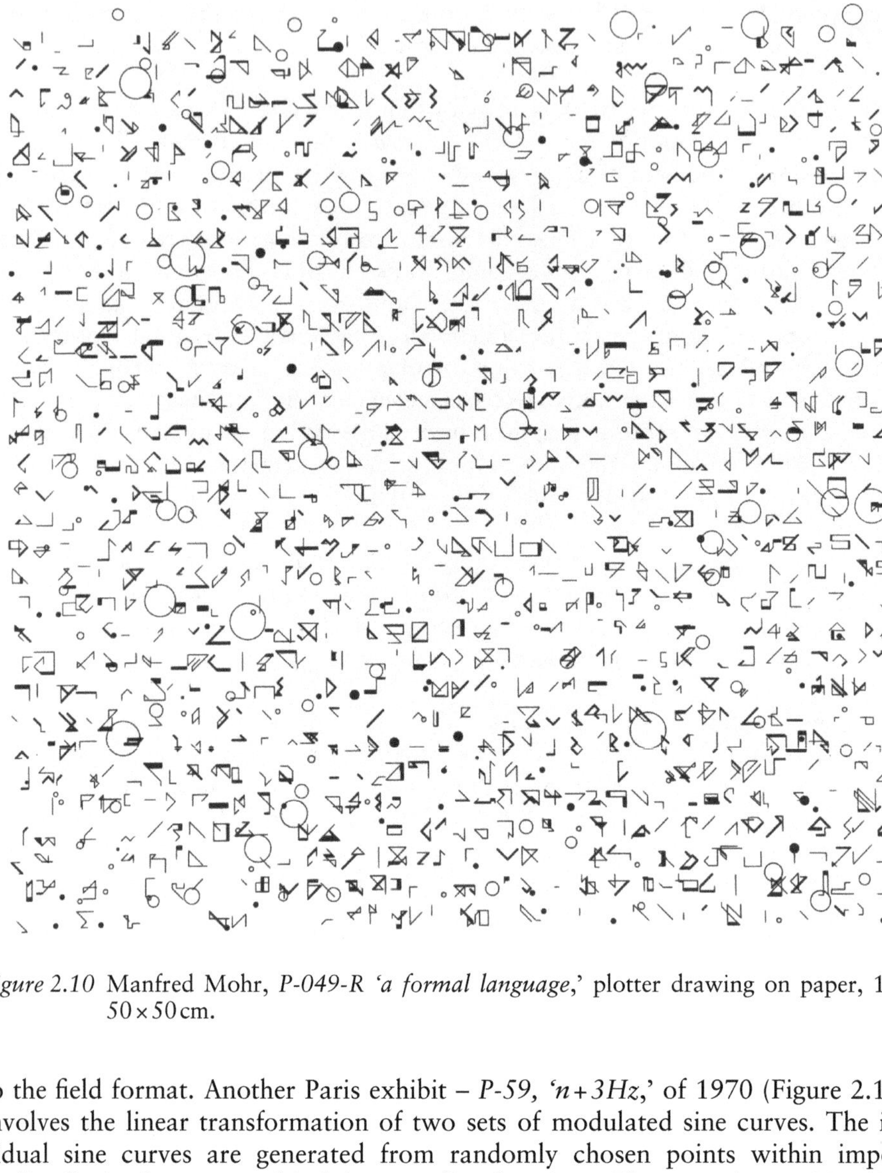

Figure 2.10 Manfred Mohr, *P-049-R 'a formal language,'* plotter drawing on paper, 1970, 50 x 50 cm.

to the field format. Another Paris exhibit – *P-59, 'n+3Hz,'* of 1970 (Figure 2.12) – involves the linear transformation of two sets of modulated sine curves. The individual sine curves are generated from randomly chosen points within imposed outline limits, by means of 3rd degree spline functions. The smooth repetitive linear oscillations are compacted and, at points, so compressed in relation to one another as to create effects of three-dimensional undulation – consistent with gentle folds in adjoining swatches of fabric, or detached areas of human skin.

One of the broader effects of works such as this (intended or otherwise) is the evocation of organic material *as* the embodiment of complex mathematical relations. An artist can represent such organic material as proportioned but, in Mohr's work, the mathematical aspect is manifest more lucidly through algorithmic methods (the implication being, of course, that the artist can profit by recourse to such methods, a point that is especially consistent with Bense's approach).

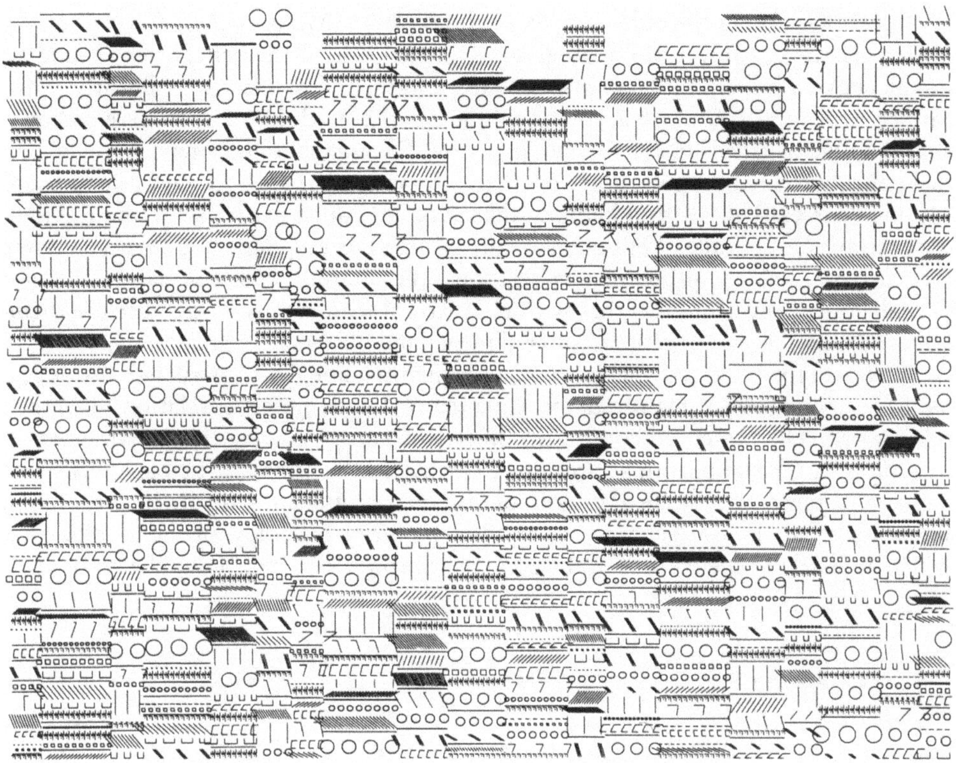

Figure 2.11 Manfred Mohr, *P-71, 'serielle zeichenreihung,'* plotter drawing on paper, 1970, 40 × 50 cm.

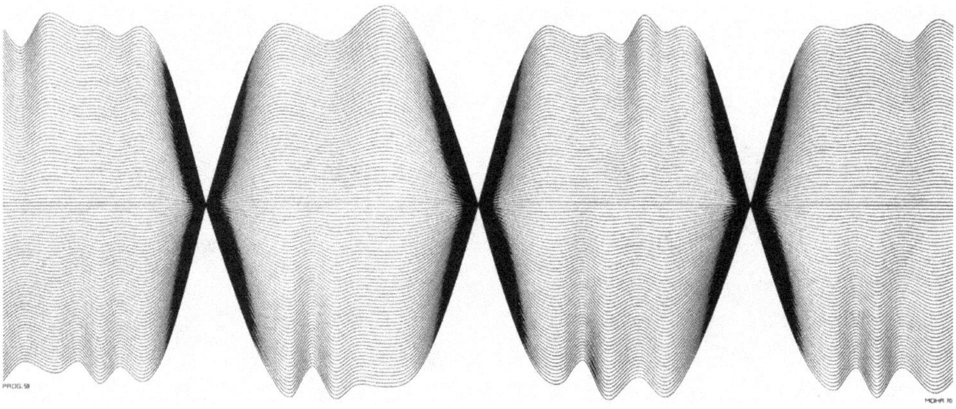

Figure 2.12 Manfred Mohr, *P-59 'n + 3Hz,'* plotter drawing on paper, 1970, 50 × 65 cm.

There is another basic format that has proven of enduring importance for Mohr. It centers on varying the cube. For example, in 1971, Mohr created *Cube Drawing P-80 a* (Figure 2.13). As Mohr observes, 'On each side of the cube, a set of random points above a horizontal line are connected and then in defined steps linearly transformed to their positions on a horizontal line.'[20] The work in question here creates a similar range of effects to *P-59*... but in a very different spatial context. In this piece, the reformed cubes appear as two cuboid boxes that have become crumpled to varying degrees. The relation between the space contained by the walls and the tight concentration of parallel – but occasionally crimped or bulging – lines that constitute their texture, sets up an interesting relation. The internal walls are darker in color than the outer ones, and together with the textural features just noted, declare themselves as representations of 'real' three-dimensional objects.

However, the way that images have been mathematically constructed also leaves its mark upon them. It manifests the same truth already noted in relation to Mohr's other work. The finite and contingent objects of nature involve exact mathematical structures in their appearance, and this extends even to those particular quirks that define an object as a *particular* example of such and such a thing. In the present work, for example, this is conveyed by the repetitive exactness of the parallel lines which are basic to the texture of the cuboids. Through this exactness, the crimped or

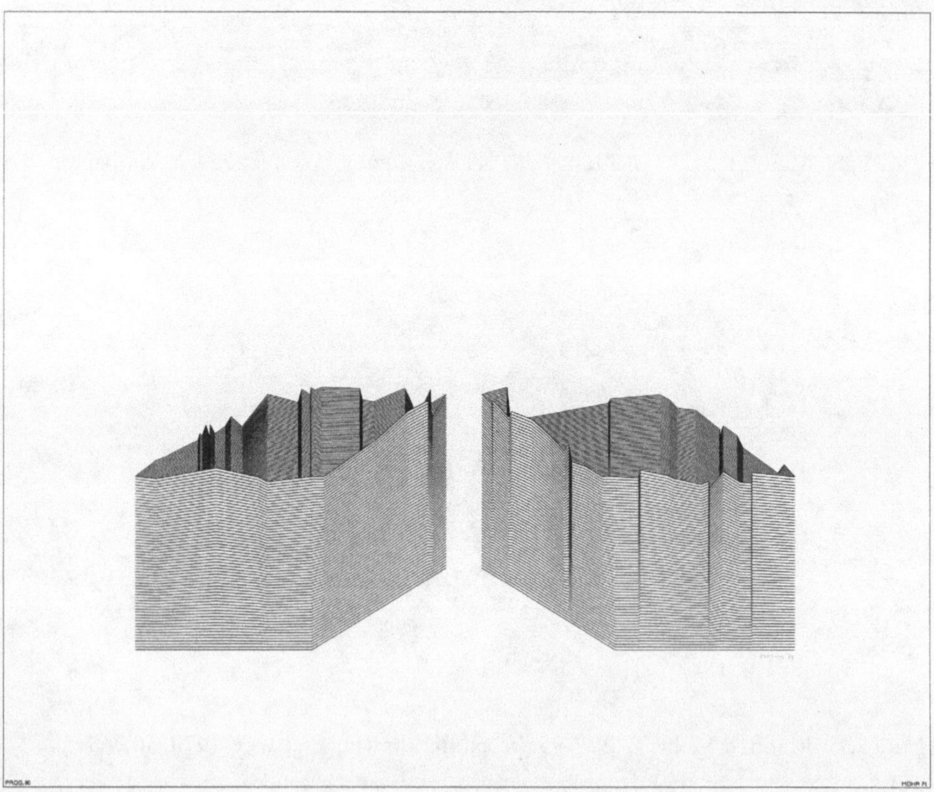

Figure 2.13 Manfred Mohr, *P-080a*, plotter drawing on paper, 1971, 44 × 54 cm.

bulging formal features are more evocative of mathematically derived transformations than they are of changes arising from physical pressure (though a faint sense of this latter possibility is also present).

The concept of 'cubic limit' came to occupy Mohr's creative activity in broader terms from 1973 onwards – linking up with the semiotic field structure approach. Indeed, one of the strongest features of Mohr's creative strategy is the progressive refinement and extension in new directions of important structures already established in his work. The digital medium allows him to make sense of the logical phases of his development with an exactness that might not be possible for an artist working with more traditional means. Here, for example, is how he describes the Cubic Limits strategy and his next phase.

> In 'Cubic Limit,' I introduce the cube into my work as a fixed system with which signs are generated. In the first part of this work phase (1972–76), an alphabet of signs is created from the twelve lines of a cube. In some works, statistics and rotation are used in the algorithm to generate signs. In others, combinatorial, logical and additive operators generate the global and local structures of the images. ... In 'Divisibility,' the cube is used again as a fixed structure to generate signs. The cube is divided into four sections by a horizontal and a vertical cut. Four independent rotations of a cube are projected onto the corresponding quadrants created by the cut. In order to visually stabilize the structure, two diagonally opposed quadrants (top right and bottom left), contain the same rotation. In the first part of this work phase (1980–84), the 'four-cut' is the basic structure with which the 'out-lines' form shapes and the 'in-lines' form signs.[21]

An example of this first 'Divisibility' phase is *P-306/O* (Figure 2.14). Interestingly, in this phase Mohr goes beyond the plotter-drawing format – having the plotter pen mark an acrylically primed canvas with liquitex paint (the surface sanded down to facilitate its marking). An interesting result of this is that the drawings take on a three-dimensional relief-like quality. Indeed, in the next stage of this phase (1984–1986) some of the algorithmically generated designs are embodied in cardboard and wood. The 'four cut' involved in the previous stage acts as a seed – with algorithms of graph patterns determining which features from the earlier generation are going to produce the new 'four-cut' form.

A decisive transition in Mohr's treatment of the cube occurs between 1987 and 1989 ('Dimensions II'), where he begins to use the hyper-cube. This is a structural relationship of eight interconnected cubes emergent from a series of rotations, and involving complex viewpoints. Each cube is presented through a square window, and four of them are shown through their frontal aspects (black) and four through their reverse aspects (grey). The algorithm deploys this separation of black and grey as a principle of combination.

This structure has proven decisive for Mohr's work hereafter down to the present. He observes,

> I first used the hypercube in 1978 in Dimensions I. I struggled for 2 years, made many drawings, but needed a few more years until my second attempt in 1987, to really understand the potential of this structure. During this second attempt to master n-dimensional structures my whole intellectual understanding changed

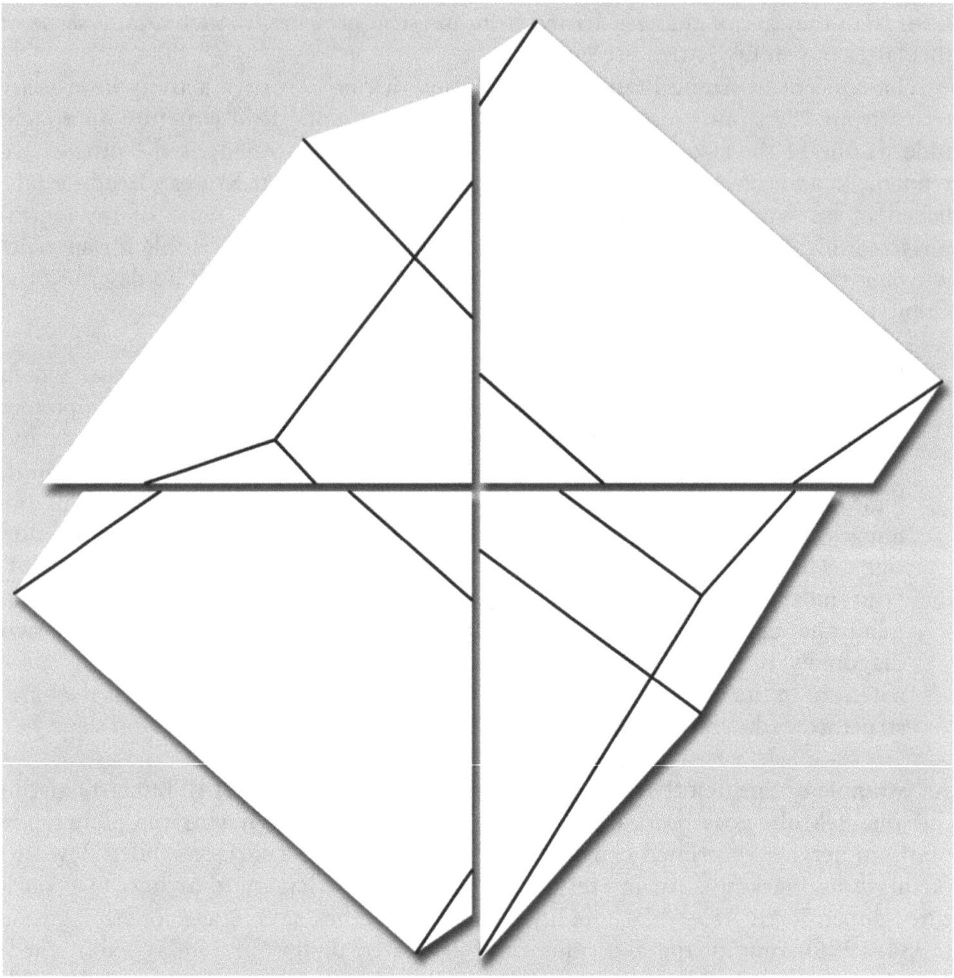

Figure 2.14 Manfred Mohr, *P-306-O*, acryl/canvas/wood, 1980–84, 250×250 cm.

> drastically and laid the foundation for a complete new approach, lasting until today. ... The structure itself as a visual whole was not of interest to me, but the potential of a complex system, a set of rules, by looking only at aspects of this structure to create semiotic signs. My reasoning was: for example, our alphabet has 26 letters, we never show all 26 of them as a system, but we carefully choose single letters and form words, sentences etc. ... I do the same with n-dimensional structures: I choose (invent) aspects from these systems and form 'sentences' with which I operate...'[22]

An example of this is *P-411/B* (Figure 2.15). Mohr's basic format – over and above digital methods – is the two-dimensional plane surface. Earlier, we noted a three-dimensional effect arising from copying the plotter-drawing on acrylically primed canvas. This has a subtle relation to the plane surface format – making it, as it were,

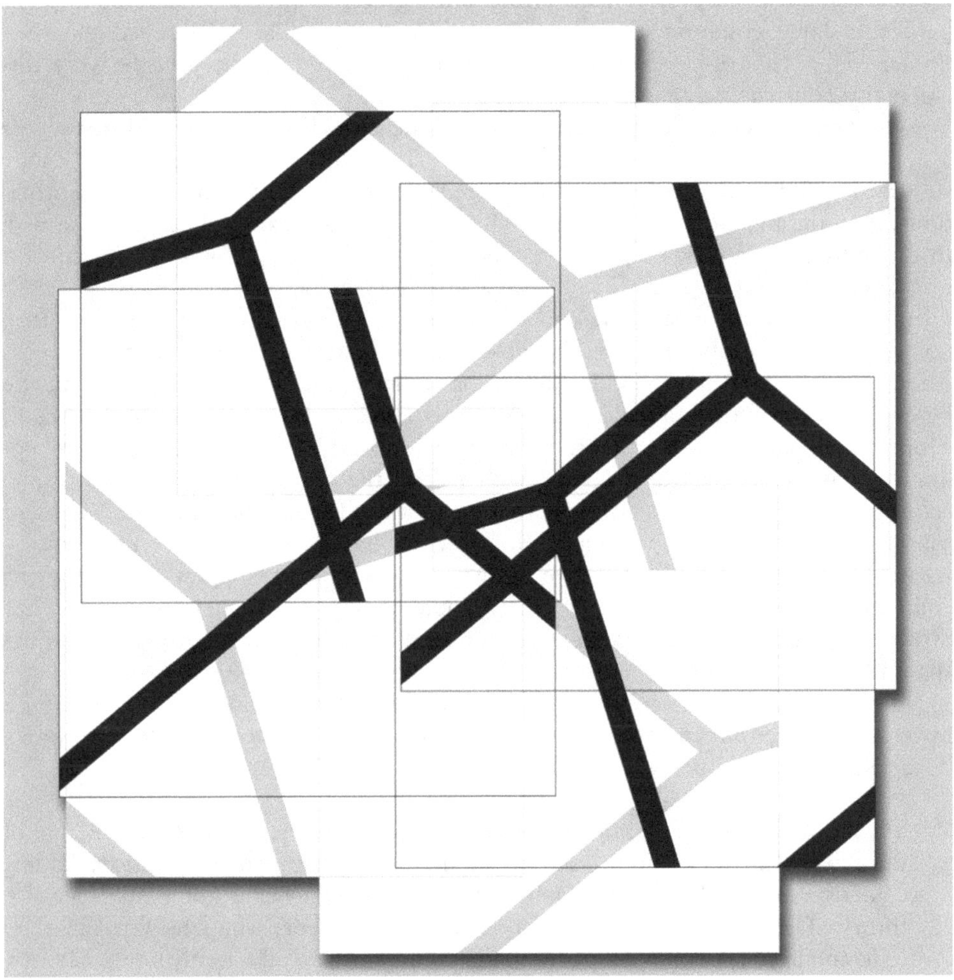

Figure 2.15 Manfred Mohr, *P-411-B*, acryl/canvas/wood, 1988, 164 × 151 cm.

more physically insistent than it would be as a drawing. But physical insistence, here, involves more than mere visual emphasis, for it is relevant to the evocation of construction and rotation as mathematical operations. The quality of paint and of the stretched canvas literally distance the formal configuration from the surrounding wall (or whatever) upon which it is physically placed. There is a notional motion of the work towards the viewer.

This optical momentum has a catalytic effect on the internal visual organization of the work. The square, and fine linear planar structures act as fixed reference markers through which the black and grey lines perform their suggested hypercube motions. At some points, the black cube-lines cover the grey ones and, at other points, the grey lines interrupt the black. This creates a curious effect of simultaneous dislocation and construction – of analysis and synthesis. Such a space is two-dimensional, but consistently creates the optical effect of three-dimensional space *in the process of its geometric production*. After all, the hypercube is constructed from a point extended into a line, then into a square, and then to a cube rotated in the perpendicular. Geometric structure, in other words, is a space of implied construction as well as that of presently given shapes and solids. Mohr's hypercube work discloses this constructive space.

However, it does so through a static two-dimensional surface – and this is where a significant problem of interpretation arises. When Mohr's hypercube variations are shown alongside one another, or if presented temporally – as animated transformations, then the hypercube structure of Mohr's conception can be broadly discerned. In the individual works, they cannot. The logic of their algorithmic construction is not visible – they appear only as geometric abstraction.

But this is by no means the end of the story. The space-in-construction effect noted above, is not only an abstract one – it carries material connotations insofar (as we have seem) even the particularities of matter such as the crumpling of a box can be expressed in mathematical terms. And this leads to the ultimate significance of Mohr's hypercube developments. Even if their exact algorithmic origins are not immediately manifest, they have, nevertheless the unmistakable precision and economy of techno-design – of something synthesized from constituent elements or aspects. Through this appearance, Mohr's cubic works evoke *space as matrix* – where basic geometrical forms are shown in a way that suggests their shifting embodiment in the emergence of microscopic or even molecular material. They evoke possible structures of appearance at levels visible only when the eye probes space through technology.

Mohr's subsequent phases take this further, coming to operate, for example, with hypercubes of six dimensions. In due course, Mohr felt the need, in 1999, to introduce color. He explains:

> The steady increase of complexity in my work forced me to reconsider the use of this b/w binary system in order to find a more adequate visual expression. Adding colors to my work describe spatial relationships which are not based on color theory. The colors should be seen as random elements, showing through their differentiation the complexity and spatial ambiguity essential to my work. My new work is shown as inkJet images, and also on a flat screen hanging on a wall presenting a slow motion animation, so that day after day different images appear.[23]

With these works, Mohr makes a random selection of four 'diagonal-paths' from a repertoire of 23,040 (32×720) possible paths. The selection is shown in two-dimensional projection, and then subjected to further complex design procedures. Ultimately,

> The hypercube is rotated in 6-dimensional space and then projected into 2-dimensional space. The resulting image overlays the color fields from front to back. Together with the 'diagonal-paths,' the resulting image creates unimaginable constellations.[24]

The phrase 'unimaginable constellations' is very instructive here. If we consider *P-701/B* of 1999 (Plate 4), we have a work whose appearance – vis-à-vis its linear sharpness and angularity, and – as it were – *sanitized* color declares it as a product of digital art. This is complemented by the visual rhythm of the work – which suggests a process of mathematical construction. Of course, images of this kind, may be produced, in principle, through traditional painting methods inspired by the look of digital images, but there is something about Mohr's color works that declare the digital style with the greatest insistency. Even if we cannot recognize the hypercube programming simply from the individual work, its composition has a sophisticated visual logic that presents itself as one moment in a constructive process. The process is too complex to be given in a single image or to be imagined by the viewer, but the color/line relation in these works has an inviting clarity that points towards its algorithmic origins – and does so, indeed, much more than Mohr's earlier cubic explorations. Indeed, his conception of color is, in essence, technoscientific. Colors are 'secondary qualities' arising from the causal impact of 'primary qualities' – in the form of space occupying bodies and forces. Colors do not describe the primary qualities themselves, but are, rather, modes of perceptual adaptation whereby the human sensorium makes the effects of primary qualities easier to comprehend. Mohr treats color in exactly this way. Colors in his work function as they do in the basic ontology of the world – to clarify order, as can be seen in another relevant work, *P-703_C* of 2000 (Plate 5).

Conclusion

Mohr's work takes the tradition of Bense's generative aesthetics to its most developed point – but, at the same time, also shows its conceptual irrelevance. The importance of generative aesthetics extends no further than being historical catalyst and general inspiration. Frieder Nake realized this, observing that

> Although some exciting insight into the nature of aesthetic processes was gained this way, the attempt failed miserably. Nothing really remains today of [the] theory that would arouse any interest for other than historical reasons.[25]

Nake suggests, in general terms, that Bense's approach denudes the subjective dimension of the aesthetic. This is true, but we can take the critique much deeper. Bense himself claimed that

> The system of generative aesthetics aims at a numerical and operational description of characteristics of aesthetic structures. ... Aesthetic structures contain aesthetic information only in so far as they manifest innovations, or rather innovations of probable reality. The aim of generative aesthetics is the artificial production of probabilities, differing from the norm using theorems and programs.[26]

For Bense, this all centers on the production of order from disorder, or from order itself, or from a combination of order and disorder. But even if we admit – as many have done – that the aesthetic involves some enjoyment of unity in diversity (or vice-versa) in how things present to the senses, it introduces variables that overwhelm Bense's approach.

The big problem is that mathematical relations and procedures do not even begin to sufficiently determine the meaning of order and disorder in the aesthetic context. Their criteria vary *massively* on the basis of historical, geographic, class, race, and gender contexts. Indeed, they are also influenced by the cultural significance of what kind of sensory manifold it is that carries the aesthetic 'information.' In the case of the arts this brings the issue to a higher dimension entirely insofar as the aesthetic response is not simply about some satisfaction in beholding sensory 'information'; rather the nature of the information – of the aesthetic meaning of the signs – is determined by how they relate to other works in that historical tradition, and by the character of our personal experience of the world. Specifically, it is *originality* in how the work presents some aspect of the world, that is decisive for our aesthetic involvement. If this were not the case, then aesthetic information would be no more than mere decorative value.

Bense himself realized the importance of originality – but only in the reduced and distorted sense of disorder, randomness, and the like. But originality in the aesthetic context involves relations between past, future, and possible ways of interpreting aesthetic information. There is no such information without that horizon of interpretation but, of course, as soon as we acknowledge this, then the concept of aesthetic information reveals itself as useless. It is centered on measurement, but what is measured is only the physical configuration of the aesthetic manifold's appearance – not its *aesthetic meaning*. This is why Mohr's work is so important. Mohr is clearly still inspired by Bense, but his own kind of generative aesthetics is based on programs that utilize motifs from his own earlier works, and thence personal historical experience (rather than some grand vision of objective aesthetic information). And the twists and turns Mohr gives to this in devising new algorithms are not mere deductions from what he has done. Some possibilities are favored over others. These may involve buiding elements of randomness in the designs, but these randomness inclusions are *chosen* and, as such, reflect a meta-creative viewpoint. They are original in an authentic artistic sense.

In effect, Bense's generative aesthetics turns out to be one of Modernist art theory's great sunsets – still hoping to shine the light of progress and advancement towards higher levels of artistic advancement, but fast sinking away. Whilst this reductive utopian aspiration was inspirational in driving early pioneers to think in terms of digital art, their actual practice goes far beyond it. Nake suggests that, whilst Bense's approach is generally a failure, it does succeed in drawing attention to the importance of the sign.We are told that

> A semiotically grounded aesthetics not only opens the discourse of Postmodernism, it also links parts of aesthetics to informatics. ... The concept of the sign is central to informatics, to aesthetics and to Postmodernism. Postmodernism is the times of enhanced artificiality.[27]

However, the notion of the 'sign' as developed by C.S. Peirce, Ferdinand de Saussure and others, is very much a part of Modernist technological thinking – seeking to analyze living communicative phenomena into their constituent parts and basic operational rules; or to put it another way, figuring out what is distinctive to them, determining what makes them work. In the cybernetic form of this investigation we go beyond the analysis of signs in the abstract, to *exploiting* them – applying them in new contexts involving the prediction and control of behavior. Far from Postmodernism being the time of 'enhanced artificiality,' its post-industrial core involves ever accelerating levels of *real* control.

The dimension of artificiality is more of a factor in the means whereby this control is developed – namely global consumerism. Consumerism is based on products – from gadgets to clothes, and 'lifestyles' – that are designed not to last, or to fall out of fashion quickly. It also depends on publicity, and the plethora of information made available electronically, which results in it being harder to distinguish between facts, disinformation, and 'false news.'

All this might be described as 'artificiality' but it is only a superstructural effect of the technological innovation that drives post-industrial production. Digital art is an aspect of this drive. It is, we will recall, literally Postmodern – in the sense of not searching for aesthetic purity in the manner of late Modernist work, but rather exploring the communicative possibilities opened up through digital space and electronic virtuality. These features are, of course, key aspects of that naturalization of technology whereby, in the Postmodern era, it becomes a kind of habitat. Even Mohr's explicit use of the hypercube as a formal alphabet goes far beyond the mere creation of signs, as such. It is a principle of generation that also illuminates aspects of space itself – as a field of hidden and yet to be constructed aspects.

We have seen examples of this explorative drive throughout the present chapter. Noll, Nees, and Nake, and Mohr, all adopt the principle of formalized reciprocity – wherein the computer does not simply follow instructions, but is programmed to create possibilities, that the programmer can choose or reject. This artistic strategy is used to generate fundamental works which – however visually basic they may seem now – explore how three-dimensions can be projected through forms that penetrate the two-dimensional plane obliquely, or by creating forms that repeat the basic planar structure recessionally. The same three artists develop field structures, where signs are distributed across the plane in harmony with its two-dimensionality.

These strategies, in fact, are characteristic of the first generation of digital artists in general – also being found in figures such as Vera Molnar and Paul Brown amongst others. They all create works with either the visual thrust of geometric simplicity, or (in the case of the fields) component elements that *look like* machines, or mathematical equations or terms, even though they are not things. Of course, Modernist artists often represent machines or their effects of mechanisms, but in these early digital artists, the technological domain is embodied and celebrated *as the basis of artistic production* as well as featuring in aspects of subject-matter. Vera Molnar, for example, realized the potential of computer-generated form as a continuation of her interest in abstract art – an area she was exploring from the late 1940s. Indeed, if one studies the development of her works, they involve an economy of compositional space, and precise character of individual forms that appear to anticipate digital space.[28] Given this, it is hardly surprising that, in the late 1960s, she learned basic coding in Fortran. In 1968–1969, this gave rise to a number of work such as *Interruptions*, where planar-orientated fields of visual signs are destabilized at various points, through the subtle placing of empty spaces. In some cases, indeed, the field of forms is constituted from barb-like angularities that both maintains and, to some degree, disrupts, the regular rhythm of the field. This tension is not the Bensian Modernist reduction of art and the aesthetic to the purity of mathematical relations; rather it is the visual manifestation of new *experiment* – the construction of digital space enabled by the computer technology that drives Postmodern society.[29] Technology is both the means and deep iconology of digital art in its time of emergence.

Notes

1 The Catalog tape is online at www.youtube.com/watch?v=TbV7loKp69s.
2 See D.P. Henry 'The Henry drawing computer' and John H. Whitney 'Permutations,' both included in Reichardt, *Cybernetic Serendipity*, September 1968, p. 50, and p. 65, respectively.
3 See A. Michael Noll's paper 'First-Hand: Early Digital Art at Bell Telephone Laboratories, Inc,' *Leonardo*, Vol. 49, No. 1 (2016), pp. 55–65. An accessible online draft version can be found at http://ethw.org/First-Hand:Early_Digital_Art_At_Bell_Telephone_Laboratories,_Inc (accessed September 4, 2017).
4 The Memo can be found online at http://noll.uscannenberg.org/Art%20Papers/BTL%20 1962%20Memo.pdf.
5 See Clement Greenberg, 'Modernist Painting,' included in John O'Brian (ed.), *The Collected Essays and Criticism. Volume IV: Modernism with a Vengeance*, 1993, pp. 85–94.
6 'Human or Machine: A Subjective Comparison of Piet Mondrian's "Composition with Lines" and a Computer–Generated Picture,' *The Psychological Record*, Vol. 16. No. 1 (January 1966), pp. 1–10. Allusion to this and other works by Noll is found in his 'A subjective comparison of Piet Mondrian's Composition with lines 1917,' included in Reichardt, op. cit., p. 74.
7 Stuart Preston 'Art ex Machina,' *The New York Times*, Sunday, April 18, 1965. The account of the 'Computer Generated Pictures' exhibition just presented is based on A. Michael Noll's paper 'The Howard Wise Gallery Show of Computer-Generated Pictures (1965): A 50th-Anniversary Memoir,' *Leonardo*, Vol. 49, No. 3 (2016), pp. 232–239.
8 See http://noll.uscannenberg.org/Art%20Papers/BTL%201962%20Memo.pdf.
9 Christoph Klutsch, 'Information Aesthetics and the Stuttgart School,' included in Hannah B. Higgins, and Douglas Kahn (eds.), *Mainframe Experimentalism: Early Computing and the Foundation of the Digital Arts*, 2012, pp. 65–89. This reference, p. 67.
10 'The Projects of Generative Aesthetics,' quoted in Klutsch, op. cit., p. 71. An English translation of this important text is included in Reichardt, op. cit., pp. 57–60. It can also be found online (preceded by the German version) at www.computerkunst.org/Bense_Manifest.pdf (accessed December 29, 2016).
11 See the interview with Nees at www.gasathj.com/tiki-read_article.php?articleId=42.
12 Some of Nees's drawings also appeared in the December 1964 edition of the journal *Grundlagenstudien aus Kybernetik und Geisteswissenschaft*, edited by Helmar Frank. His writing and work also features in Reichardt, op. cit.: 'Programming Stochastic Computer Graphics,' p. 79. Works reproduced include *23 Corners*, and *Corridor*, discussed in the present work.
13 Viewable online at http://magazin.spiegel.de/EpubDelivery/spiegel/pdf/46272435 (accessed December 29, 2016).
14 A good selection can be found in the online page of the Heike Werner Gallery for Computer Art and New Photography, www.heikewerner.com/nees_en.html (accessed December 29, 2016).
15 Quoted from an email sent by Nake to the author on January 30, 2018; with further explanatory points made in another email from Nake to the author on January 31, 2018.
16 www.vam.ac.uk/content/journals/research-journal/issue-02/computer-art-at-the-v-and-a (accessed January 2, 2017). The Klee-inspired work discussed here was one of those reproduced in Nake's article 'Notes on the Programming of Computer Graphics,' included in Reichardt, op. cit., pp. 77–78.
17 See Mohr's website at www.emohr.com/ww2_out.html.
18 Quoted from www.emohr.com/ww2_out.html.
19 Images of all the artworks by Mohr discussed in this Chapter can be found at www.emohr.com/ww4_out.html (accessed January 11, 2017).
20 Quoted from www.emohr.com/ww4_out.html.
21 Quoted from www.emohr.com/ww2_out.html.
22 Personal email correspondence with the author, January 2017. The hypercube form had already become an object of interest for digital art pioneers, through work in 1966 by Noll and colleagues at Bell Laboratories. They were the first to digitally generate the animated unfolding of such a cube. See the Noll's personal website version of http://ethw.org/First-Hand:Early_Digital_Art_At_Bell_Telephone_Laboratories,_Inc.

23 Quoted from www.emohr.com/ww4_out.html.
24 Quoted from www.emohr.com/ww4_out.html.
25 Nake, 'Art in the Time of the Artificial,' *Leonardo*, Vol. 31, No. 3, pp. 163–164, 1998. This reference, p. 163.
26 Max Bense in Reichardt, op. cit., pp. 57–58.
27 Nake, 'Art in the Time of the Artificial,' pp. 163–164.
28 Molnar's entire *œuvre* is set out in a chronologically successive order on her website at www.veramolnar.com/diapo.php.
29 For Molnar's work, see also http://dam.org/artists/phase-one/vera-molnar/artworks-bodies-of-work/works-from-the-1960s-70s.

3 Digital Plasticity and Its Objects

In the previous chapter we saw how early developments of digital art under the influence of Bense had a predominantly abstract orientation – distributing signs as fields in alignment with the picture plane, or creating three-dimensional optical effects through forms projected obliquely from the plane. The realization of a fully developed virtual three-dimensional digital space, however, proved elusive. One might suppose that the breakthrough in this respect would come from those digital artists whose interests were figurative. This turned out not to be the case. In the next chapter, indeed, we will see the painstaking explorative development of early linear digital figuration, but will note, also, how this did not attain any high level of development until the mid-1980s.

The real breakthrough towards three-dimensional digital space occurs in artists whose work is mainly abstract, and who took advantage of the invention of the color frame-buffer – a complex tool which enables real time work upon the emerging digital image. This allows the artist to work much more efficiently on those nuances of color, shading, and texture, which create emphatic three-dimensional illusion. The artist can negotiate the visual stuff of three-dimensionality. Let us call these three-dimensional experiments *digital objects*.

Of course, in the field of abstract painting, many artists have used three-dimensional plastic elements akin to the digital objects just described and some key artists, indeed, have composed primarily in terms of 'realistic' presentations of such abstract forms (for example, Yves Tanguy and Roberto Matta). However, in the computer context this has a special significance. Digital space is – potentially – a systematic alternative to both that of ordinary perception *and* that of conventional pictorial art. But the distinctiveness of this alternative is something that demands the digital *imprimatur* – the sheer *look* of digital origins that we discussed in the Introduction to this book. The two-dimensional configurations of early digital art have this, but the idea of digital space as a radical alternative needs the third-dimension also, presented in more insistent terms. It needs plasticity with a distinctive digital *imprimatur*.

Now, it is interesting that Tanguy's and Matta's abstract paintings not only have three-dimensional content per se, but often a realism that suggests *systematic* alternative worlds. This anticipates the distinctive virtuality of digital objects. Such objects are abstract but – both individually, and in their relations with one another – can have a three-dimensional plasticity whose realism exceeds Tanguy's and Matta's. In its most developed form, this digital *imprimatur* can involve systematic *trompe-l'œuil* effects. As noted earlier, this allows artists to create forms that exemplify the formative basis of objectness per se. And, of course, once this strategy is established, it can easily be adapted to figurative ends, enabling the virtual representation of ordinary kinds of visual thing and/or states of affairs.

In this chapter, then, we consider the origins of digital plasticity and its objects. Part One, addresses early steps towards this taken in the 1970s by Edward Zajec, and also by Ruth Leavitt and Duane M. Palyka. Part Two explores the amplifications of this in David Em's innovations of the 1970s and 1980s and beyond. Attention is then paid to William Latham's evolutionary programs. Finally, some further sophisticated expressions of digital plasticity and the virtual object are considered in the work of Gerhard Mantz.

One

By 1968, Edward Zajec had turned to computing as a way of solving compositional issues in his painting – arising from the repetition of shape. His more specific problem was to find visually challenging ways to create a visual whole out of discrete units.

An important breakthrough occurred in 1971, with a project entitled *The Cube: Theme and Variations* (Figure 3.1).[1] The matrix of the project is an extended

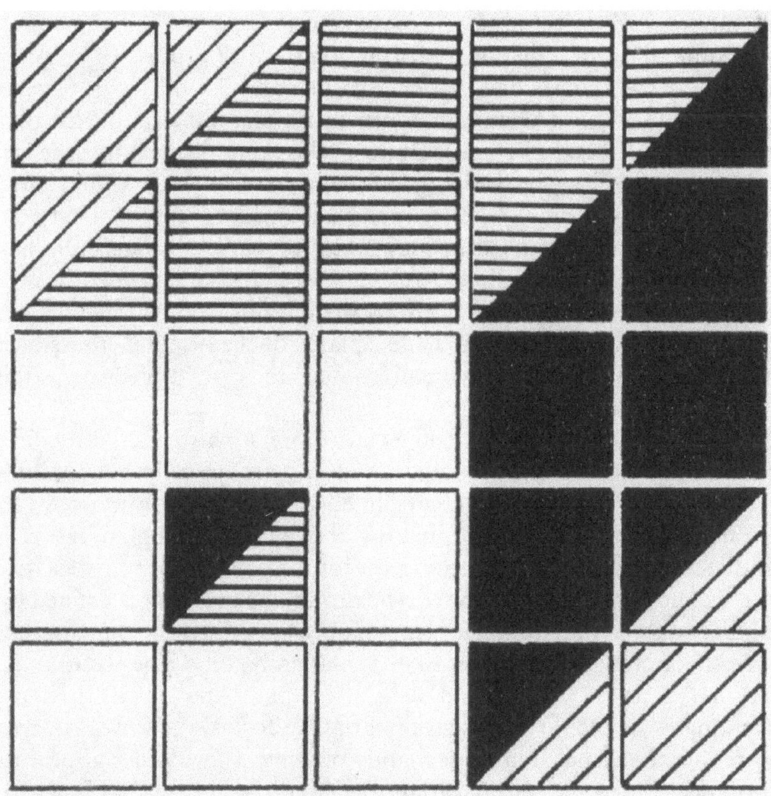

Figure 3.1 Edward Zajec, *The Cube: Theme and Variations*, 1971, image from page 17 of the 1971 TVC exhibition catalogue at the Palazzo Costanzi in Trieste Italy.

hollow cube that projects obliquely towards the viewer. The face of the cube is white; the roof and visible interior floor is composed of densely packed horizontal lines; its side elevation is presented in black. Areas not occupied by the cube are presented through diagonal lines. However, the vital point is that this visual whole is constituted *entirely* from a grid of twenty-five equally sized squares. The eight that define the cube's face are plain white. Its optical three-dimensionality (external and internal) is suggested by supplementary squares – some of which are entirely black, some of which are composed entirely from the densely packed horizontals or from the diagonal lines, and some of which combine these (half one and half the other).

Initially, Zajec tried to derive compositions from this structure by simply rearranging the units on the basis of computer-generated random probabilities. However, he felt that the outcomes of this strategy were poor – in his words, 'If you have seen one, you have seen them all.'[2] In effect, he was trying to create compositional 'sentences' by the random juxtaposition of the alphabetic elements in his system. Zajec felt that what was needed instead was an approach using a more consciously linguistic model. On these terms, the white squares would be programmed to function as words – as formative elements. The other squares from the original structure would be programmed as a grammar for 'sentence' construction – functioning either as connectives, or as supplements. Through this, the computer would generate possibilities for distributing white squares; and for possibilities of developing these through different combinations with the secondary squares.

The mainframe computer that Zajec was working with during the TVC project allowed two output modes – a linear one that created pen and ink drawings using a computer-controlled plotter, and a computer-controlled alpha-numeric device that printed characters in shades of grey. These output modes were devised in order to deal with the computer's inefficiency in filling out solid areas (which would have required color for optimal rendition).[3] Let us consider some examples. First, *tvc 28223* (1971). This is one of the plotter drawings. In it, the basic cube structure has been multiplied into a number of smaller, extended examples, independently presented. Indeed, these examples seem to be, in effect, the interior of the original cube, extracted and transformed into a solid. The white squares of the original cube's face have been rearranged to form connecting structures – in three cases appearing as the exterior of partial bridge or tunnel.

The work *tvc 78478* (Figure 3.2) has a somewhat more sophisticated structure. The white squares are modified to define extended cubes with optically hollow interiors. These are arranged in a repetititive crennellated format in the lower row. A similar structure starting at the right edge of the row above it is interrupted by a rectangular prism and stepped wedge prisms sitting on top of one another (a structure repeated above the second of the crenellations). The ground of the form is defined by evenly distributed diagonals – constituting a plane upon which the three-dimensional cube extensions are sited. However, there is a key visual ambiguity. The white crennelations have regular squares that extend below the base line of the pattern. Whereas the other squares define three-dimensional optical forms, the lower squares in the second row render the visual statement slightly opaque. They do not appear to serve any clear form enclosing function. A variant opacity arises in *tvc 87892* where the white square and the rectangle in the top right corner are incompletely defined to their left boundaries.

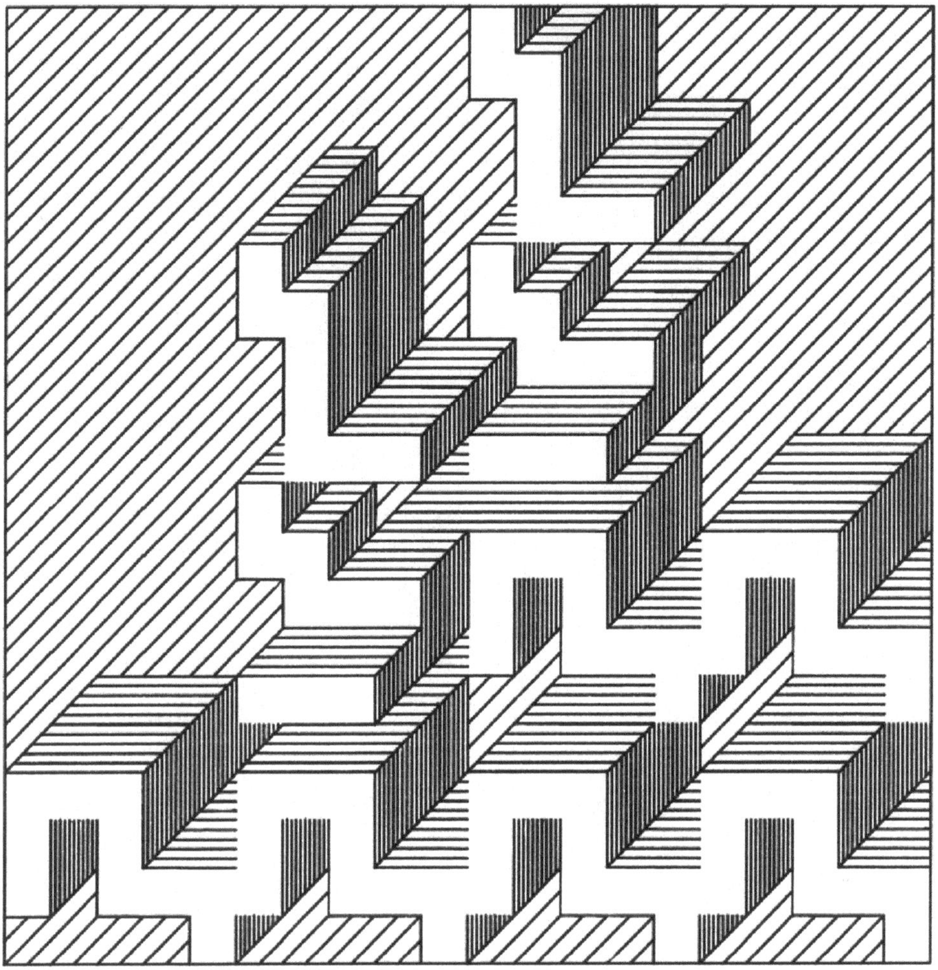

Figure 3.2 Edward Zajec, *tvc 78478*, 1971, produced on an IBM 7040 computer using a 563 plotter (India ink on paper), size: 14 × 14 inches. Created at the Computer Lab Centre of the University of Trieste.

Three-dimensional form and presence is – ironically enough – less ambiguously defined in an alpha-numeric work. An example of this is *tvc 38839* (Figure 3.3). The irony arises through the fact that whilst the image is a manifest composite of dots and numbers, their optically composite character is suspended by the vigor with which the whole allows *space as volume* to be declared. This effect is, in part, enabled, through the extended cubes and cube-prism combinations being presented as pure solids with no interior.

Now, we must recall that in these different works, the basic units (the face of the cube in white squares, and the horizontals, diagonals, and blacks which define its extension) are rearranged by the computer to make different statements about the basic cube structure. There is something extremely formal about this strategy – that

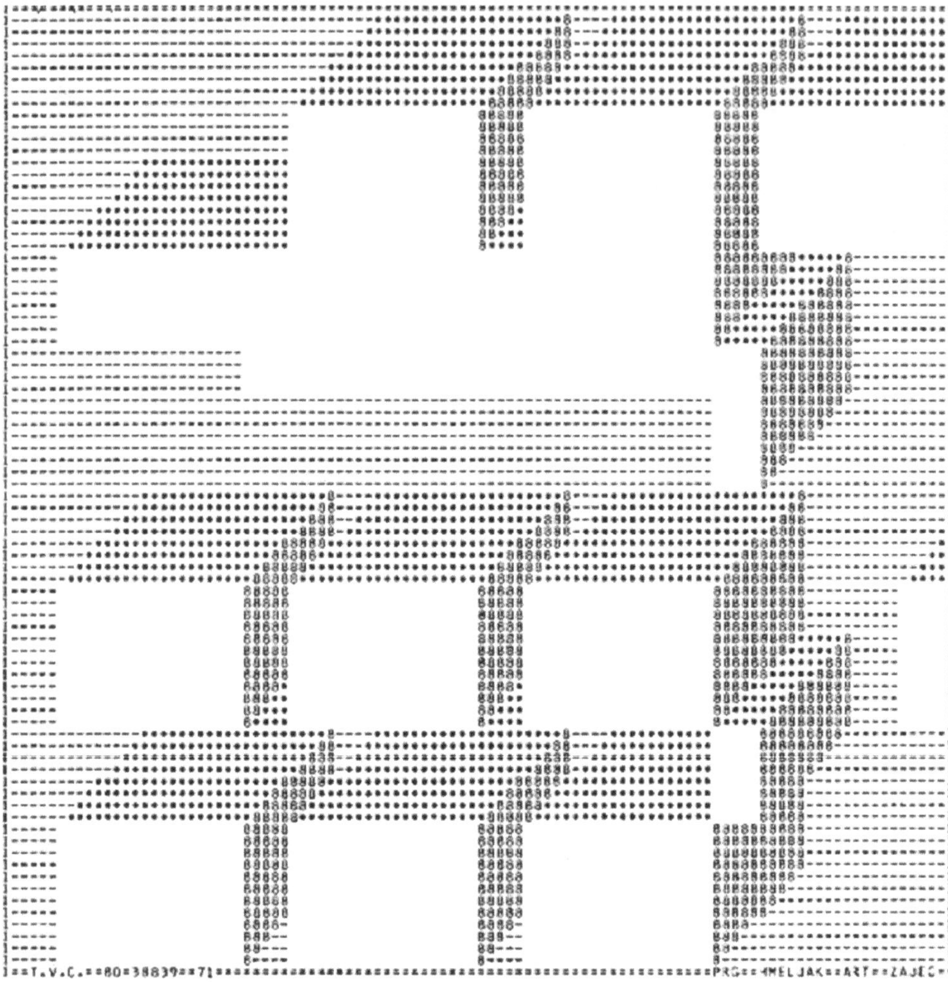

Figure 3.3 Edward Zajec, *tvc 38839*, 1971, produced on an IBM 7040 computer using an alphanumeric line printer (typewriter ink on paper), size: 16 × 11 inches. Created at the Computer Lab Centre of the University of Trieste.

links it, in practice, to the Bensian tradition. However, the decisive point is that Zajec is finding a digital vocabulary for the description of three-dimensional space. Sometimes it is literal; in other cases it has opacities – in which case it is exploring the optical possibilities for expressing three-dimensional space-occupancy. And this means, in effect, exploring its aesthetic potential.

The importance of this strategy is that instead of three-dimensional digital space being posited as some zone or container for objects, it is created as a space of meaning – of configurations which are autonomous formulations of a spatial language, and which both describe it with literal structures, and more opaque ones (in the sense noted earlier). This represents an important break with the two-dimensional fields and/or oblique creations of three-dimensional illusion that characterizes the artists discussed in the previous chapter. For one thing, the distribution of white squares in the tvc works is often closely aligned with the ground plane, so that there is a counterpoint between the affirmation of the plane and the contrary motion towards recession. For another thing, in using diagonals, tightly packed horizontals and verticals, and black, Zajec creates *shading* effects from visual devices that also have a strong decorative loading. Both these features, of course, are realizations of the aesthetic potential noted above.

Of course, Zajec's patterns look like the ambiguous 'see it like this, or see it like that' figures which are often used to represent the optical ambiguity of perceived configurations. However, it is one thing to use a pattern to illustrate a theory, and another thing entirely to generate such a spatial possibility by digital means – playing-off on probabilities and possibilities in the programming. In the latter approach, space is generated rather than consciously populated. It is the opening up of a world of visual possibility.

However, this comes at a price. In 1976, Zajec himself noted of his previous works that

> When the output of these programs was exhibited as stills in the form of computer graphics, I realized that the structure of the underlying process was of little or no relevance to the viewing public. This opened up a whole set of new problems which could be summed up by saying that no relevant contribution can be made by using the computer in the arts unless the public can be coinvolved as an active participant.[4]

Zajec's subsequent work, accordingly, is orientated mainly towards various interactive features of computer art, rather than the plasticity issue being presently considered. It is interesting that in the influential volume *Artist and Computer* by Ruth Leavitt (1976) the issue of plasticity is not developed much further. Exceptions to this include Leavitt's own work, and that of Duane M. Palyka.

Leavitt came to computing from a background in abstract painting and, gaining access to computer technology, began to experiment with its artistic potential. Using a pre-existing program

> I drew and shaded pictures on a cathode ray tube using a light pen attachment. The program had features which made it superior to drawing by hand. But after 6 months I was frustrated with it. Everything I drew so freely on the scope was ultimately resolved into a grid. This dissatisfaction, coupled with the fact that I now knew more about how computers worked, led me to think of my own idea for a program.[5]

These remarks are especially important for present purposes, as they show Leavitt's recognition of the constraints of the two-dimensional grid, and yearning for a more plastic virtual space. She took steps towards this by devising her own program.

> My idea was to use the computer to simulate a rubber sheet and to stretch any patterns I wished to draw. Initially my patterns would be hard-edge, constructivist in style. But after distortion they would have the lyrical quality of abstract expressionism imparted to them. I have explored several patterns with this

> program, a linear one, one dealing with mass, a 3-dimensional projected figure, etc. Each series is unique, comprises a new style, and even requires its own method of stretching. I have used this 'stretching' program to create graphics and paintings.[6]

The fruits of this strategy can be discerned in a number of Leavitt's works from the mid-1970s. The *Prismatic Variation* and *Diamond Variation* series, for example, introduce virtual plasticity through the distribution, compression, and release of facetted forms.[7] *Inner City Variation II* involves trapezoid prisms with smaller protruding cubes, all of whose shapes are stretched slightly. The stretching changes these from regular geometric solids into more ambiguous bodies whose spatial identity is that of a virtual space-occupying item as such – i.e. a digital object.

Leavitt's compositions were executed mainly as screenprints, and, in works such as *Diamond Variations II*, involve colored structures. However, the real breakthrough in terms of digital plasticity involves shading effects based on more optical *gradations* of light rather than visual declarations based on mere difference of densities in how lines and dots within a grid are distributed or stretched.

Important work of this kind is found in another artist featured in the Leavitt's book, namely Duane M. Palyka. As far back as 1967, Palyka devised computer programs that created works on line-printer paper using a LP-12 line-printer (driven by a Bendix G-20 computer). This *CMU* series involves works constituted by field structures with contrasting densities and distributions of elements. These produce arrays of linear and/or angular and concentric forms. However, a major contribution towards digital plasticity is achieved through basic elements of tonal gradation. These emerge through the computer being programmed to print out text characters on top of one another at specific points in the field – as in *CMU 1* of 1967 (Figure 3.4).[8]

In 1974, Palyka took another major step forward through the use of color in a work called *Patterned Bubbles* (Figure 3.5). In this work, a colony of spheres with concave depressions (each with the apparent pupil of an eye at its base point) appear to be stretching the restraints of the netted forms that enclose them. The key feature here is how the concavity and other recessional features are evoked by nuanced optical gradations of shadow. Indeed, the three-dimensional loading arises as much from the elasticity suggested by these gradations as it does from the volume of space occupied. Of course, there is something of the biomorphic about this imagery – by virtue of the eye association – but the spatial refinements vis-à-vis the concavity and stretching effects make it more of a virtual object in the sense described at the beginning of this chapter. In his words,

> It was created by putting red, green and blue filters in front of a cathode ray tube, where each point was drawn by the computer one dot at a time and exposed to the film through each filter. Chance dictated the placement of the sphere-like forms, which pulled their surface patterns from the background grid. Patterns were also created randomly on the surface of the forms. Saturated color was an artifact of this new process of recording color images directly from the computer.[9]

The three-dimensional illusion involved in this use of color was based on a linkage of video and computer technology. The video factor allowed color effects to be

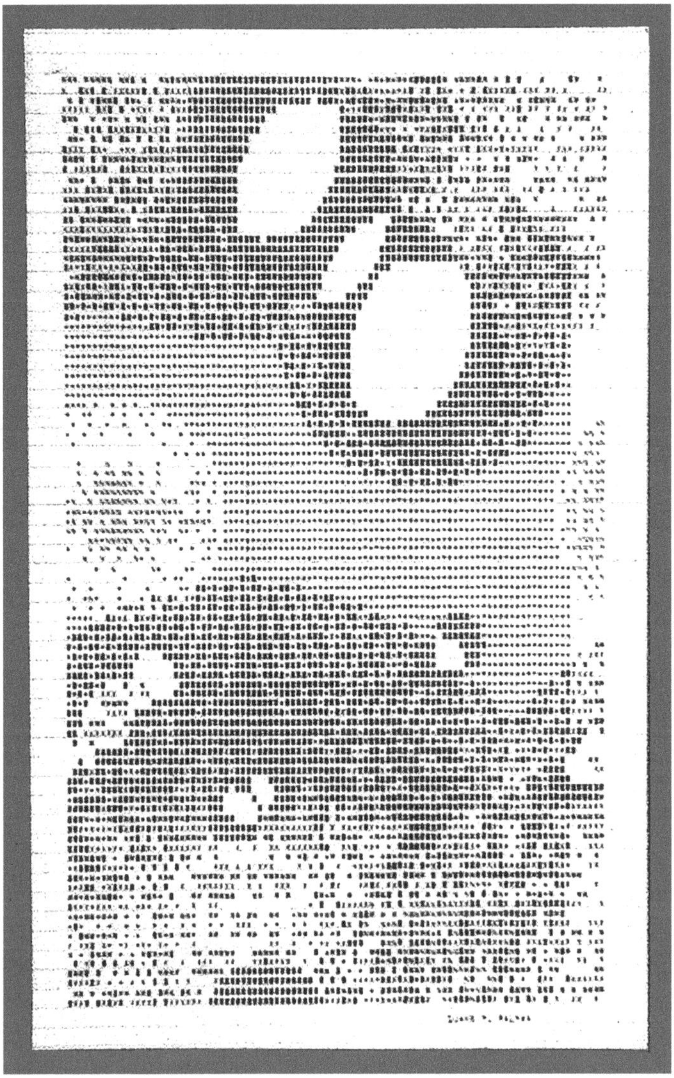

Figure 3.4 Duane M. Palyka, *CMU 1*, 1967, 9.5 × 16 inches (internal size of image).

synthesized in complex ways. However, around the time of Palyka's experiments in the mid-1970s the color factor in digital imagery was taken to an entirely new level by the invention of the frame-buffer. This device allows a single frame of video data (i.e. the content of a full video screen) to be both stored and displayed in real time, so that the artist can work directly on the image.

This offers, in effect, a blank virtual canvas which can be painted upon, electronically. As Palyka notes

> one can have the computer simulate a traditional art medium with which the artist is familiar and leave it to the artist to make the transition from the medium

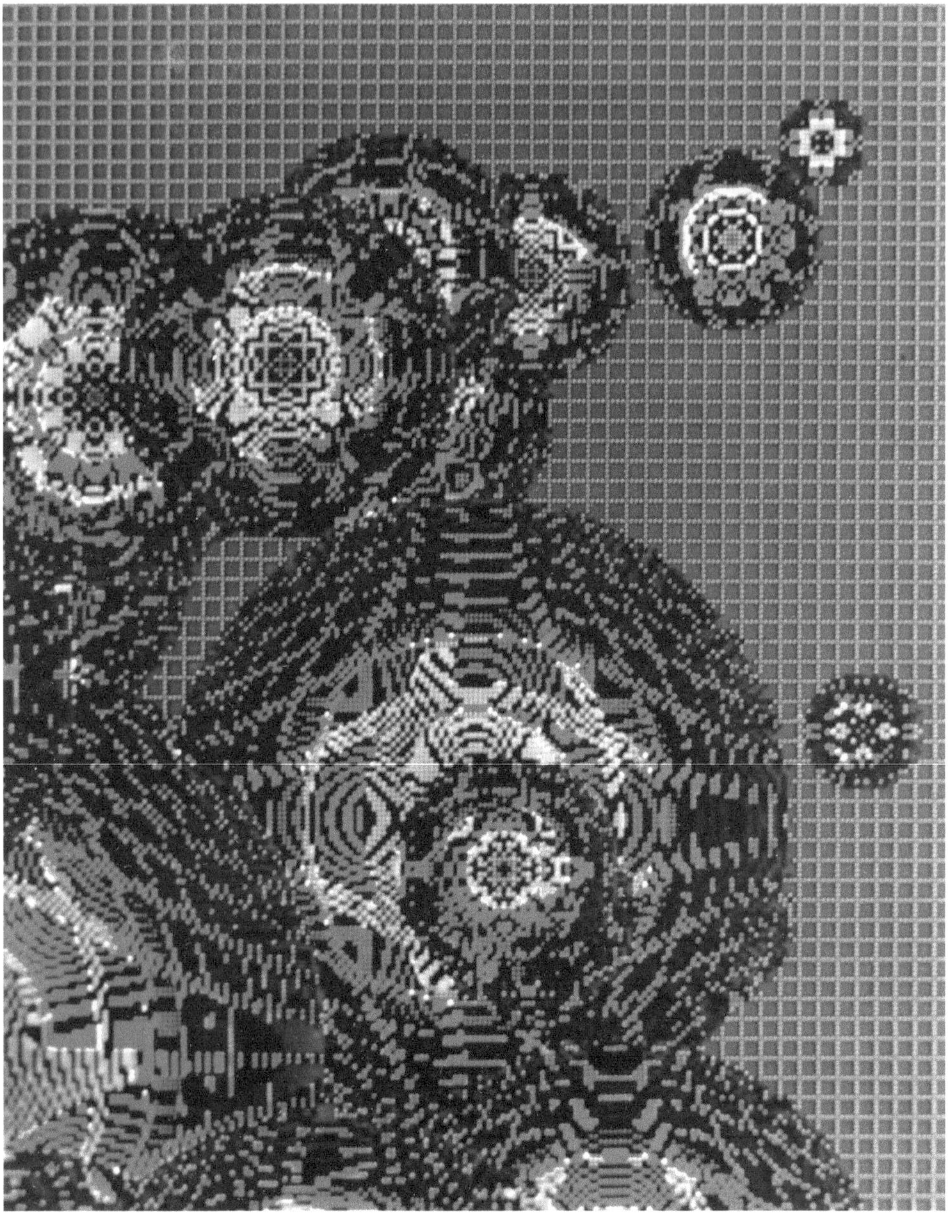

Figure 3.5 Duane M. Palyka, *Patterned Bubbles*, 1974, 8 × 10 inches (internal size of image).

he knows to the new medium on his own terms. The computer is very good at simulation and, coupled with a frame-buffer, this particular simulation is simple to implement. Using an electronic pen and tablet for input, the artist can be provided with a medium similar to acrylic painting. He can watch on a TV monitor a flow of color reflecting his hand and pen movements on the tablet. In fact, he can even select the brush sizes he wishes to use.[10]

Palyka's own work from 1975 includes some interesting untitled digital paintings which develop the *Patterned Bubble* thematic using the frame-buffer.

Interestingly, another artist – David Em – had himself begun modifying buffer-frame technology in 1975. It his work we now consider.

Two

A short biographical account of Em's career is, at the same time, a very effective way of revealing the technical creative issues that determine his work. He attended the Pennsylvania Academy of the Fine Arts in Philadelphia, where he studied painting. He became interested in the possibilities presented by acrylic paints, and had useful contacts with local manufacturers of the plastic base used in such paints. These helped his work in molding plastic-based paint into three dimensional structures. Unfortunately his instructors at the Academy could offer little help in these areas of interest. In an interview, he notes that 'I was told what I was doing was not art because it was made with the assistance, the intervention, of technological means.'[11] Hardly surprisingly, Em left after his third year. On moving to California he met the owner of a plastics factory who had artistic interests, and who cooperated with Em's creation of highly textured plastic sculptures. This led to an important breakthrough. In Em's words,

> I spent a lot of time lighting the pieces I was creating on the industrial machines, and after a while I began to think of them as three-dimensional canvases that I was composing with light instead of paint. The arrangement of highlights and shadows was the central focus of each piece.[12]

Em's exploration of these ideas was given a further boost when he acquired an old color tv set that still worked but had interesting distortions of color which could be altered vis-à-vis hue, saturation, and brightness. In following up ways of further controlling these effects through analog video synthesis, Em was led, eventually, to contact with the Xerox Research PARC in Palo Alto. Alvy Ray Smith – a scientist there, working in the field of digital imaging – had developed a paint program for a computer-controlled frame buffer (originally created by Dick Shoup at PARC). This allowed total control over hue, saturation, and brightness effects. Smith showed Em how to use the program –

> which consisted of an electronic stylus that could create lushly colored and exotically shaped electronic brush strokes on a color computer screen. Moving the stylus across a digitizing tablet controlled the location and movement of the electronic brushes on the screen. Up to this point no-one from a fine arts background had sat at the controls of the system. But the stylus and tablet setup were easy for me to adapt to because of my traditional painting background and my familiarity with video tools, and an hour later I had created my first computer image.[13]

Unfortunately, Xerox closed down its computer graphics lab soon after. However, Em then collaborated with a satellite engineer Larry Templeton working in video synthesis, to build a color frame buffer of his own utilizing Shoup's general architecture. A low-res version had been completed by the end of 1975.

Em was able to form a connection with the Jet Propulsion Lab of California Institute of technology. Here, Bob Holzman – a technician with an interest in the arts and Em's work – obtained funding for a computer graphics lab. However, despite Em's involvement with this, progress on his imaging projects was slow because of many practical operational difficulties. Fortunately, by 1977, some significant steps forward had been made, especially through the participation of Jim Blinn – who had devised programs for realistic simulation in digital imaging by presenting objects in terms of precisely textured surfaces. The Jet Propulsion Lab graphics section also achieved widespread recognition through their involvement in realizing the images transmitted to earth from the Mars Viking Lander expedition, and the Voyager flybys of Jupiter and Saturn.

All these factors influenced Em both technically and inspirationally. Over the next few years, for example, he was able to adapt Blinn's programs for his own purposes. In his words,

> The system's ability to manipulate vast amounts of picture information with great speed and flexibility allowed me to develop new working procedures. Ideas came up that would not have occurred to me otherwise, and the images began growing into and out of each other. Eventually I was able to use the computer intuitively, and as the tool became more and more transparent to me, I began to explore the unique qualities of the computer as an art medium, to see where it obeyed my commands and where it controlled my actions.[14]

For Em, the great advantage of the computer medium was the way it allowed him to work in formal areas very different from one another, by switching programs. He was able to study symmetry and geometric arrangements, and alternate between the current stage of the image's progress and considerations based on its stored previous formats. His entire sense of what it meant to compose an image underwent change because of features distinctive to the digital medium. Again, in his words,

> When a creative fork in the road appeared, I could save the current stage of the image in memory, explore one path, then come back to the stored image and explore the other, a process not possible in traditional painting. Images could be built up in layers, and elements of one could be combined with elements of another. A detail from one painting could become a texture wrapped around an object in another work, and the objects could be scaled to any size and viewed from any angle. I had always been interested in sculpture and architecture as well as painting, and now I was able to explore elements of these disciplines through the computer's keyboard, as well as investigating the properties of an entirely different medium.[15]

One especially interesting lesson Em learned, arose as a side-effect of adapting programs originally created for scientific purposes. These would sometimes lead to errors that, nevertheless contributed accidental but visually useful effects. Indeed, Em found these errors so fruitful that, even when the programs were running without problems, he would introduce occasional random numbers to create some element of unexpectedness in the visual outcomes.

Let us now consider a couple of key examples. In *Caligari* of 1978 (Figure 3.6), we find a single virtual object – a development interesting in itself, as early digital plasticity usually involves groups of objects rather than single items. The visual character of the object is subtle – appearing as a white plate-form that may have once been in a more elastic state – e.g. confectionary icing, or an unusual ceramic, or a simple organic life-form.

These complex effects are generated from two main formal devices. The plate itself has subtle gradations of tone suggesting an uneven concavity. This converges on a button-like indent in the dead center of the plate. The button, indeed, is the locus of the second key formal device – a radial network of concentric chocolate colored webbing. The webbing radiates either outwards or inwards from this indent in a web whose rhythm of patterning appears to have been disrupted by some centrifugal force. This creates a further visual association – of a magically transformed impact crater.

All the visual effects just described center on Em's use of random numbers to create formal 'accidents.' A rather more 'perfect' realization of visual proportions is found in Em's first masterwork of digital plasticity – *Transjovian Pipeline*, created in the summer of 1979 (Plate 6). The pipeline form itself thrusts obliquely from the right-hand corner into the upper left, before foreshortening dramatically and plunging into the distance at two different successive angles. There is a curious fibrous quality to the pipeline's surface, and contrasting zones of quite subtle color (at some

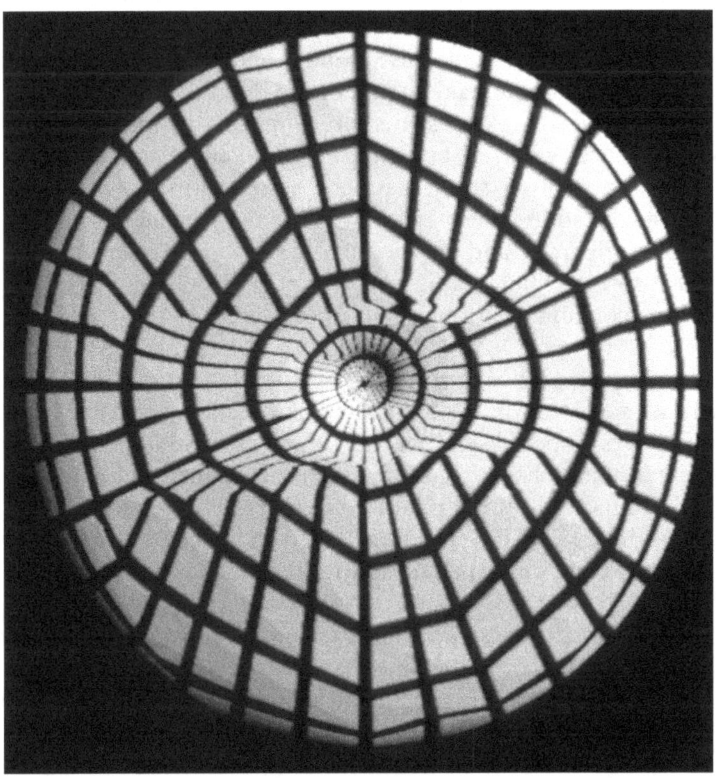

Figure 3.6 David Em, *Caligari*, 1978.

points with quasi-iridescent effects). The nuances of the fibrousness are such that individual striations are rendered in clear visual relief – a plasticity of texture in addition to that of the pipe's volume.

There is also a deeper drama of virtual space in more general terms played out in this work. The pipeline recedes into a dark ground covered in dots of varying color – suggesting, of course, a position in outer-space. However, there are two – almost monolithic – masses that intervene on this in different ways. The first is a kind of carpet or tablecloth of patterns separated by grey orthogonals. These move from the left and center of the work, receding away from the viewer. As they do so, the patterns undergo color and formal changes according to the phase of recession. The carpet or tablecloth analogy is especially apt here, because these visual effects considered on their own are far more evocative of surfaces in a domestic interior, than they are of outer space. They also appear to affirm the enduring solidity of that which they cover, or are the surface of.

The second monolithic mass is much more extraordinary. It occupies the upper right quadrant of the image, and the lower left of its mass is traversed optically by the pipeline itself. It is a rectangle enclosing a red rhombus and diagonals that themselves center a red diamond-shaped lozenge with slightly curved sides – giving the effect of a star surrounded by protecting force lines. The structure is internally energized by arrays of colored bead forms – linked in intricate 'wires,' sometimes in straight lines or perpendiculars, and other times linked in curves and concentric structures. These untoward 'traceries' have the ambience of both organic presence and uncovered clockwork, about them.

Now, even though in recessional terms this second monolith is further away from the viewer, the effects just described make the tip of the red star appear to approach the surface plane of the image. The same spatial area, in other words, is coming and going simultaneously. Hence, what, at first sight, is an exercise in 'normal' three-dimensional recession is actually a subtle aesthetic restructuring of virtual space. This should be considered also in relation in relation to the pipeline, its outer space setting, the carpet/tablecloth areas, and the spectacular red star lozenge and its array. They create a coherent formal whole but it is one whose compelling visual/imaginative power arises from potential tensions or incongruities between these features, individually considered.

In one sense this is an exemplar of the fact that any good artist can integrate individually incongruent elements of form in a satisfying aesthetic whole. However, the digital *imprimatur* involves a special sense of this. When an abstract painter such as Tanguy uses strange and unfamiliar three-dimensional forms their individual configuration is not usually found uncanny, because, *qua* painting, we know that it is a product of artistic imagination. Now, in the case of digital objects – whether individual ones such as *Caligari* or spatial states of affairs as in *Transjovian Pipeline* – there is a reversal of this. We know that the work is a product of human artifice, but the digital means create a level of realism which, at one level, subverts such knowledge. The *trompe-l'oeuil* character of the object presents it as existent even though it most certainly is not. When such an effect is achieved by representing a familiar kind of perceived object, it is enjoyed mainly as a pleasing trick. But when the object is very different from ordinary ones, the intensity of its presentation *as* existent is – to say the least – *uncanny*. It is as though a genuine alternative reality is intruding on our own. However, it is important to note that, whilst this uncanniness may suspend our sense of the digital object as a product of artifice, it does not eliminate it – we do not mistake the image for a reality, no matter how persuasive its presentation may be. This means that we can enjoy the image's uncanniness as an aesthetic experience – as something with an element of the negative (like the sublime) but which is contextualized by our admiration for the artist's ingenuity in programming.

By the early 1980s, then, Em had developed his own large three-dimensional databases, and developed interests in painting with electronic light. At this time, the available technology was undergoing important changes. Em notes that

> Through 1984, working in 3-D and color simultaneously was a challenge. Until then, frame buffers ... could only display 8-bits of color per pixel, a setup that yielded access to a total color space of 16.7 million colors, but only 256 of those colors could be displayed at one time. I had to organize those 256 discrete hues into color maps in such a way as to incorporate shading for the 3-D.[16]

However,

> All that changed in 1985 when I started working with a 24-bit frame buffer that could display all 16.7 [million] hues simultaneously. This resulted in a series of pictures that spanned 1985–1986 in which I explored fluid digital color spaces in ways I'd been thinking about for years.[17]

An interesting example here, is *Mar* of 1986 (Figure 3.7). The spectacular painterliness of this work is very different from the geometric and architectural precisionism of *Transjovian Pipeline* and many other of Em's alternative virtual worlds, but such painterliness is an equally important and recurrent feature of his *œuvre*. *Mar* clearly looks for inspiration to the space exploration images that Em encountered at the JPL. However, as well as visual features akin to the gaseous plumes of the Jovian atmosphere, there is a luster and vibrancy of form that suggests concealed totemic figures and spatial process magically transformed into fluid jewels of color and shape. Certainly, the extraordinary color range made available by the new technical innovations is celebrated here with the greatest *élan*.

Around this time, Em also paid more attention to the qualities of the digital medium itself. In his words,

> In the mid-eighties, my focus shifted from building virtual worlds to perceiving the work as data structures that could be tinkered with. Making small changes to a few numbers sometimes produced radical evolutionary progressions. Most were blind alleys, but periodically they returned gold.[18]

An impressive work in this respect, is *Guadelope* of 1998 (Figure 3.8). Here, Em's creative strategy extends into something that is, for all intents and purposes, a semi-concealed visual *symphony* of texture. At first sight, we see an unknown form of vertical orientation rendered with trompe-l'oeil plasticity in the form of patterned greyish folds and coils. On closer scrutiny, the patterns on this ceramic like substance resolve into tiny dots or ovoids of brown, green, and black, investing the surface with a subtle damascening effect. This has the further effect of suspending our interpretation of the form between three different materials – seeing it as a

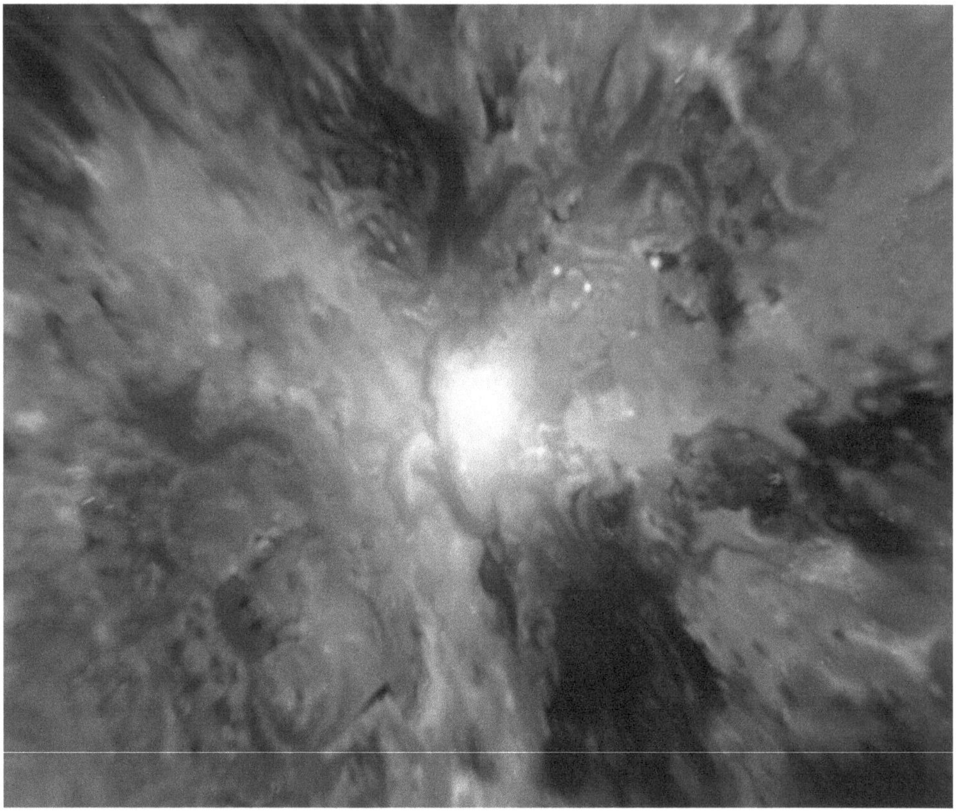

Figure 3.7 David Em, *Mar*, 1986.

ceramic, or a plastic, or as a metal cast with a fine decorative matte finish. It is this hovering between which gives the work its quasi-magical aesthetic power.

Em's power as a digital artist is shown by the stylistic range of his compositions. They extend from digital objects rendered with Zurbaran-like quiddity, to the most ethereal painterly effects. There are also many works where such precisionism and painterliness are combined in a complementary way. Consider, for example, *QED* of 1998 (Figure 3.9). The overall impression is of a field of centrifugal and centripetal vortices whose joint gravities both explode and arrest a billowing whirl of forms. The bulk of these are dull orange irregular trapezoids, with a host of similar smaller shapes in blues, yellows, browns, and rose. There is an extended area at the right of the image, where the forms are mainly rose colored in varying densities. At three points there is a suggestion that the field of forms is mainly in front of a light blue ground. However, as well as concealing most of this ground, the field of forms also appear to have a more intimate link with it – as though it were a gestating energy.

A third of the way along the lower edge of the work is a concentration of structures that give the impression of deep spatial descent – revealing that the billowing field is actually composed from many layers of such forms. The layering and frontal distribution suggest a field of debris – organic or of exploded technology, that is

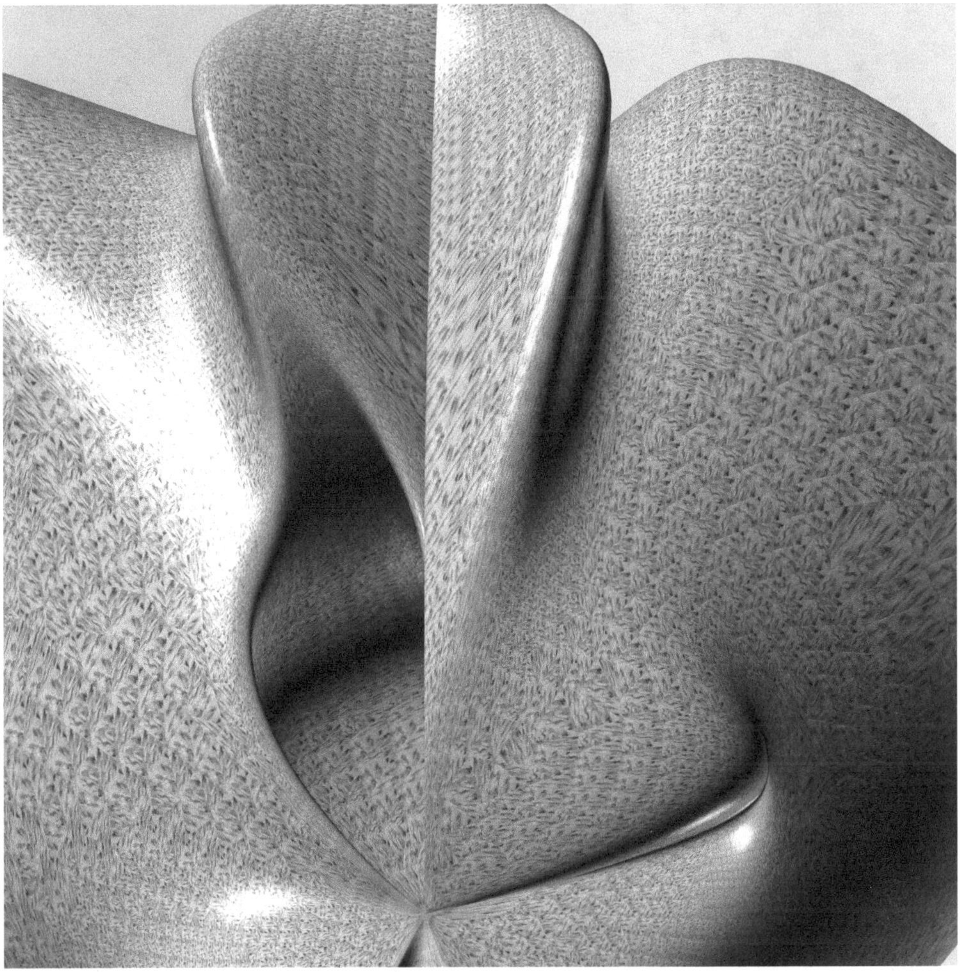

Figure 3.8 David Em, *Guadelope*, 1988.

being held in place by the gravitational forces. However, this factor is, perhaps, secondary to a very different association – of festiveness. The image evokes celebration and ceremony – the billowing materials having been launched but held in place until a grand moment of dissolution (as when fireworks explode into pattern). At the heart of this positive mood is the relaxed harmony of the color scheme, and the trapezoids' rather flimsy two-dimensional substance.

Em's work, then, explores the sheer scope of digital media. It does so by both projecting alternative worlds comprised of digital objects and relations, and by painstaking investigations of the intrinsic properties of the relevant technologies. This latter point cannot be emphasized enough. Em's entire career shows what is ultimately at issue in the artistic use of computers – a willingness to explore the properties of digital media, to understand both their advantages and limits in relation to traditional art media, and to use this as a basis for new creations.

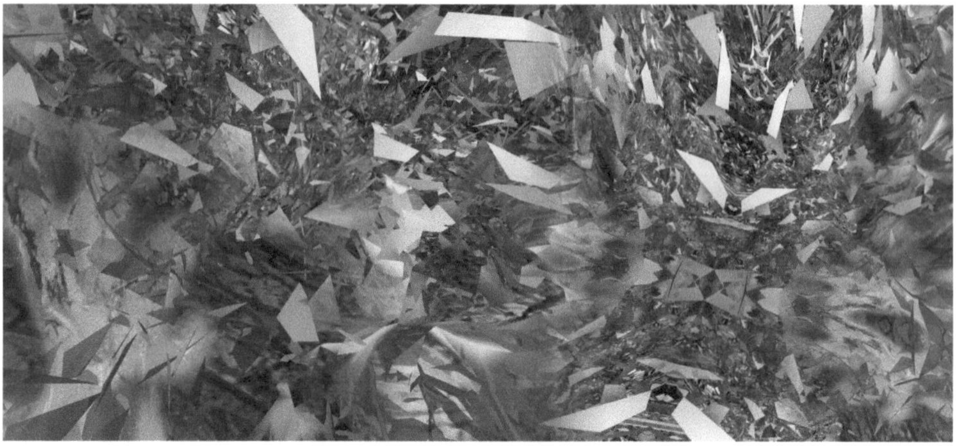

Figure 3.9 David Em, *QED*, 1998.

We turn now to another artist, whose career has involved attentiveness to these issues but from a very specific theoretical perspective – that of how organic forms evolve. The artist is William Latham.

Three

In the 1980s and 1990s Latham employed digital idioms based on algorithms mimicking evolutionary processes. These resulted in digital objects of the most striking plasticity. Latham was inspired by Mandelbrot's work on fractals, and the cognate ways in which natural systems frequently create complex structures through the repetition of very simple steps. Of special importance in this respect was the time he spent at the Natural History Museum in London during his student days. Thinking of the brain as a kind of computer, he was able to eventually devise his own 'Form/Synth' drawing system using large-scale depictions of evolutionary transformations of specific visual forms. The principles of transformation involved operators such as beak, bulge, twist, scoop, grow tendril, and stack.[19]

Latham worked as a Research Fellow/artist at IBM Research Laboratories from 1987 to 1993, and had access to mainframe and super computers. He also met and collaborated with IBM mathematician Stephen Todd for five years. Working together, the two devised three complementary artistic systems based on the notion of artificial life. In their words,

> *Form Grow* generates lifelike forms using geometric rules; *Mutator* is a system based on mutation and natural selection which helps the artists explore the world of these forms; and *Life Cycle* animates these forms by rules of birth, growth and death.[20]

The actual creative process of this 'evolutionism' involves two major stages. Again, in Todd's and Latham's words,

> The artist first creates the rules of the virtual world, applying whichever physical and biological rules he chooses: light, colour, gravity, growth and other rules of his own invention. The artist then becomes a gardener within this world he has created; he selects and breeds sculptural forms as a plant breeder produces flowers, and records the evolutionary process in animations which show skeletal forms unfolding and surreal lobsters breeding.[21]

Let us consider the digital art film *Mutations*.[22] In cooperation with his production team, Latham first decided what ideas would work in a film illustrating life and natural selection. In the first instance, this involved detailed discussion of many hand-drawn sketches – with the computer only used incidentally to determine whether ideas would work or not. The next major step was to engage the *Form Grow* program (written in ESME) whereby relevant primitive structures – such as, in Latham's case, pumpkin shapes, oryx horns, shells, tusks, and many mathematically generated forms were transformed. The 'transforms' included new instructions such as 'Bend,' 'Twist,' 'Stack,' 'Branch,' 'Ribcage,' and 'Web' which gave the generated three-dimensional forms a much more natural appearance. In effect, *Form Grow* acts as 'an evolutionary fruit machine' with which Latham could breed and cross-breed mutation variants.

In the case of *Mutations*, the decision was made to confine the program's application within a subsystem 'which creates a related family of forms and artworks each with its family style.'[23] The style in question was that of the lobster form, and ribcage structure. Interestingly, Latham's understanding of the these features was not based on naturalistic observation, but more loosely from the studies of animal skeletons (mentioned earlier) that he had done at the Natural History Museum whilst a student.

Given the selected *Form Grow* computer models, techniques of coloring and texturing would then be applied using the Winsom CSG solid modelling software (developed by Peter Quarendon and John Woodwark at the IBM UK Scientific Centre). This enables the models to be visually realized with photo-realist levels of visual specificity. Once the relevant possibilities have been so rendered, Latham selects which families of form are to be used. On the basis of these choices, *Mutator* is employed to generate aesthetically attractive new family members (using the 'transforms') mentioned earlier. As Todd and Latham note, 'The artist sees the forms [on screen], makes judgments which he communicates to *Mutator*, and *Mutator* then uses this feedback to produce new forms.'[24] More specifically, digital 'genes' (i.e. the software code sustaining the form) are altered so as to create, in general, nine variants. One of these is then selected for further mutation, and the process repeated again and again until some culminating 'whole form' emerges that strikes the artist as an aesthetically fitting outcome to this process of quasi-natural aesthetic selection.

Finally, the *Life Cycle* operator takes the selected forms through a repertoire of changing structures appropriate to various stages of formal growth, maturity, and decay. Again, the artist's choice would play a key role here, through the use of a lower-level control program – *Director*. This program gives the artist

> many options to allow for the generation of a quick preview of an animation looking at individual frames and so on. The artist makes several experiments at this stage to get the precise timing and flow of the scene as he requires it, modifying *Life Cycle* definition and timing parameters as necessary.[25]

Now, whilst the animated *Mutations* sequence has extraordinary visual power, the stand-alone images that Latham derives from it and makes into prints are just as powerful and more widely accessible to a viewing public.[26] Indeed, it is impossible to appreciate the full poetics of the *Mutations* process without an aesthetic engagement with the individual features and stages of this process. Whereas, for example, seeing a still extracted from a film can help illuminate how the film is composed, the relation between still image and process in the case of *Mutations* is much more complex. For here we are dealing with a reciprocity – the individual 'frames' are what the process is 'about' – it is of interest not as a mere visual fact, but as a process-of-becoming, defined by its specific moments and not only the flow from one state to another. Indeed, the sequence is artistically constructed from these individual frames in a way that film as a medium hardly ever is. But, at the same time, the full visual identity of the individual frames is dependent on their place within the process. This gives them an aesthetically paradoxical character. Existing as individual prints, the frames do not seem to have been snatched from a process of vision as, for example, individual photographs do. Rather they have a curiously timeless appearance – massively organic but, as it were, elevated beyond transience, through the aesthetic impact of their individual appearance. This metaphysical *stillness* is more than a photographic snatched moment because it is itself evocative of the process of growth and decay of which the individual is a part.

Even though this process is not depicted literally in the individual frame, it is evoked through the extraordinary visual rhythms and relations of Latham's virtual life-forms. Their open unity – *qua* spatial objects – is a flowing complexity of scanning possibilities for the viewer. These arise from the sometimes astonishing relations of shape and texture aspects vis-à-vis the whole organism. Especially potent in this respect are the whorls, curves, details within details, and radiating rib and spine structures that are so central to the morphologies of these virtual creatures. The viewer does not simply register them, but is drawn into a process of perceptual exploration that provides a symbolic analog of the process of which they are part.

Another interesting feature of *Mutation*'s aesthetic paradoxicality (and a creative departure from any Darwinian element) is its capacity to sustain 'marriages' between a form and any of its progenitors, so as to achieve especially complex outcomes. In one case, for example, we have a form presented simultaneously as being born and giving birth.[27] This is, at least, another example of the importance of the individual pictorial frame – in being able to present two temporally incongruous aspects of a form simultaneously. Perhaps also, it is this temporally incestuous element and its biological associations that gives Latham's organic configurations their occasionally ugly or nightmarish ambience.

Let us consider some of these points further, in relation to specific works by Latham – starting with some created before *Mutations*. *Twister 1* of 1988 (Figure 3.10) involves twisted segments of contrasting sizes that are wrapped around one another. Its basic color is a mix of scarlet red with faint purple tinges. This 'skin' is mottled by irregular white blotches – some of them with black edging, and some containing further black or red blotches. A sequence of low protruding peg-like shapes form a spine. This follows the visual circumference of the structure, from the top right, descending from the structure's apex, to end halfway down, on top of a group of tightly bunched segments. The tightness of this configuration gives the impression of a claw – curved so as to protect and/or hide something. The claw's

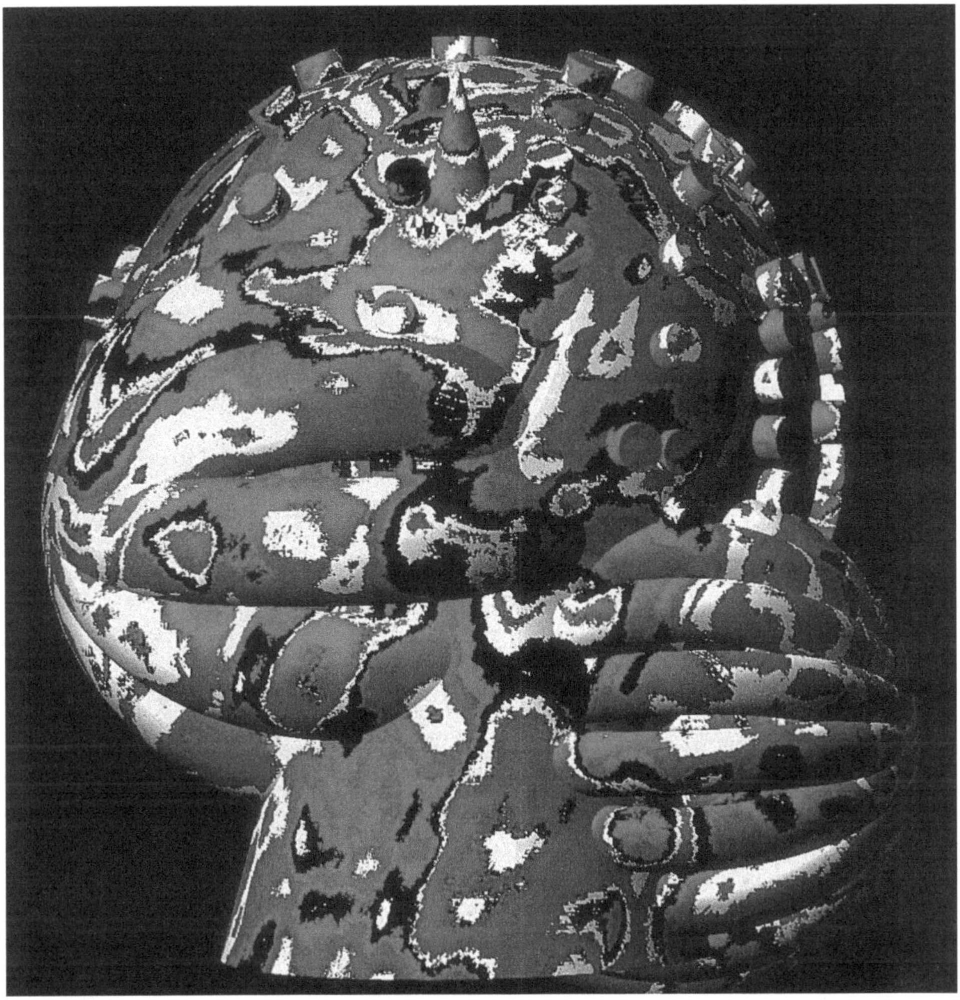

Figure 3.10 William Latham, *Twister 1*. IBM UK Scientific Centre 1988, Computer/Cibachrome. 103 × 103 cm.

Source: © William Latham 1988.

visual momentum is rightwards spectatorially speaking; but a group of larger (and fewer) layered segments occupying the left central mass of the structure, have a more ambiguous momentum. The white mottling seems to point leftwards in immediate optical terms, but this is gathered up by the broadly configured segments in a covering action.

All these shapes, colors, and optical motions, suggest, then, a visually determinate creature, but of an unknown kind. Its twisting coils appear to protect, or to shelter, something that will eventually be released. There is, as it were, a stillness that is, nevertheless, pregnant with possibilities of becoming – biological or behavioral, or, of course, both. Indeed, an element of potential menace is evoked through the chaotic effect of color and shape in the textures. They give the impression of skin-forms that might come alive and jump out at different angles from the surface.

Tube Horn with Egg of 1988 (Figure 3.11) is very different. It centers on a relation between two physically distinct virtual forms, whose character is aptly represented in the work's title. The tube horn is a broadly lipped orifice formed from smoothly textured and successive concentric segments that constitute the structure's volume, and diminish in perfect proportions vis-à-vis the viewing position. The main form converges on the aforementioned orifice, but has a major portion that continues leftwards to form another concentrically defined major limb. Between the main horn body and its limb, an irregular spherical 'egg' form is located – appearing indeed, to be gently lodged in place. Both the egg and the secondary limb have a surface texture – like a deposited vitreous film that has dried and lost its lustre.

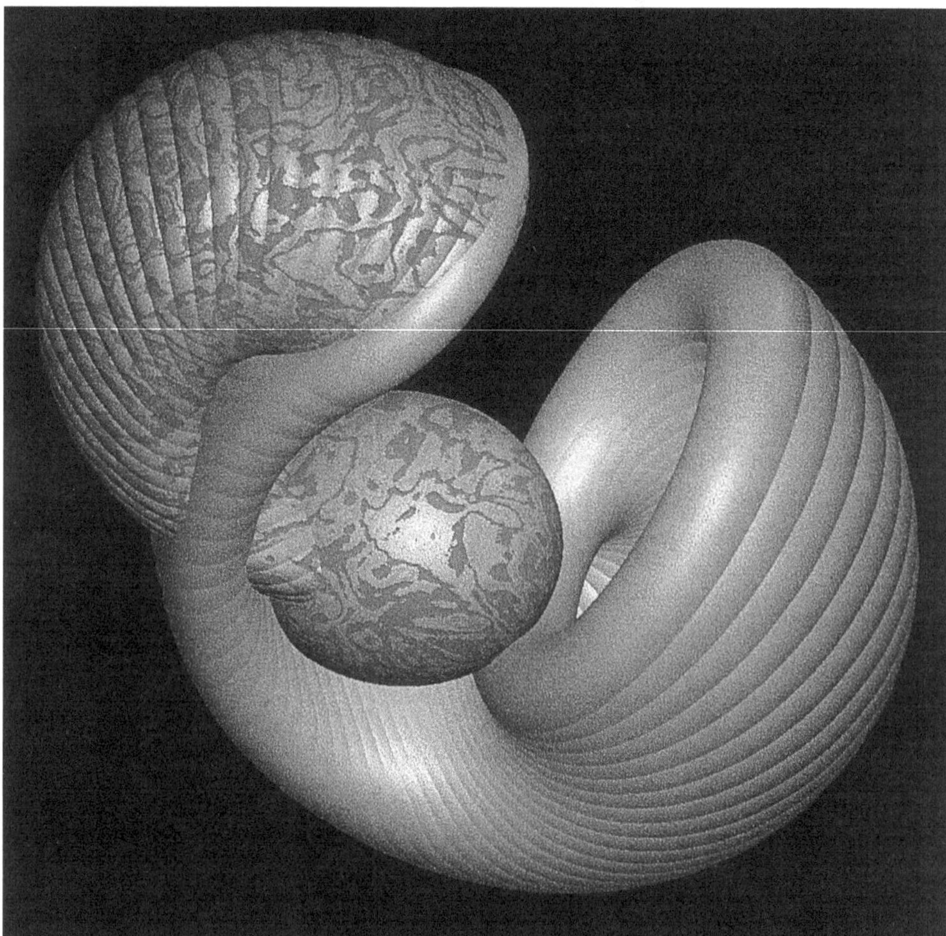

Figure 3.11 William Latham, *Tube Horn with Egg*. IBM UK Scientific Centre 1988, Computer/Cibachrome. 103 × 103 cm.

Source: © William Latham 1988.

Whereas, in *Twister 1*, the intense colors and textures of the work invest it with a kind of subdued violence, in *Tube Horn...* the opposite is the case. All the main features are formally tranquil with an almost religious purity of color, proportion, and formal articulation. Indeed, the material substance of Latham's *Tube Horn...* is deeply enigmatic. Its very finely granulated surface texture and tight disposition of segments suggest, at once, the fixity of a ceramic body, yet also, the elasticity of rubber. These two opposing features cancel one another out in an *aufheben* that suggests an – again – highly determinate but unknown life-form. Its visual presence creates a kind of lower key version of the *uncanniness* of physical presence that can be found in Zurbaran's still-lives (and which is also found in Em's work). This effect is amplified by the egg's visual inhabiting of two opposite vectors of possibility. With equal justification, it can be seen as on the verge of being drawn into the main form's orifice, *or*, as having just issued from it.

The two works just discussed precede *Mutations*, and are not part of an animated sequence. But their visual identities – with their powerful suggestions of things about to happen or which have happened – are entirely consistent with *Mutations*' logic of the individual as part of broader evolutionary structure. Let us, then, now consider how this is shown by individual frames from the *Mutations* work itself.

In this respect, it is useful to compare *Mutation X Raytraced* (Plate 7), and *Mutation Y 1 Raytraced* (Figure 3.12). Both works are presented in an evolutionary space that is literally black. They are not shown in visual relation to anything except themselves and their unfolding process. This in itself, has a symbolic value. The broader sufficient context which allows life-forms to evolve at all (i.e. efficient causation by environmental factors in relation to the physical composition of the organism) are not sufficiently explicable to us. The origins of life and the reasons for its development are ultimately *mysterious*, and it is this very mystery which is tacitly acknowledged in the darkness from which Latham's *Mutations* emerge and transform.

Mutation X... is especially deeply shadowed. It has a nautilus shell-type central structure composed of a mildly lustrous extending main tube. The main tube is composed of tightly chained segments, enclosing radial ribs. The ribs are, in turn, made of circular chained segments linked also by narrow external spines of raised peg forms. These two main features gravitate around a black hole at the lower right-center of the image. This hole is partially surrounded by what appears to be an organic growth, composed of many 'fingers' each reaching about halfway up the individual ribs, or in the case of the lower ones, moving between them. One such finger penetrates into the hidden area beyond the ribs. The growth's entire surface mass growth consists of a red ground with uneven linear and ovoid patterning in white.

The main tube itself originates as an end-rib that curves upwards and left towards the viewer before brushing the frontal plane and curving backwards and away into the distance. This receding motion, in effect, transforms the receding tube into a tail, thus completing the nautilus structure by presenting it as a spiralling coil. The active motion of the coil is accentuated through the main tube acquiring a spine of vermicular wavy elements as it presents to the viewer and then recedes into the distance. This recession is accentuated further through three or four sub-tubes that emerge from the top of the main tube – pushing upwards to join with the outer points of its tail phase.

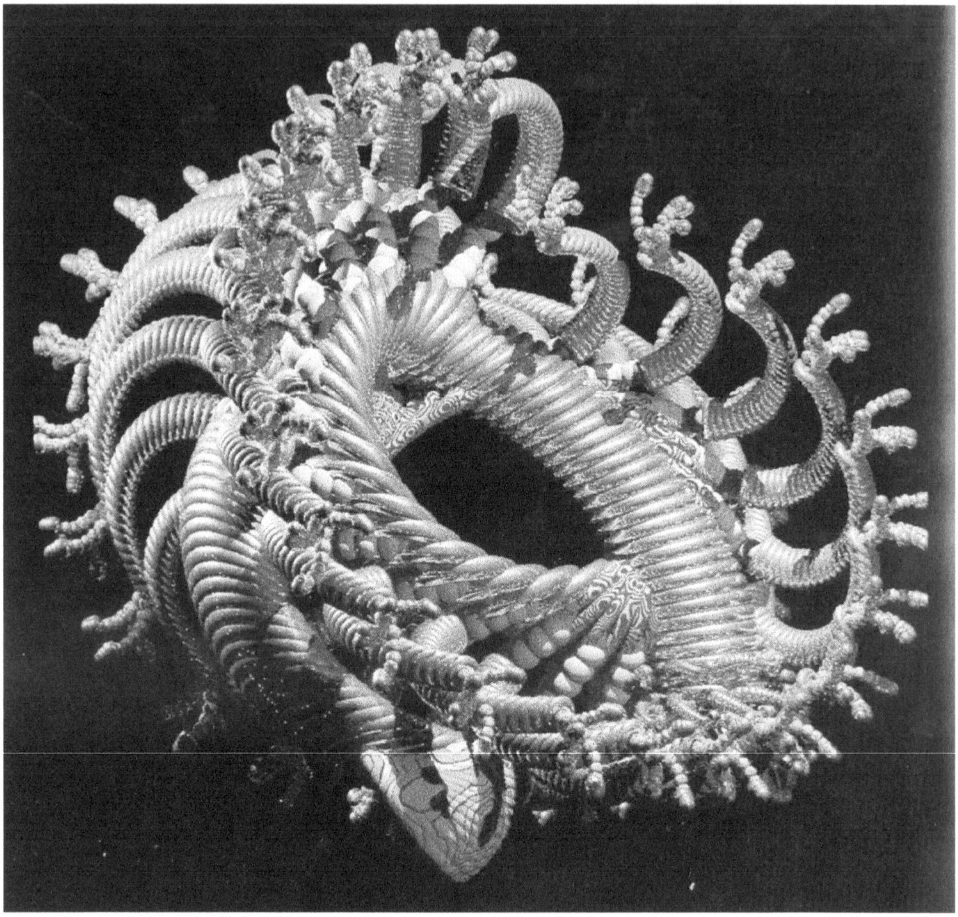

Figure 3.12 William Latham, *Mutation Y 1 Raytraced*, IBM UK Scientific Centre 1992, Computer/Cibachrome. 56 × 56 cm.

Source: © William Latham 1992.

A second important figure also emerges, to the left of the sub-tubes. It is a proboscis of tight oval segments – lurching towards the viewer – with a head tapering upwards to form a smaller, secondary proboscis. The head is an orange ground, patterned with white bands forming irregular linear and ovoid shapes. A similar pattern (albeit it with a red ground) is found in the quasi-umbilical cord which ties the major proboscis to the nautilus structure. This appears to be a continuation – with the color scheme inverted – of the organic growth partially surrounding the black hole at the nautilus center.

It is important to emphasize that *Mutator X* is *spiralling* in an active sense, and not simply a spiral shape. This spatio-temporal dynamic again presents structure as one phase in an active process of becoming. It is interesting that this effect is created, in part, by the oblique angle of the main tube's emergence from the rib stage towards the viewer. But, in terms of the viewer's interpretational perspective this oblique animation is ambiguous (on lines encountered in the other Latham works considered). We have described the structure very much as emergent towards the viewer. However, the visual dynamic could equally well be read in opposite terms – as starting with the tail's furthest point as the structure's actual point of emergence from distant space or from nothingness. On this reading, the nautilus forms into shape before the viewer, rather than the complete structure being given as a starting point, with the tail moving away the distance.

These alternative readings give the main proboscis different implications. If the nautilus is given at the start, with the tail beginning to pull it towards the distance, then pulled away from the viewer into the distance, then it appears as though something has been brought to fruition, and the proboscis is, in effect, an offspring that has been successfully delivered. If on the other hand, the nautilus has surged from the distance to create its full form before us, then the proboscis is a part of an ongoing process. It may have been launched as a probe or attacking limb, or, again, it might be a very process of giving birth.

This ambiguity means that – even though it is generated by an artist – its meaning is resistant to a single sufficient interpretation. Indeed, there are further aspects to this resistance. The dark is not just a background against which the form is defined, but one that presents the structure's black hole and the radiating ribs *under a shadow*. This tends to distract from the important organic growth at the bottom of the ribs, and emphasises the visual coldness of the structure as something created in and dwelling in space-as-a-vacuum. Yet the overall form appears organic, and so the ambiguity develops further. The nautilus's dull lustre makes it appear halfway between shell and metal. This creates an impression of coiled elasticity – an uncanny rigidity that connotes strength through restraint rather than brittleness. The form has not only the potential to change, but also control over when and how the happening will occur. This relates to the ambiguity of the spiral itself – in signifying meaning that the viewer's interpretation cannot fix in place.

All these things are, in effect, emblematic of something more general – biological process's independence of the human will. Experimentally we can create the conditions whereby natural phenomena do things that we want them to do; we can even create conditions whereby they behave abnormally. But the mechanisms that make these conditions operate, and which make organic material respond to them, involve principles of efficient causation whose workings are themselves independent of our will. Why they work the way they do remains an enigma. The enigma might be resolved if human beings could transcend the present epistemological limits of human cognition, but if that happened, we would no longer be specifically human life-forms, and the question would cease to matter. *Mutator X…* affirms the realm of both visual and conceptual *mystery*.

Let us now consider *Mutator Y 1 Raytraced*. The main form is presented at only a slightly oblique angle towards the viewer, and carries no suggestions of spatial-temporal motion in the way that the previous example did. Indeed, the slightly oblique angle of presentation is creatively compensated for in a creative way. This is through the alignment of chained links in the lower section of the main tube (immediately beneath the central black hole) which twist slightly away from the viewer.

The configuration involves many such formal balancing features. Its composition focuses on the aforementioned tube which is actually a single entity but with two different aspects. The first is the one just referred to – the section with the slightly twisting links. This curves abruptly rightwards near the center of the structure and transforms into a sequence of more numerous, tightly compacted links with narrower, sharper edges. Towards the bottom of the structure this intersects with florid beaded radial 'arms' that move in two directions. The upper one is a spine composed of wavy tubular forms akin to the dancing arms and hands of a Hindu deity. The lower sequence gives way leftwards to a multitude of obliquely emergent individual tubes. These end in an array of tubes on top of one another, each with an individual downwards motion away from the viewer, suggesting the rear part of a head. The downwards motions of these forms again is beautiful counterpoint to the waving arms on the top right of the structure.

If *Mutator X…* suggests potential activity, *Mutator Y1…* presents potential realized through a fully developed structure. It is a self-contained network of basic tubular forms whose kinship gives way to complex variations of intricacy and motion. Especially striking is the impression of energy transmitted in complex ovoid rhythm – a rhythm bonding all the elements as players in a higher-order aesthetic unity.

At the heart of this are two features that give visual stability to the rhythm in a discreet way. At the very base of the structure is a tongue-like form that has the same orange-white color scheme as the aggressive proboscis from *Mutator X*…. However, it is here playing a support role – offering a careful touch of polychrome to anchor the ovoid rhythm. And equally discreet is the second feature – namely the red-white patterned cord that links the proboscis to the main nautilus structure in *Mutator X…* In *Mutator Y1…* it appears – almost incidentally – where the twisting links join with the more tightly compacted ones in the lower right center of the structure. However, it also continues – as a twisting cord – above the compact links, eventually moving beneath them to re-emerge and join with the lower tube of broader twisting links.

It is formal devices such as these that make *Mutator Y 1…* into an aesthetically highly evolved virtual life-form. What might have ended up as a cross between a mask and a basket, or a dreary repetition of waving forms becomes something far more effective. In complete contrast to this highly controlled structure is the final work by Latham that I will consider. It is *Breeding Forms on the Infinite Plane*, of 1992 (Figure 3.13). Here a group of segmented horn structures are linked in ways that suggest that each is emerging from one of the others – in effect, the overall structure is both being born and giving birth. The superabundance of small crustacean-like creatures with pearly/metallic segments heighten the overall impression of fecundity. However, the heavy contortions of the other forms fix much more on the process of giving birth itself. There is a pervasive awkwardness and asymmetry of the 'limbs' even though they have some shapes in common.

Many of Latham's virtual life-forms are baroque in the way that their different formal aspects play off against one another in aesthetic terms. However, *Breeding Forms…* is almost counter-baroque. It is a nightmare horn-of-plenty where the burgeoning substance of the breeding material overwhelms the individual morphologies that arise from it. This creates a similar effect to that experienced by the character Roquentin in Sartre's novel *Nausea*. Roquentin is overwhelmed by a tree root he sees in a park.

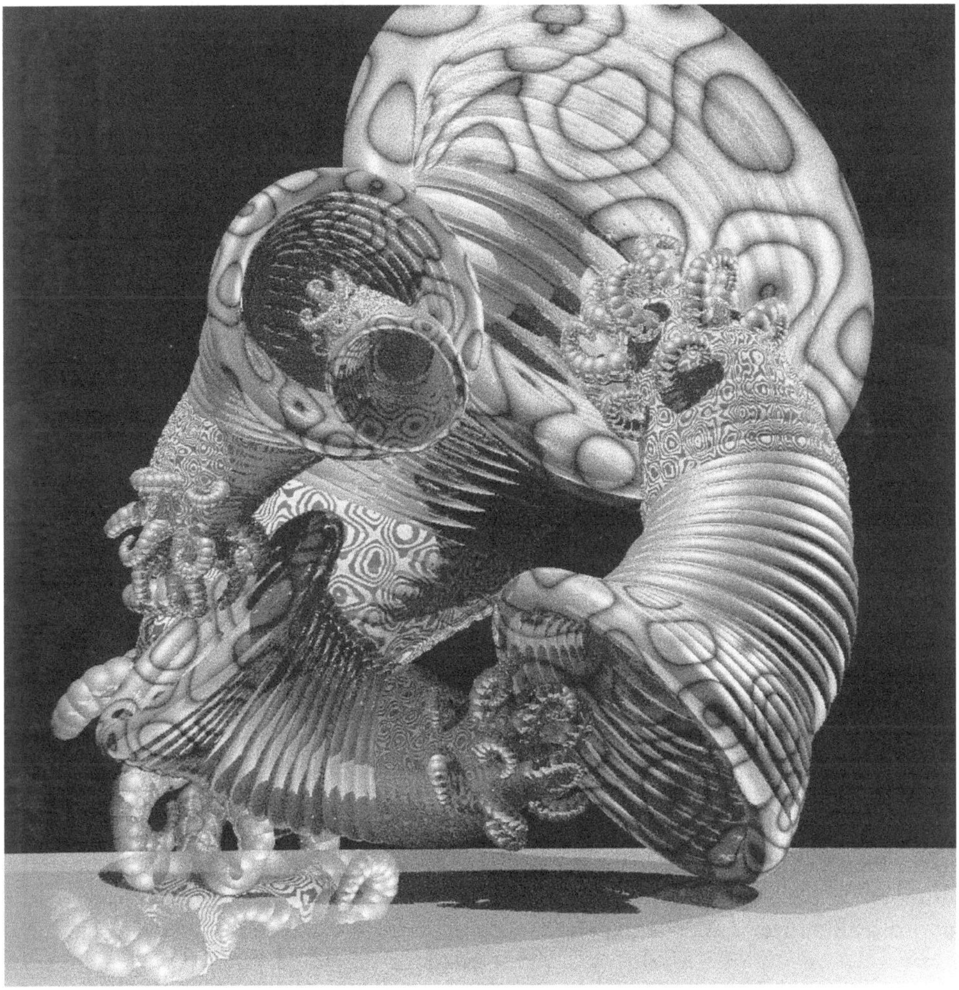

Figure 3.13 William Latham, *Breeding Forms on the Infinite Plane*. IBM UK Scientific Centre 1992, computer image.

Source: © William Latham 1992.

> And then, all of a sudden, there it was, as clear as day: existence had suddenly unveiled itself. It had lost its harmless appearance as an abstract category: it was the very stuff of things, that root was steeped in existence. Or rather the root, the park gates, the bench, the sparse grass on the lawn, all that had vanished; the diversity of things, their individuality, was only an appearance, a veneer. This veneer had melted, leaving soft, monstrous masses, in disorder – naked, with a frightening, obscene nakedness.[28]

Latham's virtual creatures are always precisely rendered, but in *Breeding Forms* ... the preciseness – the clarity of visual form and its categorization – is overwhelmed by the evolutionary surge into existence, by the very power to generate being. Visual detail overloads itself and looses its bearings 'leaving soft, monstrous masses.' In this work, the generative power of becoming existent is evoked in a kind of raw state. In the *Mutations* film we see the process of evolution enacted successively. In an image such as *Breeding Forms...* the processual character of the process is compressed *within* the individual image.

At the heart of all this is a complex notion of metaphysical contingency. The superabundance of *Breeding Forms...* involves a curious absurdity or meaninglessness. All this generation – but why? Why should anything exist at all; and given, that it does, why does it have just this form? One might invoke the necessity of natural laws as explanations of why things have the form they do. But this cannot answer the question of why things should exist in the first place, and – even within its own terms – it invites the question of why scientific laws work in just this way, rather than some other.

Now, whilst a work such as *Breeding Forms...* invites these questions in pressing terms, there is a sense in which they are at issue in all of Latham's *Mutator* works. His strategy is more than evolutionary as such, it offers a space of alternative outcomes to those evolutionary processes which provided the original visual data for his digital transformations. The virtual life-forms created by Latham are based on artistic strategy, but they point questioningly back to the whys and wherefores of evolution itself. The beauty of this is that the nature of the questions raised varies according to the artistic character of the individual virtual form.

Now, Latham's evolutionist works blur the distinctions between human creativity, natural creativity, and computing, but there is more to them. If anything they articulate what is involved in any creative artistic process – namely inspiration from nature and/or technological factors (in the broadest sense), and the reciprocal modification of natural and technological material through creative direction. However, as we have seen throughout this book, in the Postmodern era the interactions between technology and other fields of activity have become massively overt – engaging both the content and means of artistic creation.

Latham's evolutionist works amplify and dramatize what is at issue here at many different levels. He describes his works as 'sculptures.' This is, in part, due to the photo-realist three-dimensional effects that arise from using the Winsom technology. However, we *know* that this sculptural effect is created from a two-dimensional plane surface. Indeed (as we have seen), the individual two-dimensional frame makes its own aesthetic contribution to the interpretation of what is represented. The real significance of the sculptural effect in Latham's work consists in how it changes the relation between abstraction and figuration. His virtual life-forms are creatures who never existed (even though their visual lineage has its origins in the artist's original studies of animal skeletal form). But, of course, they have the appearance of living organisms.[29] Such 'biomorphic' suggestion is traditionally the province of certain forms of abstract art. It involves the evocation of possible forms of organic life other than those of the actual natural order. This tends to be done allusively – by suggestion – much more than by depiction. Latham's virtual life-forms, however, are very different and offer a much more direct presentation that takes the biomorphic to levels far beyond abstraction and traditional figuration – be they pictorial or sculptural. They are digital objects with the most manifest digital plasticity. Traditional artistic divisions are here assimilated and transcended through the technological development of Latham's original studies. Digital space affirms the distinctiveness of its potential. The techno-habitat of the Postmodern era is expanded further still.

In the final analysis, the hyper-precision of Latham's virtual life-forms involves a paradoxical de-literalization. For their insistently real appearance is at odds with the fantastic and unlikely character of their physical configuration. In the tension between these, the idea of alternative organic forms – of new realities – is opened up *for the imagination*. They are uncanny in the positive sense described earlier.

Technology here naturalizes itself through the projection of alternative possible life-worlds, on the basis of techniques of evolutionary generation that appear to mimic nature. But, no matter how 'natural' the resulting forms appear, they equally affirm their origins as expressions of technological development. This gives them a curious second affinity with organic form. There is the hint of an ineluctable *telos* in all forming – be it natural or rational – that shows itself through process, but which cannot be sufficiently explained.

Four

We turn finally – albeit at less length – to a mode of creating visual objects that seems to occupy a different universe from those of Latham's *Mutator* phase, but which overlap in some respects with aspects of Em's *oeuvre*.

Gerhard Mantz was trained at the Karlsruhe Academy of Fine Art from 1970 to 1975. Having established himself as a sculptor, in the mid-1990s he began exploring the possibilities of computer technology for the realization of plastic forms. Between the second half of the 1990s and 2000, he created a series of three-dimensional 'virtual objects' (or 'digital objects' as they have been called in the present chapter) presented in physically two-dimensional formats, such as cibachrome prints. Mantz describes his basic strategy as follows.

> In my prints I aim to research the field between non-representationalism and recognizable materiality. I design objects and environments that show space and material without the familiar objectivity. ... Unlike photographs of real objects, virtual objects are defined in three dimensions. Every point of an object is defined by its co-ordinates in space, and its specific materials. All parameters can be adjusted, even beyond realistic values. At this point the computer calculates views from this data. Only these renderings visualise the mathematically defined structure. In cyberspace bodies can intersect each other without mass and weight. Thus constructions are possible on the edge of imagination. Things that are real yet from unknown materiality.[30]

It would be hard to come up with a better formal description of the ontology of the digital object than this. It involves the virtual occupation of three-dimensional virtual coordinates by objects whose mode of projection is determined mathematically. In this digital space, real physical properties of mass and weight are suspended. We are shown objects that appear to have mass and weight etc. but have so *only* at the level of visual possibility. But, of course, this level of visual possibility is actually a very compelling one.

Consider, for example, *Seltenes Gluck* (*Rare Luck*) of 1998 (Plate 8). The character of the object is highly ambiguous. It could, for example be a reptilian eye; or the egg of an unknown creature; it could be made from a plastic or ceramic material;

the substance could be solid or viscous. It has an apparent interior, and it seems also that this is enclosed by some kind of casing.

Such ambiguity is basic to how abstract artworks mean – they function by creating allusive possibilities of meaning. One such level may be dominant, in other cases, the different possibilities may be associationally equal. This is all down to the personal style in which the artist presents form. It invites the viewer to make associations guided by the work's appearance. In the case of Mantz's digital objects the situation is transformed because of the insistent realism of the image *qua* digital. The object is quite visually specific – it seems a definite kind of real thing, but is, of course, unlike any real thing that actually exists. The associational meanings just suggested are present, but the concrete realism of the object's presence seems to suppress them. This ambiguous unambiguity of presence makes it uncanny in an intriguing way.

This is reinforced by the way the objects are presented in absolute stillness. This is more than not moving. It is the occupation of an atemporal universe. There is nothing external to the object – only a background space with no items which one would be able to describe it in relation to. Without such a frame of reference we cannot determine the top or bottom of the represented object; we cannot determine the purpose for which it might exist, or even whether it is an artifact at all. We can recognize its parts as having a spatial relation to one another, but this is left at the level of appearance only. There is no clue as to how the parts might operate in relation to one another.

Ontological mystery is also found in *Local Revolt* of 1998 (Figure 3.14). It involves a structure based on three spheres. The larger (green) one acts as the ground, and a black one occupies the high center of the image. Both these spheres seem to be semi-opaque inside but with surfaces that are highly reflective. The main source of these reflections is a third sphere which is like the veined body of an eyeball, or an unusual planet. The system of reflections in the green and the black sphere is rendered complex by a number of light sources – which could be deep inside the spheres, or reflections of a light source behind or level with the viewer.

In this image all sense of efficient causality is suspended. The spheres may just be present to one another, or they may have some kind of organic or material interaction that cannot be discerned. They may relate to the space of the viewer, but equally well they may not. Their 'reflections' might even be interpreted as not reflections at all, but rather forms showing through from the translucent depths of the spherical bodies. Again, Mantz's mode of presentation does not provide the relational context where we could identify the spheres as specific kinds of things or states of affairs in a way that would allow us to infer the character of the materials from which they are meant to be composed. Their mass and weight is optical rather than causal, and hence can sustain the weight of positive imaginative ambiguity.

These features are also heavily to the fore in *The Sound of Passing Trains* of 2000.[31] In this work, extended glassy forms and items that appear to be optical tools of one sort or another are configured in a three-dimensional counterpoint of transparent masses and light. Here, it is impossible to distinguish between optical rhythm and materials intersecting with one another, between mere interaction, and collisions, or even processes of growth. The boundaries between technological and natural effects are erased – or, better, absorbed – within the particularity of the individual digital object. Here we have a configuration that seems to involve causally interacting elements but with no clues as to what this interaction means.

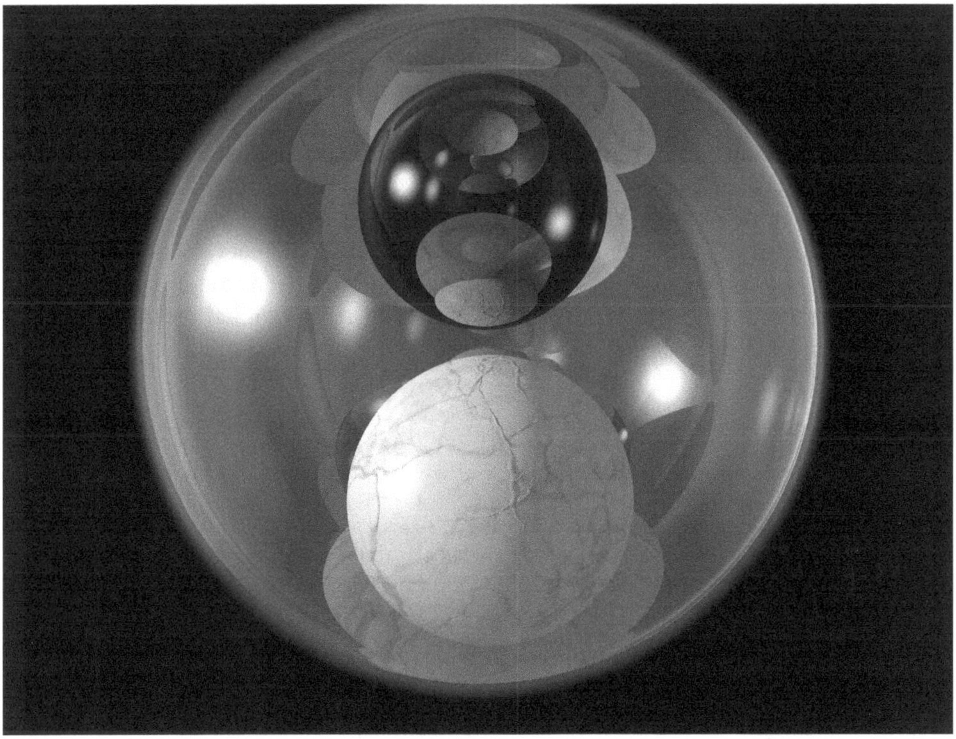

Figure 3.14 Gerhard Mantz, *Lokale Revolte (Local Revolt)*, 1998, Cibachrome, Diasec 120 × 160 cm.

Now, as we have seen Mantz affirms that he designs objects and environments 'that show space and material without the familiar objectivity.' True. But it is important, nevertheless, to underline that his alternative to 'familiar objectivity' is not the absence of objective identity, but rather ambiguous possibilities of it within the same configuration. The realism of his means is what renders the outcome so uncanny.

Conclusion

In this chapter, then, we have considered, in effect, the rise of distinctively digital space. It centers on the achievement of plasticity. However, this is not the three-dimensional illusionism of figuration, but something more distinctive – a mode of illusionism which centers on the generation and connection of forms that are similar to those of the familiar perceived world, but which do not fit into its conceptual grid of recognizable kinds of things or organic life forms. What is presented, rather, are different forms of objective unity and relations – ways in which new material or organic things might cohere in alternative worlds of space-occupying objects and states of affairs. Some abstract painters such as Tanguy evoke such worlds, but digital plasticity and its objects do so in much more systematic ways, and with extra-ordinary levels of visual realism.

It is this realism which declares digital plasticity and its objects *as* digital. This has a dual significance. On the one hand, its presentation of unreal forms as if they were real is a kind of intrusion of alternative reality into our own. This gives it an uncanny quality. On the other hand, this uncanniness is aesthetic and pleasurable precisely because we also know – even if the object's realism pressures us otherwise – that this intrusion of alternative reality as digital in its origins. We know that its uncanny beauties disclose the vision of the artist's programming gifts.

In the final analysis, then, this realm of digital plasticity and its objects is perhaps the most distinctive achievement of computer created art. The level of complexity in composition and 'finish' in the digital object is of an order that might be achieved in traditional media – but only if the creators were assisted by digital means. This creative achievement is distinctively Postmodern.

Notes

1 Information taken from the artist's website at www.edwardzajec.com/tvc4/pil/index.html.
2 Zajec, ibid.
3 Information by email from the artist, April 10, 2017.
4 Ruth Leavitt (ed.), *Artist and Computer*. Considerable effort has been made to trace Ms Leavitt with a view to including some of her work in this chapter. She has not been traced.
5 Untitled article by Leavitt in *Artist and Computer*.
6 Ibid.
7 These works are reproduced in Leavitt's own article in *Art and Computer*.
8 Works of this kind were discussed in the article 'Computer Prints' by him in *Cybernetic Serendipity*, *Studio International* Special Issue, London and New York, 1968, pp. 92–93.
9 See Palyka's site, www.pal-katoonz.com/early_art2/early_art2.
10 Quoted from www.atariarchives.org/artist/sec18.php (accessed 13/04/2017).
11 Interview with Em at www.technocultures.org.uk/davideminterview.html.
12 Most of the biographical information provided here derives ultimately from Em's 'A Note about my Work,' included in *The Art of David Em: 100 Computer Paintings*, Harry Abrams, New York, 1988, pp. 14–20. This is the first ever dedicated volume on a computer artist. For convenience, I will quote from the online version at http://digitalartmuseum.org/essays/em01.html.
13 Em, http://digitalartmuseum.org/essays/em01.html.
14 Em, Ibid.
15 Em, Ibid. Em observes, also, that in 1979, his entire artistic orientation had arrived at a new stage. In his words,

> by being able to actually immerse myself in the virtual space, my whole notion of what defines 'composition' was forever altered. Once I entered the image space's (often unstable) database, it became possible, for example, to turn 180-degrees around inside it and be completely surprised to discover what was there.
> (Personal email correspondence with the present author, April 24, 2017)

16 Em, personal email correspondence with the author, April 11, 2017.
17 Ibid.
18 Em, personal email correspondence with the author, April 7, 2017.
19 For more information on William Latham, see the online resource http://latham-mutator.com; and Stephen Todd and William Latham, *Evolutionary Art and Computers*, 1992, p. 2. Latham's own homepage is http://doc.gold.ac.uk/~mas01whl/index.html (accessed 21/04/2017).
20 Todd and Latham, op. cit., pp. 11–12.
21 Ibid., p. 12.
22 William Latham's original *Mutations* animation can be seen online at www.youtube.com/watch?v=7sadS5wuOjU.

23 Todd and Latham, op. cit., p. 20.
24 Ibid., p. 24.
25 Ibid., p. 29.
26 Latham is, himself, highly attentive to this stand-alone character, emphasizing that 'With gallery prints the viewer sees a virtual sculpture from just one viewpoint, and so this must be very carefully selected to make the most of the sculpture's three dimensional aesthetic qualities' (ibid., p. 30). Indeed, there is an important distinction in how he realizes his work in two-dimensional formats vis-à-vis the notions of 'raytraced' and 'raycast.' Latham explains as follows:

> Raytraced means that when rendering the 3D scene, virtual rays are in effect cast from the eye, and bounce around the scene thereby generating reflections on shiny services and cast shadows. The challenge is that this is computer intensive, and on the old IBM mainframes we were using then [during the creation of *Mutations*], a raytraced image would take several hours. Raytracing gives the most naturalistic effect, in that the lighting is what we see in reality. Alternatively many of the images we produced then were raycast, which means only a shadow would appear on surfaces of a form, not facing the light, with no cast shadows, and this was quicker to render.
> (Quoted from personal email correspondence with the author, April 21, 2017)

27 See, for example, Todd and Latham, op. cit., Plate 21.
28 Jean-Paul Sartre, *Nausea*, trans. Robert Baldick, 1971, p. 183.
29 The present author has previously interpreted them as an idiom of biomorphic abstraction, but – for reasons which will become apparent – now regards this as a very restricted interpretation. See his discussion 'Abstract Art and Techno-Nature: The Postmodern Dimension,' included in Paul Crowther and Isabel Wunsche (eds.), *Meanings of Abstract Art: Between Nature and Theory*, 2012, pp. 217–240. This chapter is reprinted as Chapter 10 of the present work in a revised form – without discussion of Latham.
30 Mantz's website at www.gerhard-mantz.de/wp/text/virtual-objects (accessed April 16, 2017).
31 Accessible online at http://dam.org/artists/phase-two/gerhard-mantz/artworks-work-phases/virtual-objects (accessed February 6, 2018).

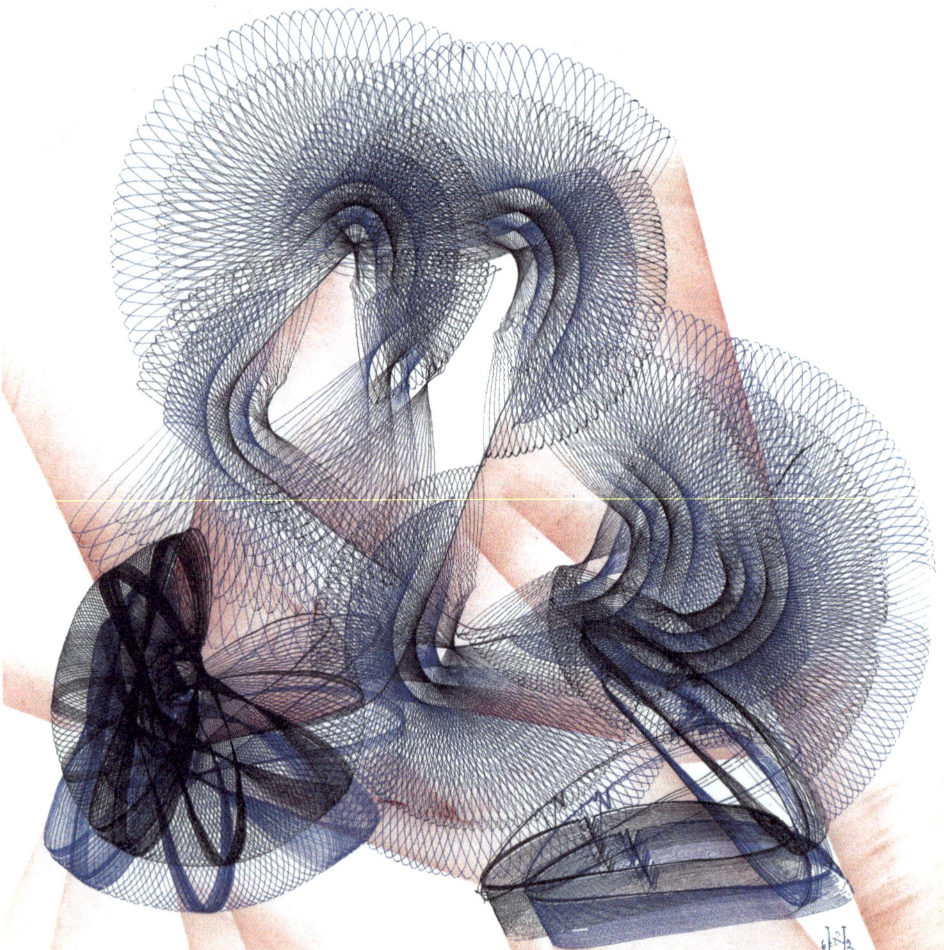

Plate 1 Desmond Paul Henry, *1962 no. 656*, 31 × 26 cm, biro on thin card. background shading.

Source: Image by courtesy of Elaine Ohanrahan.

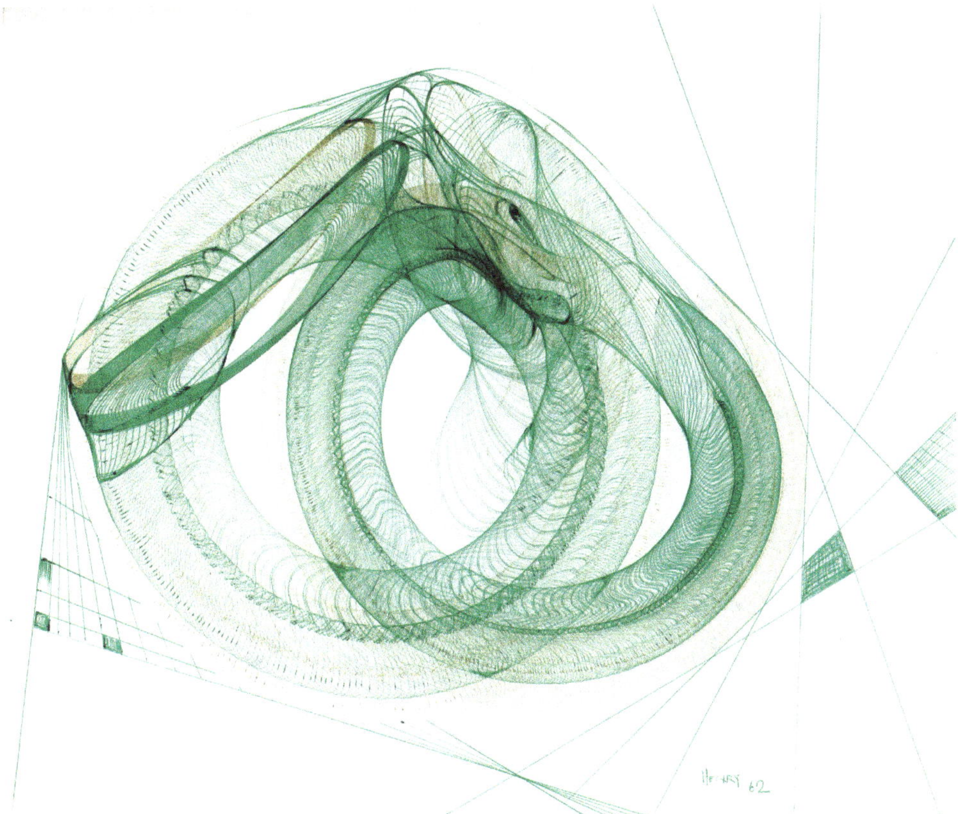

Plate 2 Desmond Paul Henry, *1962 no. 670*, 31 × 26 cm, biro on paper, hand embellishments, hand-drawn lines and shading.

Source: Image courtesy of Elaine Ohanrahan.

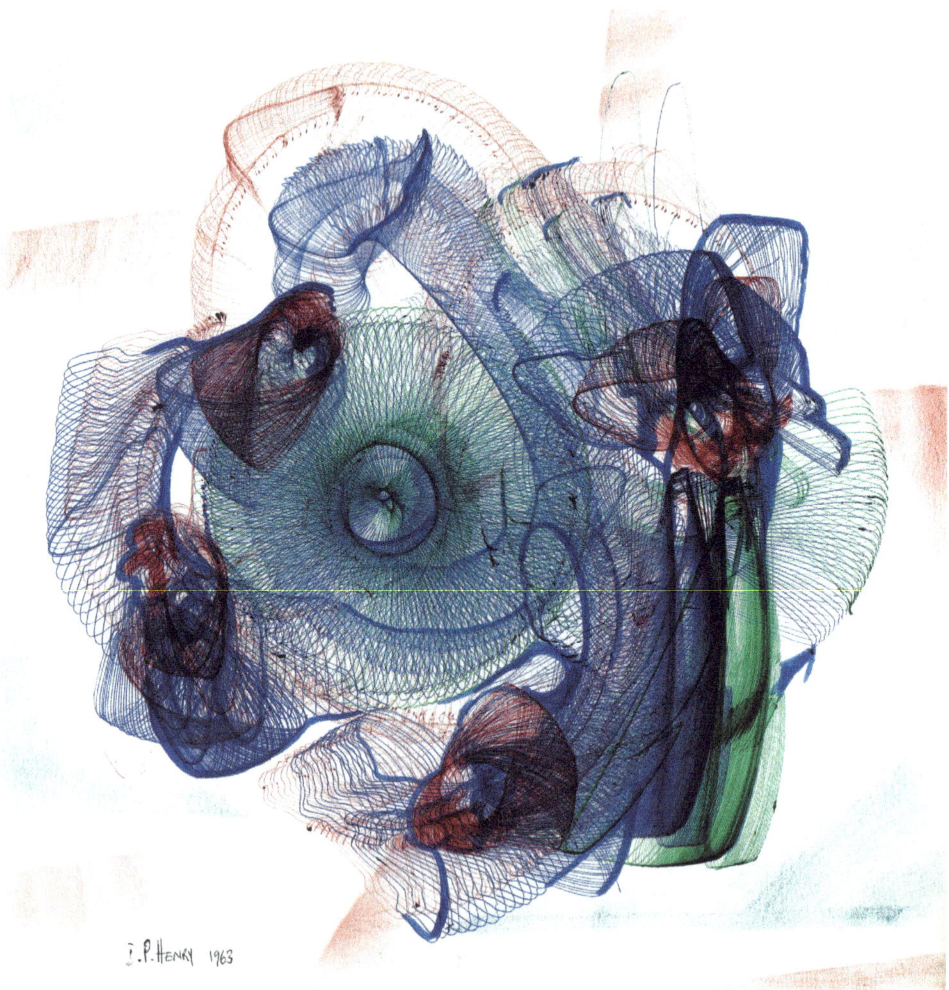

Plate 3 Desmond Paul Henry, *1963 no. 258*, 25.5×25.5 cm, biro on paper background shading, hand embellishments in felt tip.

Source: Image courtesy of Elaine Ohanrahan.

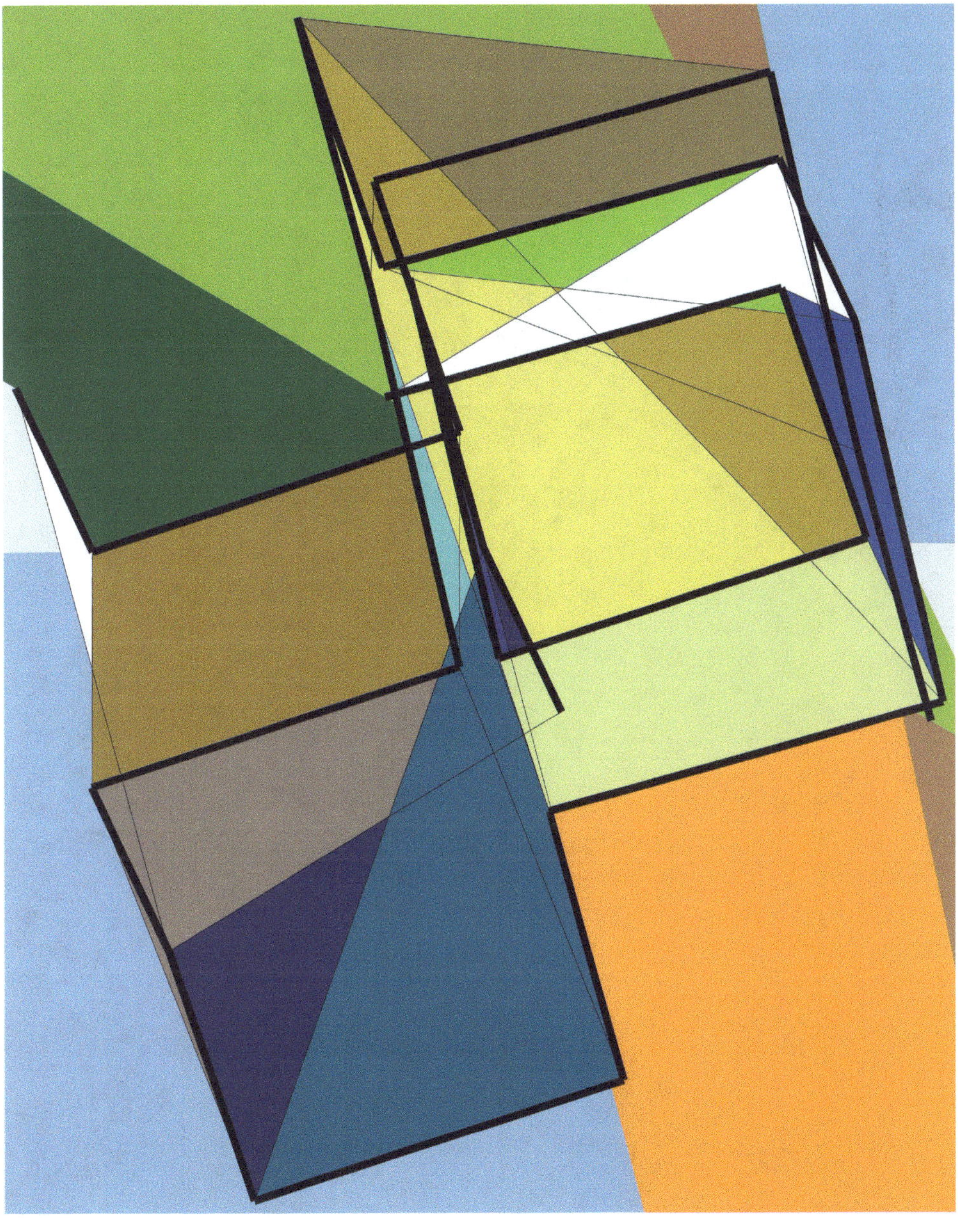

Plate 4 Manfred Mohr, *P-701_B*, pigment ink on canvas, 2000, 141 × 114 cm.

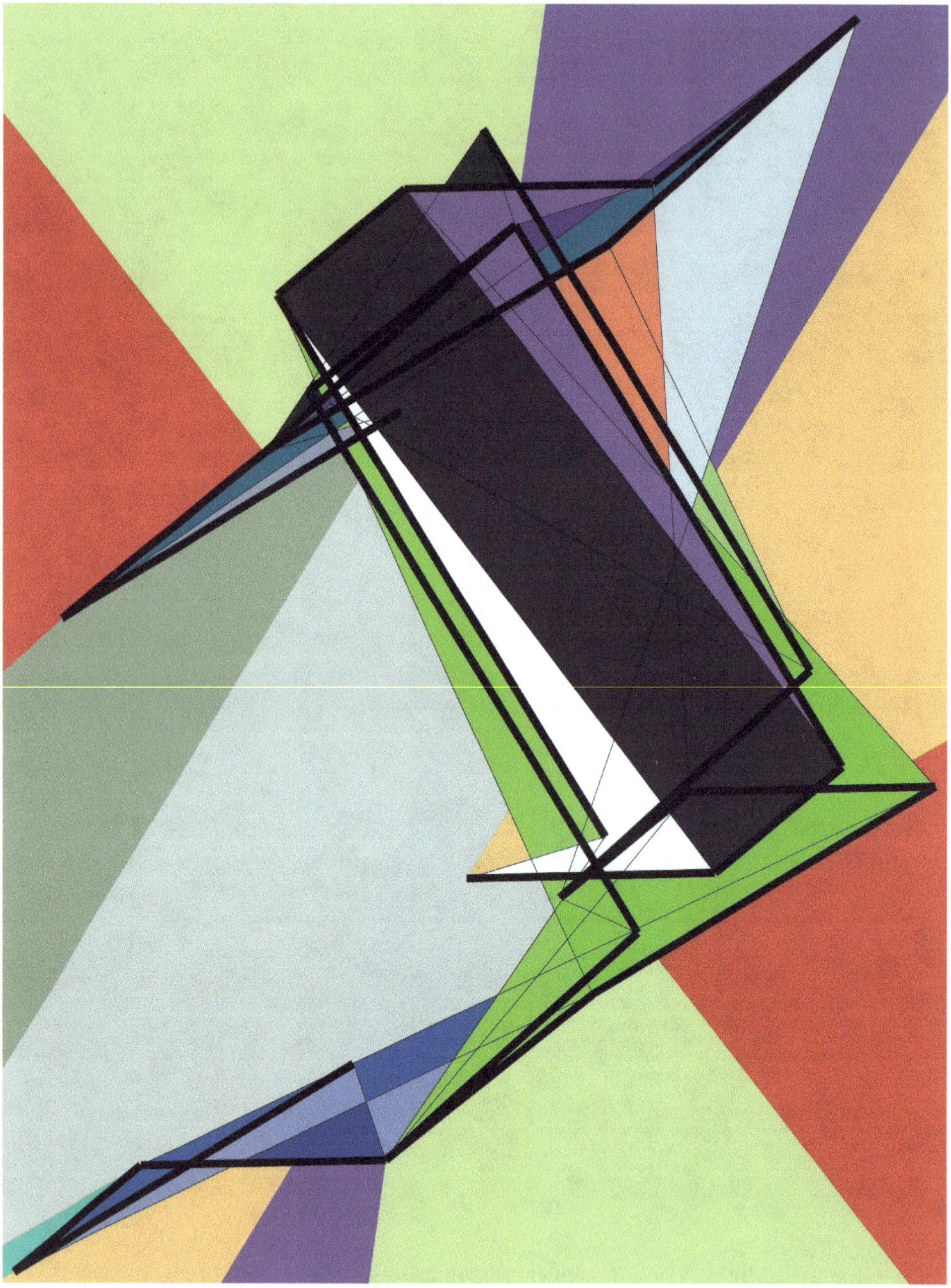

Plate 5 Manfred Mohr, *P-703_C*, pigment ink on canvas, 2000, 152 cm × 114 cm.

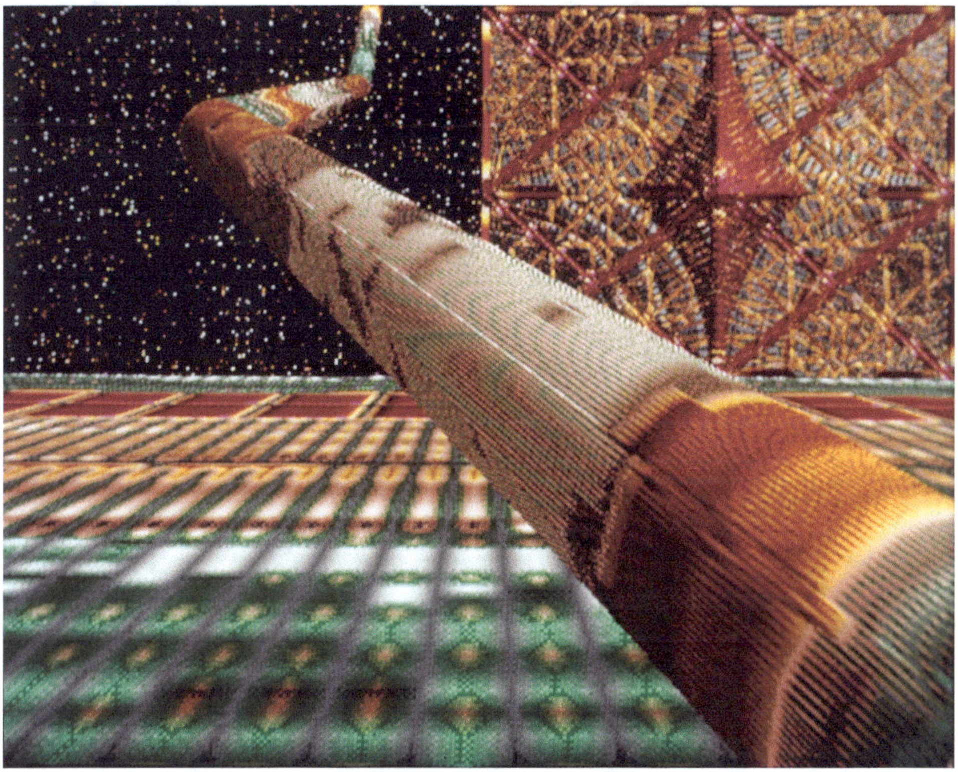

Plate 6 David Em, *Transjovian Pipeline*, 1979.

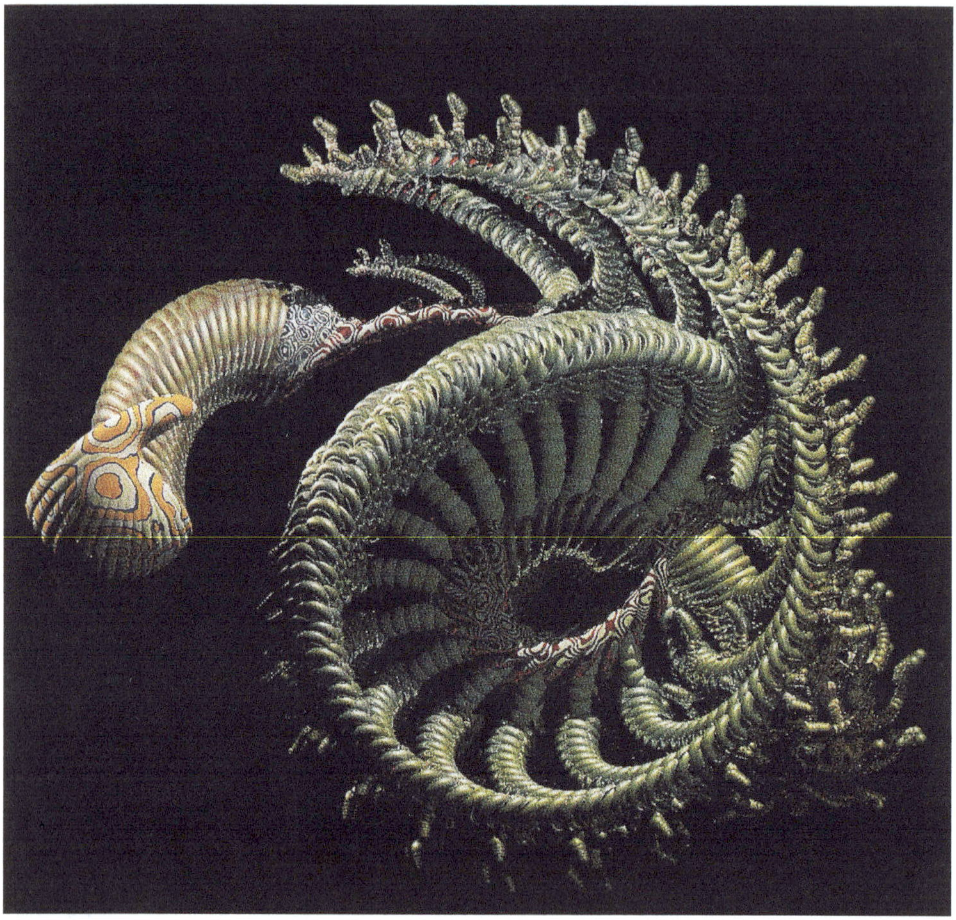

Plate 7 William Latham, *Mutation X Raytraced*. IBM UK Scientific Centre 1992, computer image.

Source: © William Latham 1992.

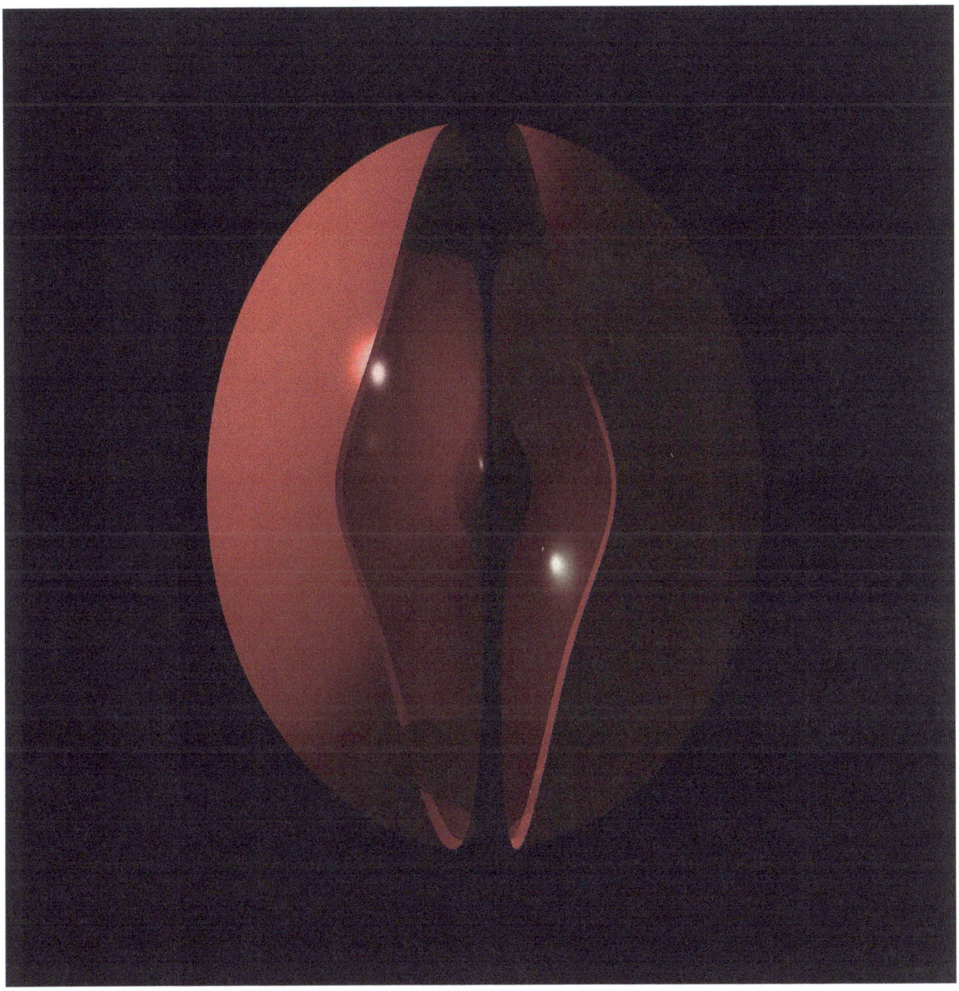

Plate 8 Gerhard Mantz, *Seltenes Glück* (*Rare Luck*), 1998, Cibachrome, Diasec, 120 × 155 cm, 1998.

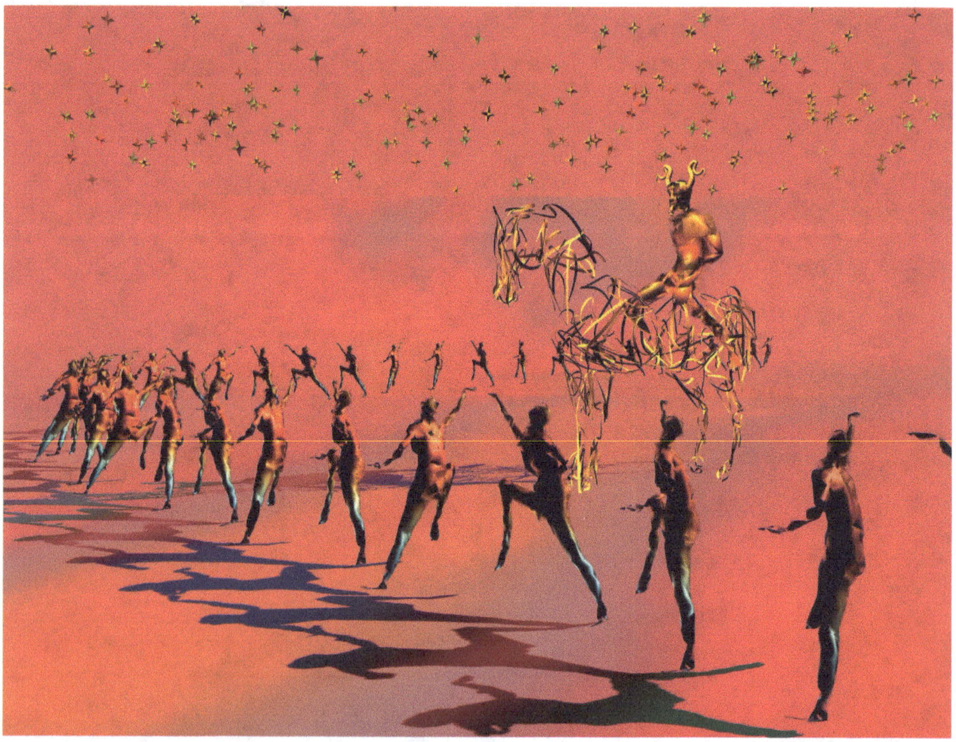

Plate 9 Charles Csuri, *Root of Evil* (aka *Ritual*), 1998, inkjet on canvas, 60 × 40 inches.

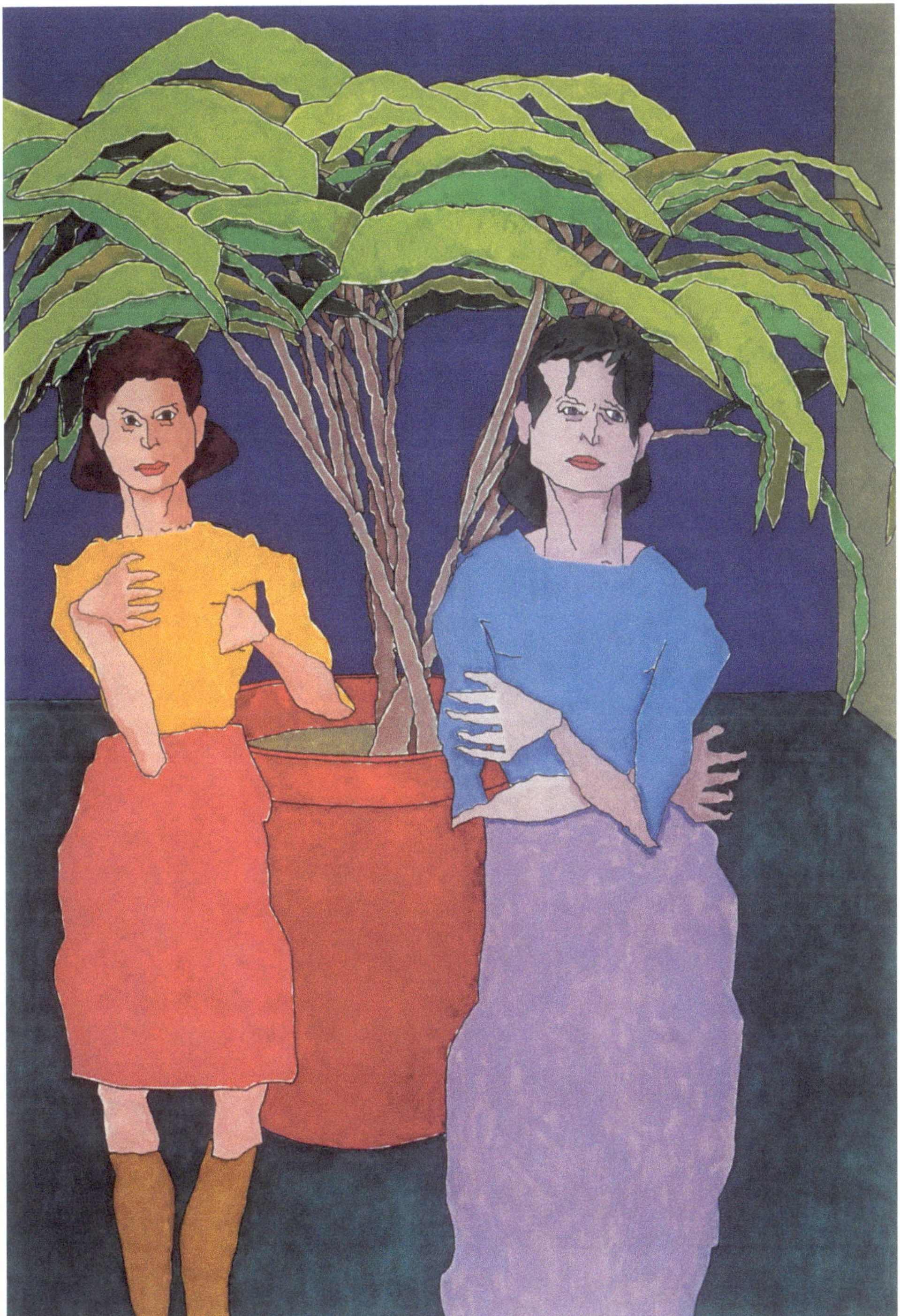

Plate 10 Harold Cohen, *Mother and Daughter*, 1997, 54 × 57 inches, oil on canvas.
Source: Image courtesy of the Harold Cohen Trust.

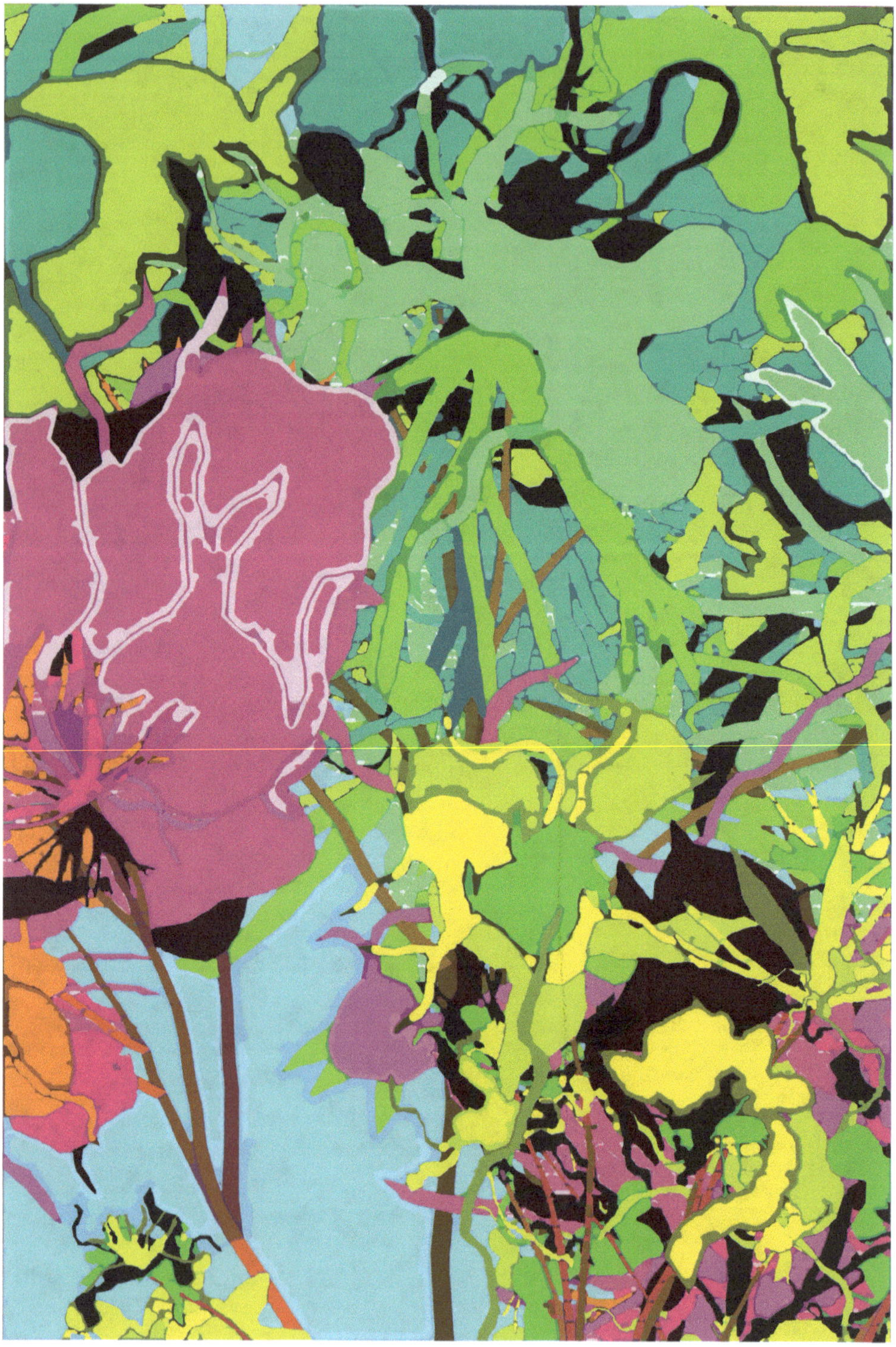

Plate 11 Harold Cohen, *0305–08*, 2003, 45 × 65.75 inches or 114 × 167 cm. Pigment ink on paper. Digital AARON image, Harold Cohen Trust.

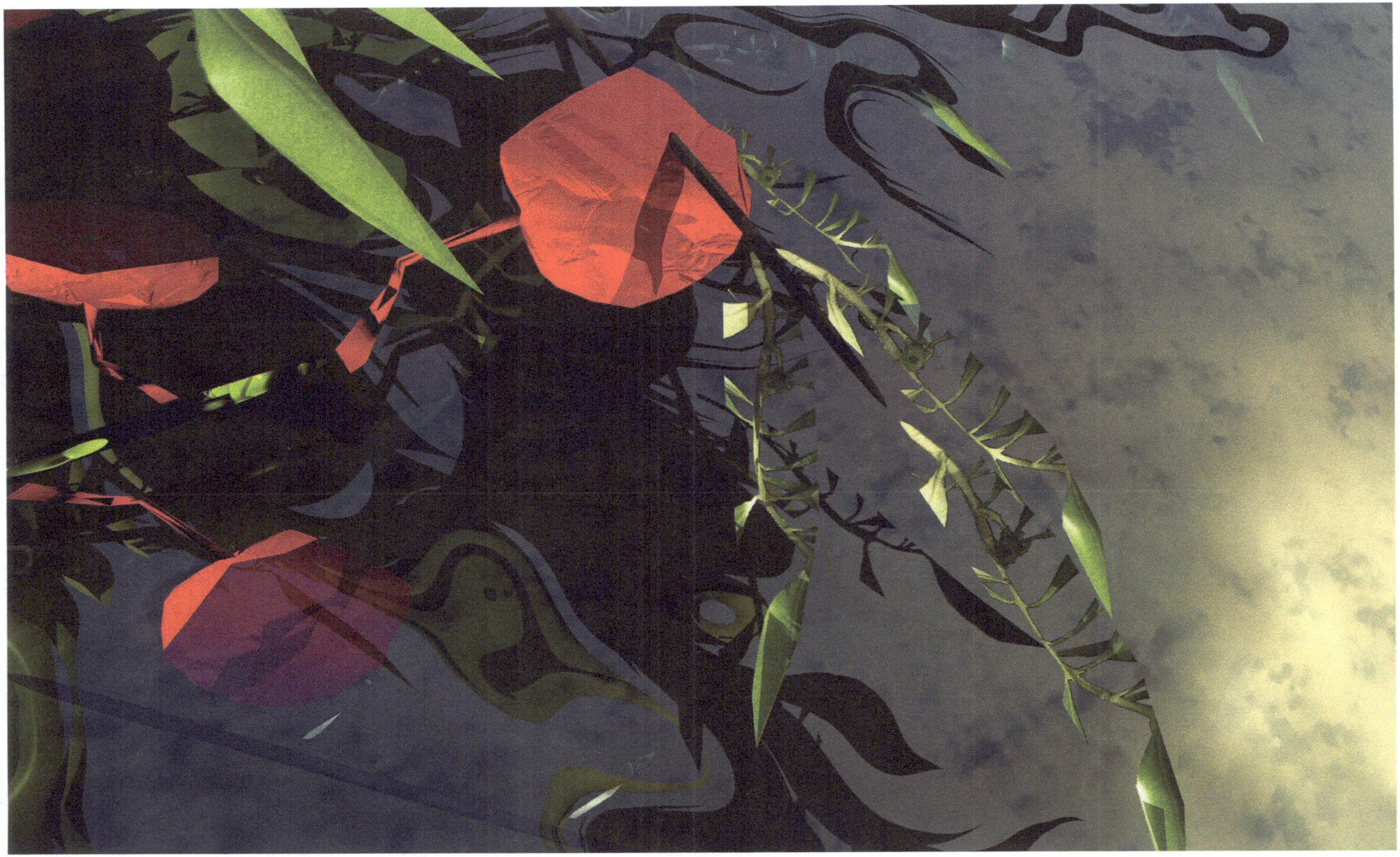

Plate 12 Gerhard Mantz, *Einleitende Begrüßung* (*Introductory Address of Welcome*), 2005, inkjet on canvas, 100 × 170 cm.

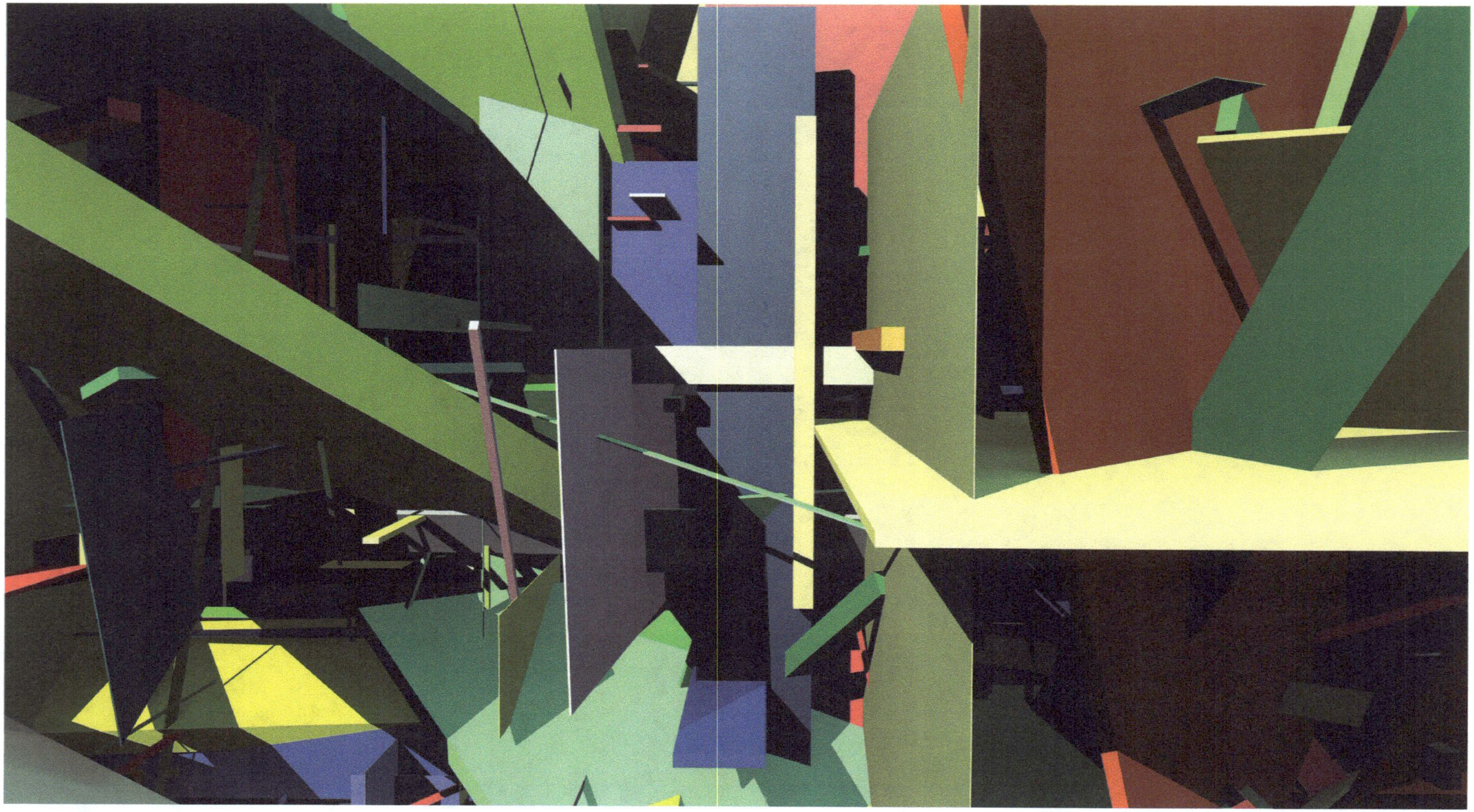

Plate 13 Gerhard Mantz, *Latente Toleranz* (*Latent Tolerance*), 2006, inkjet on canvas, 60 × 100 cm.

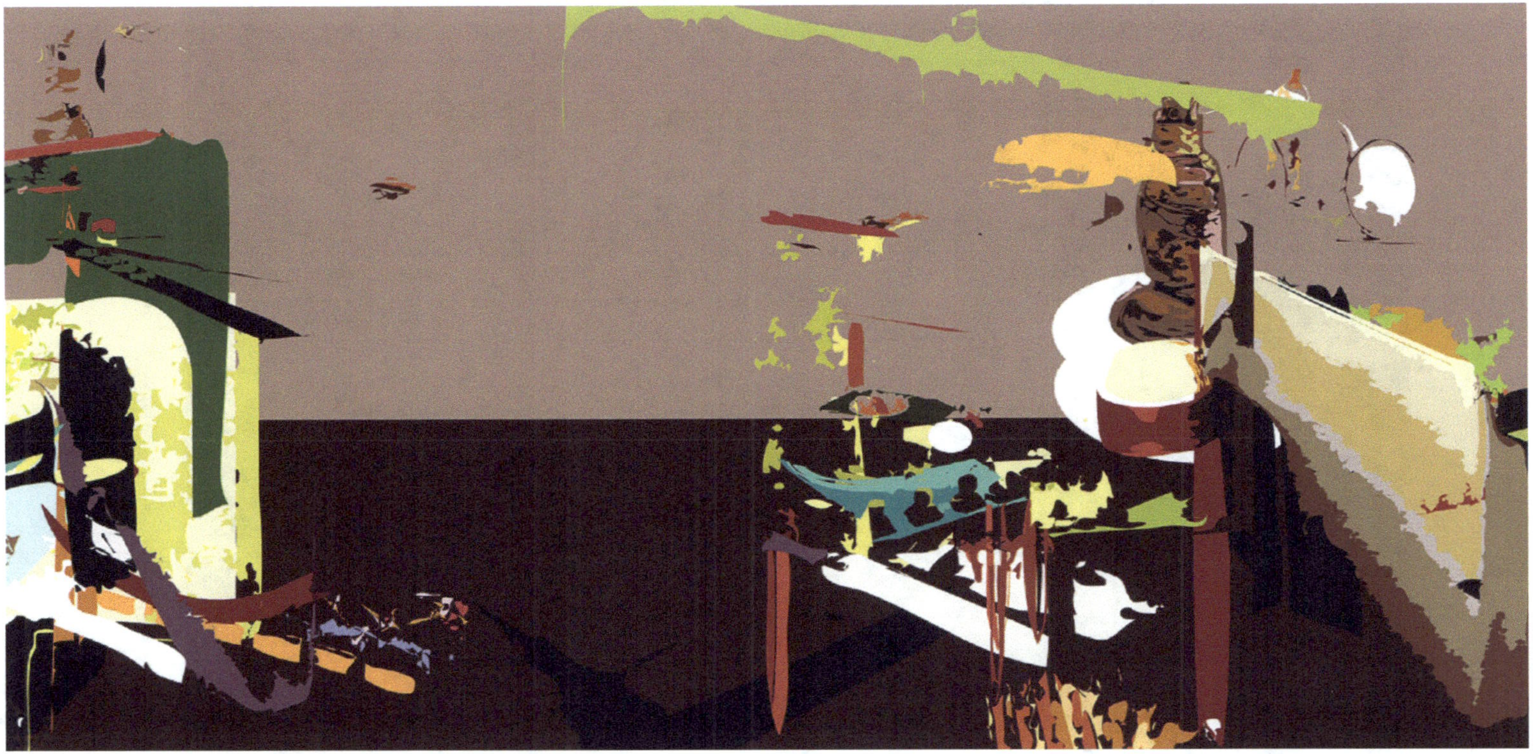

Plate 14 Chris Finley, *Goo Goo Pow Wow*, 2001, enamel on canvas over wood, 90.5 × 180 × 2 inches (229.87 × 457.2 × 5.08 cm).

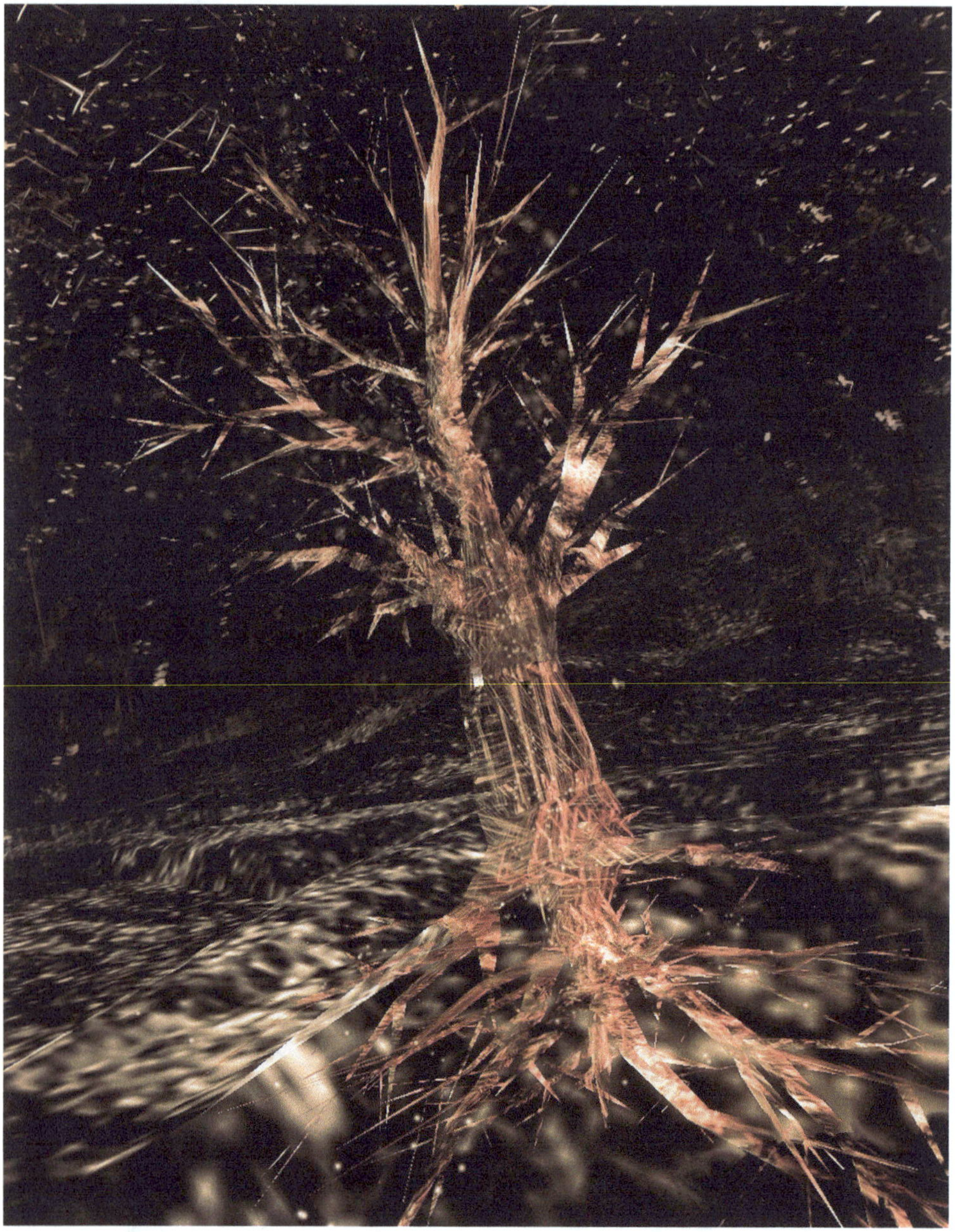

Plate 15 Char Davies, Vertical Tree from *Osmose*, 1995. Digital still captured in real-time through head-mounted display (HMD).

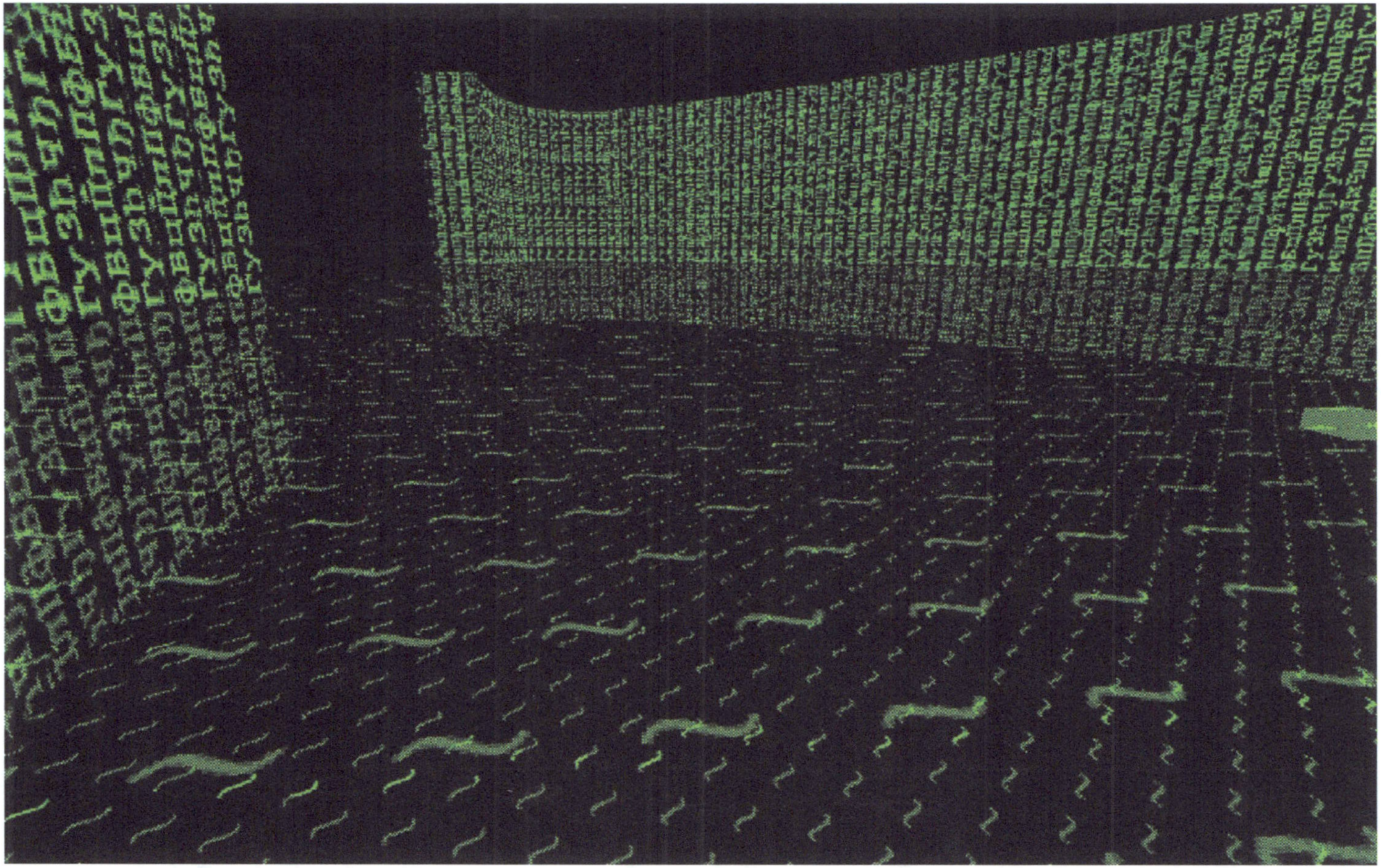

Plate 16 Vuk Cosič, *ASCII Unreal*, 1998; programming by Igor Kolbas, produced at Ljudmila.

4 Echoes of Nature, Enhanced Realities

The Rise of Digital Figuration

In previous chapters, we saw, first, how the emergence of digital art centered on the idea of the semiotic field and/or a mathematically based aesthetic. Its main orientation was towards abstraction. We saw, then, how this orientation was reinforced through the development of digital plasticity and a virtual space based on digital objects and relations between them. None of these innovations involved a Modernist aesthetic of the purity of the medium, but was geared, rather, towards exploring the possibilities of digital space as a source of new ways to project visual form and objects.

The development of figurative digital art was equally explorative and took a surprisingly long time. A number of early experiments in this direction were done at the Bell Laboratories. Kenneth C. Knowlton and Leon Harman, for example, developed a method for digitizing pictures, and converting them into a series of gray-scale values, with a pixilated image assigned to each such value. This was rendered using a microfilm plotter. The most celebrated example of this is *The Nude* created in 1966 (with the choreographer Deborah Hay as the model). It was shown in The New York Times (October 11, 1967) and, subsequently, in the exhibition *The Machine as Seen at the End of the Mechanical Age* held at the Museum of Modern Art, New York from November 27, 1968 to February 9, 1969. Another important contributor to that exhibition was Lillian Schwartz, whose subsequent achievements are scattered across many digital-related fields.[1]

The present chapter, however, focusses on more specialized practitioners of digital figuration, with a view to illuminating their creative strategies. We address, specifically the work of Nancy Burson, Charles Csuri, Harold Cohen, Gerhard Mantz, and Kenneth Feingold. Burson's most significant contribution is centered on the digitization of images per se. Csuri devises programs that use digitized material as, in effect, the basis of a visual vocabulary from which new works of digital figuration can be composed. Cohen achieves his mode of figuration by exploring the relation between programming and how humans perceive images; Mantz develops figuration into advanced realism for a specific range of visual/psychological effects; and Feingold leads sculpture into the AI field. By investigating these artists, accordingly, we will be able to understand key aspects of how digital figuration has been developed and gain insights into its artistic scope.

One

Let us begin with digitization. As we saw in the introduction to this chapter, the first digital figuration was based the digitization of existing images. In conceptual terms, it is the ground level of digital figuration. However, even this most basic form has been developed in its own right as an artistic tool, and we must consider its significance in this respect, before addressing more advanced modes of digital figuration.

Digitization – through scanning programs – is now a commonplace function available in almost all home or commercial computers. Its artistic potential is realized mainly when the digitization process itself involves, or leads to, creative transformations of the image's appearance. Indeed, this is the basis of an ontological feature which is unique to digitized imagery, namely *morphing*. This is where one visual form is changed into another without the final image showing any perceptible gaps or abrupt changes that might indicate that it is the outcome of such a process. An analog version of this is found in those 'Identikit' images used by law-enforcement agencies. These are composite visuals involving transparent images physically layered over one another. But the morphed digital image generates its final composite through a single, *continuous* electrical/mathematical process.

An important innovator in respect of this is Nancy Burson. She has held visiting or adjunct teaching posts at Kansas Institute of Art, Harvard University, Tisch School of the Arts in New York, and the New York Film Academy. In the early 1980s she began digitally scanning photographs so as to 'morph' them into composite images. Christiane Paul observes that

> Burson's work has consistently addressed notions of beauty as defined by society and culture: her *Beauty Composites* (1982), which merge the faces of film stars Bette Davis, Audrey Hepburn, Grace Kelley[sic], Sophia Loren, and Marilyn Monroe (*First Composite*) and Jane Fonda, Jacqueline Bisset, Diane Keaton, Brooke Shields, and Meryl Streep (*Second Composite*), are investigations into beauty that focus on the constituent elements of culturally defined ideals. The face literally becomes a typographical record of human aesthetics, a document of and history of standards of beauty that at the same time suppresses individuality.[2]

Burson's morphed composites clearly raise issues of the sort noted by Paul, but if cultural politics were all they were about, then they would be little more than part of the mainstream techno conceptualism where computers and digitally created imagery are used to criticize one thing or another, or to stimulate awareness of societal problems. However, in addition to this, some of Burson's composites have prophetic originality. For example, her *Androgyny (6 men and 6 women)* morphing male and female images (Figure 4.1), and combinations of animals such as *Lion/Lamb* of 1983, not only anticipate (and, in a sense, enable) morphing across lines of biological difference, but, in so doing, also become congruent with a key feature of Postmodern technology – namely its capacity to induce biological transformations with far-reaching outcomes for gender and genetics.

Burson herself has developed the morphing dimension in important interactive dimensions that feed back as static images. *The Age Machine and Composite Portraits* exhibition at MIT in 1990, for example, was an interactive video project that issued in static images. By scanning the participant's face, and referring to its database of typical ageing effects, The Age Machine was able to print out a portrait projection of how that person might appear twenty-five years in the future.

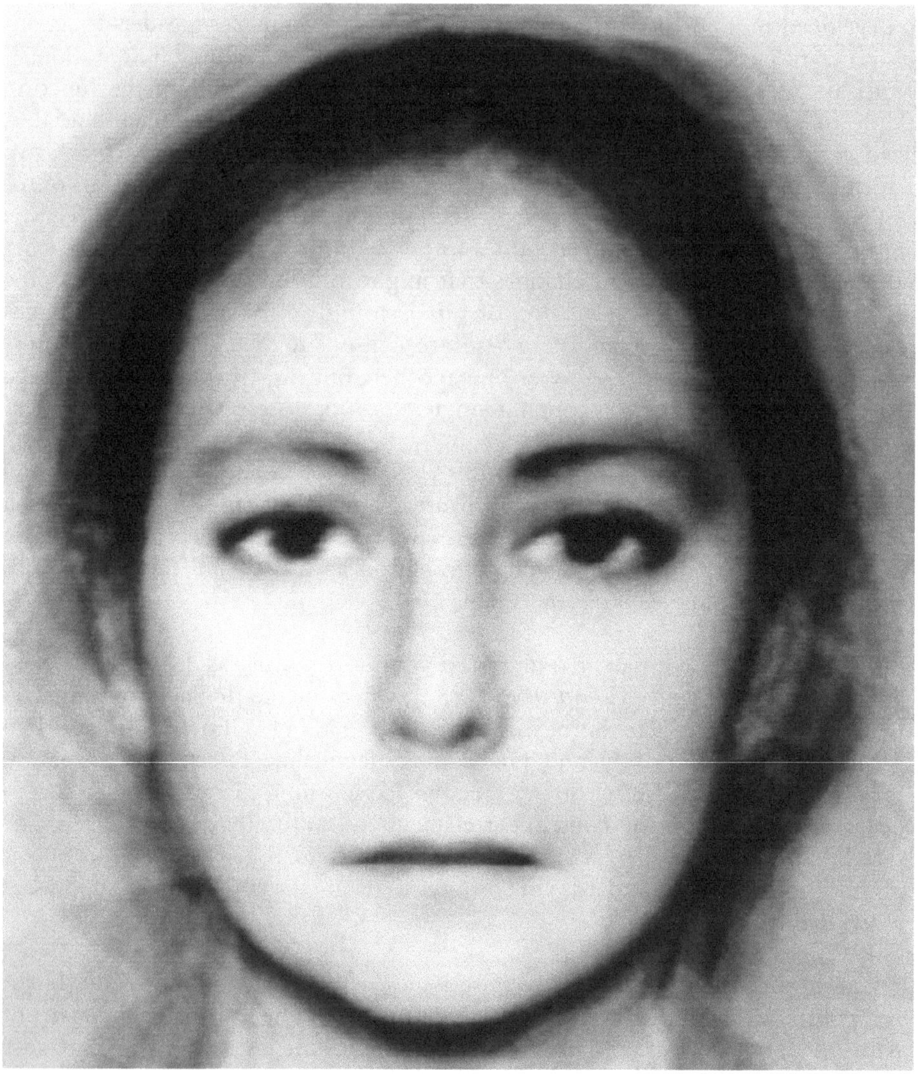

Figure 4.1 Nancy Burson, *Androgyny (6 men and 6 women)*, 1982.
Source: © Nancy Burson.

Now the process of physical ageing is seamless – it happens as an outcome of the continuous occupation of time. In *The Age Machine*, the final composite is an image that is also generated through a seamless process. This interesting outcome is grounded in the phenomenology of morphing. The resulting images are visually freed from any sense of having been constituted from disparate original elements. Non-digital composites can be described as visual mixtures, but the morphed digital image involves material scanned and programmed into a whole which is more than the sum of the original scanned parts. This *holistic visual structure* is *intrinsic* to the digital mode of generation.

Whilst digitization is a technique that has been artistically used on a relatively large scale, it is (as noted earlier), the conceptual ground floor of digital figuration – insofar as it is a technique dependent on a specific pre-existent image. The attempt to go beyond this – to produce more autonomous techniques of figuration – proved to be a complex process. A key figure is Charles Csuri. He taught art at Ohio State University, and began experimenting with computers as a means to artistic creation in the early and mid-1960s. His use of them always emphasizes the primacy of artistic significance, even though his developmental work has involved frequent cooperation with scientists and projects funded by scientific bodies (including the American National Science Foundations).

Margit Rosen suggests that there are analogies between Csuri's approach and the aesthetics of Bense insofar as Csuri felt that it might be possible to construct a mathematical description of an artist's style.[3] But this is actually the decisive difference between Csuri and the Bense school. For Csuri, the mathematical description involves analytic clarification of the details of the artist's style and the use of digital means to synthesize images from such details. The Bense approach in contrast, seeks forms that exemplify mathematically derived universal aesthetic laws. The artist's individual vision, in effect, drops out of the picture.

This profound difference between Csuri and Bense is well illustrated by Csuri's emphasis on the notion of *transformation*. The emphasis arises, in part, through the influence of Darcy Wentworth Thompson's famous book *Growth and Form*, and in particular, the use of a two-dimensional grid structure, to change the appearance of a given drawing.[4] Csuri worked with computers as a vehicle for transformation as early as 1963, when he used an analog device to revise drawings done by himself (copies of paintings by old masters). The revisions were executed by adapting the stylii of a pantograph (usually employed for copying plane figures to a desired scale). This allowed him to create key variations upon the scale of the original drawing along the x or the y axes, and to reverse its spatial orientation.

By 1964, Csuri had realized the potential of digital computing and graphic plotters as a means for the artistic transformation of given material. His first digital works date from that year. Csuri describes the cumbersome technology involved as follows.

> These images were generated with fortran programs which ran on an IBM 7094 computer. This computer was much slower than today's personal computers and one had to submit a job for processing. For computer graphics the 7094 had as output cards about 4 × 7 inches with holes in them which contained information to drive a drum plotter. Boxes of cards could represent a single image. The cards were entered into a card reader on an IBM 1130 computer with a plotter device. These punch cards had the information to move the pen and pick the pen up or down as well as programmed instructions for end of line, etc.[5]

The upshot of all this is well illustrated through one of Csuri's most important early themes – the human face. It is found in a number of his analog variations on works by the old masters, and is a recurrent theme in his early digital drawings. Of particular importance is the image of a bearded man. In the plotter drawing *Five Faces* of 1966, this image is repeated five times, each figure intersecting and overlapping with the one adjacent to it. The horizontal axis is slightly tilted upwards-left at an acute angle to that of the plane. This has the effect of tilting the group as a whole – a kind of wilful spatial 'flaw' that makes it different from digital experiment of a purely scientific kind. The reason for the difference is that even though the configuration is mathematically regular throughout, the tilting helps engender a slight disorientating effect – it is slightly out of synch with the normal horizontal orientation of how pictures present to visual perception.

Also implicated in this is the very character of the aforementioned regularity. The fact that each figure overlaps exactly with the next one in the same plane means that there is no sense of recession between them, i.e. of one being behind another. If there had been such a pictorial device, the arrangement could have been made sense of as phases of motion, as successive appearances of the face through time. Without this device the regularity of the arrangement in a single plane makes the figures appear to crowd in on one another. There is a psychological and visual *jarring*. The face is multiplied and overlapped fivefold simultaneously in a spatial and temporal manifold that is visually abnormal.

Interestingly, this effect is achieved through an important digital innovation – *instancing*. This involves the creation of a *mesh* (a whole composed of vertices, edges, and faces) that represent a recognizable three-dimensional polyhedral body. The advantage of the mesh is that it can be generated repeatedly across the digital pictorial plane, with more individual characteristics programmed in as the job requires. In the case of *Five Faces*, the repetition is simple, and, as we have just seen, the insistent invariance of the face's repeated and overlapped instances are a key to its visual impact.

The instancing effect was not Csuri's only way of transforming the image in his early work. Consider *Sine Curve Man* (Figure 4.2) created in cooperation with programmer James Shaffer and exhibited in 1967. It emerged through a complex process, and exists in at least three later variants, over and above the version considered here. During 1966, Csuri created sketch book drawings of this subject, seeking, especially, to determine the kind of frequency and phase changes that might result from variations on the *x* and *y* axes, and changes of the subject's position in three-dimensional pictorial space. Through this, Csuri, seems to have realized that aesthetically significant structures based on evocations of *vision as process* were achievable by digital means.[6]

The upshot of these explorations was the *Sine Curve Man* presented here.[7] This image is based on the line drawing of a bearded man, digitized, and then transformed mathematically. This involves the *x* axis being kept constant whilst the *y* axis is subject to a sine curve function. The upshot is an oscillating portrait.

It is interesting that some important early analog computer images created by Ben Laposky and Herbert Franke in the 1950s, and by Desmond Paul Henry in the 1960s also present (albeit in contrasting ways) oscillographic forms – sometimes of great beauty and complexity. Indeed, over and above their aesthetic impact, such forms have established themselves in late Modern and early Postmodern visual folklore as the kind of things we expect scientists to be looking at when they conduct their experiments.

However, in Csuri's and Shaffer's *Sine Curve Man*, the oscillating variations are put to work digitally – to vary the shape of the original face-drawing. The results are startling. It has been suggested that 'Csuri's abstraction of the face suggests parallels with early Cubist movements and manages, without having the advantage of color,

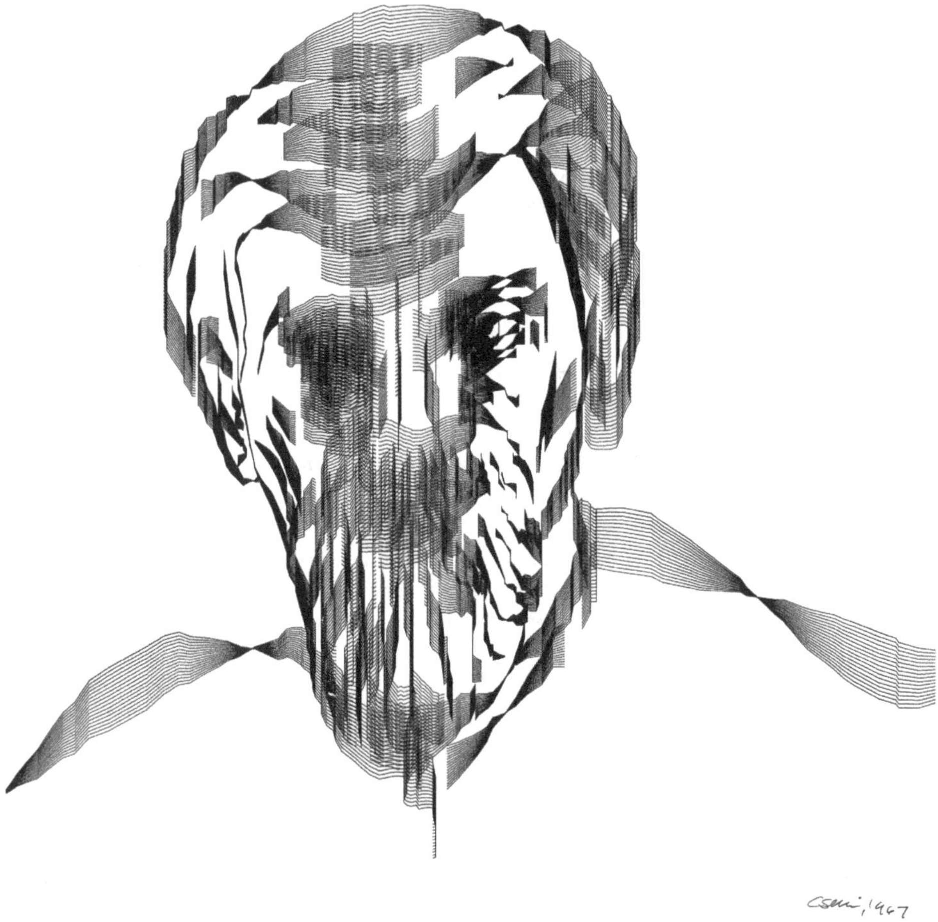

Figure 4.2 Charles Csuri and James Shaffer, *Sine Curve Man*, 1967, ink drawing on paper, 32 × 32 inches.

to invoke some of the emotive qualities of Expressionism.'[8] The comparison with Cubism is not helpful. In a work such as his *Portrait of Ambrose Vollard* of 1910, for example, Picasso changes our normal expectations of how a portrait presents its subject, by fragmenting it into facets. The facets are not linked in mathematical regularity, and are rather the artist's blending of the subject's volume with the planar features of the medium to create a new aesthetic configuration.[9] The resulting manifold is optically animated, but this does not involve the suggestion of movement in any specific temporal direction. The *Sine Curve Man* has no significant affinity with this, nor, for that matter any other phases of Cubism.

The link to Expressionism is more viable, though by no means straightforward. Drawings or paintings of any subject-matter change how that subject-matter appears – and this is the case no matter how 'realistic' the picture may be. The changes are there and are highly creative, but are not usually emphasized with rhetorical swagger or violence vis-à-vis style in composition or handling. In Expressionist artists, however, the act of painting is often emphasized in the most emphatic terms through the extremeness of the visual transformations enacted by it. Francis Bacon's portraits, for example, dislocate or throw the relation between bodily forms out of synch with one another, through composition and/or handling that smears, smudges, and distends. As a direct testimony to gesture this certainly evokes the *act* of painting more directly at the level of visual perception more than traditional works. There is a suggestion of temporal progression – but not temporal flow (in any directional, potentially measurable way).

This is the proper context for understanding the *Sine Curve Man*. Here, the bearded face has been deformed in a way that suggests a smudging or melting process vaguely moving towards the viewer. Indeed, this is psychologically unsettling insofar as it evokes the face decomposing or collapsing in upon itself through some unspecified trauma. However, what makes this uncanny is that the effect is not achieved through the artist's handling of the medium in any gestural sense. It is a mathematically expressible process of oscillatory transformation – a process of *morphing*. But, the fact that it is a drawing of a face which is thus transformed changes the significance of this very process. Our lives are *measured out* through successive moments of time, time's measuring is something we live in. Of course, we can think about the process as a concept, and become frightened of it when we visualize its outcomes, but in the *Sine Curve Man* – through the progression of oscillatory forms from the background of the figure to its foreground – the process of time through transition, *as* something measured is presented at the level of perception itself. There are clear hints at the outcome of the process, but, at the same time, the work itself is an intervention upon this. It makes it into something shared – with the artist's insight and with other spectators of the work. Here, the digital medium has been set to handle the drawing in a way that engages with the kinds of experience that Expressionist techniques in art do, but with the burden of meaning displaced from the process of making to an aesthetic of the *existential* mathematics of perception and temporal flow. This is the *intuitive* and distinctive artistic lining to *Sine Curve Man*.

Some of Csuri's most important work in the late 1960s and the early 1970s involved animation in computer graphics, and real time computer generated images that brought an interactive dimension into play. One of the most important examples of the former is *Hummingbird* (created in 1967 and first shown publically in 1968). The animation was derived from line drawings of a hummingbird with movement sequences consistent with its pattern of flight. Over 30,000 images and 25 motion sequences were digitally generated, with selected images and sequences recorded directly on to film by a micro-plotter. The frames were transferred to 16 mm film, and the resulting work was widely shown in the United States and Europe (winning an award at the Fourth International Experimental Film Competition in Brussells). The Museum of Modern Art in New York purchased the work for its permanent collection.[10]

One of the most interesting features of *Hummingbird* is the way it is composed not only from recognizable line drawings of the bird, but also from scattered details – some of them fragmented and abstract – that cohere to constitute aspects of the recognizable bird form, only when enough of them are linked together. This recalls a point mentioned earlier – namely the importance assigned by Csuri to the mathematically analyzed details of the artist's style as a source for constituting larger-scale images.

Csuri began important work on real-time objects between 1969 and 1973. For example, *Butterfly Dance*, *Lost Fish*, and *Mythical Creature* were done between 1970 and 1973. They are relatively simple visual structures whose animation is based on the object's axis of rotation being controlled by buttons and switches, and a path generated by a light-pen device. What is especially interesting is how Csuri links interactivity to the conditions of perception itself. He observes, for example, that

> ... real-time computer art objects are designed so that the aesthetic experience is realized by the user through participation. The passive 'viewer' must become an active 'participant' in the actual context provided by the system. A case can be made for the idea that art can alter perception, and that since perception is an active organizing process rather than a passive retention-of-image causation, only by actively participating with the art object can one perceive it – and thus, in perceiving it, change one's reality structure.[11]

On these terms, then, Csuri takes interactive digital art to offer an important insight into the conditions of artistic perception. Because visual artworks are mainly static objects, the temptation is to suppose that our aesthetic response to them is likewise passive – a case of registering pleasurable responses to given stimuli. However, the example of perceiving dynamic images actually points back to a dynamism in the perception of of static images, also. This is because the unity of spatial objects is, in ontological terms, open. A contrast with temporal events can show what is at issue here. The unity of such an event is only intelligible insofar as its component episodes (i.e. parts) are experienced in a linear order where each one leads directly to the next. The unity of a spatial object, in contrast, can be perceived in non-linear terms. We can explore it from up to down, left to right, back to front, or front to back, or whatever. To understand what kind of thing it is, spatially speaking, any such combination of perceptual approaches will do the job. This means our perception has an open character. And, of course, if the form is of aesthetic interest, our perceptual exploration will be even more open – seeking to comprehend possibilities of structure determined by the particular details of the phenomenal whole as well as its general features.

Now, there is not any suggestion in Csuri's observations that dynamic digital images are superior to those of other spatial art media. Rather his point is that interactivity is a factor that is distinctive to digital art, and can disclose something that more static idioms tend to conceal – namely the dynamism of aesthetic perception. It is interesting also that Csuri still emphasizes the role of the artist's individual vision in all this. The viewer must make an active contribution, but the scope of what can be contributed is determined by the hardware and software that the artist and programmer have devised.

Of course, the particular real-time works created by Csuri and Thomas DeFanti in the early 1970s now seem very basic. Indeed, by 1975, another digital pioneer – Leslie Mezei – noted that

> Computer Art, as many new endeavors, has reached a plateau of stagnation after an exhilarating start full of promise. The computer specialists who first played with these possibilities soon exhausted their ideas and their interest. They merely did what was easy and obvious with their hardware and their even more

> limited software. Since they were first the results were unique and interesting, but generally 'artless,' and not very innovative.[12]

However, in the decade after Mezei's remarks the silicon chip revolution transformed the entire situation. In Csuri's case, after a break from dedicated artistic work (he formed a computer animation company doing commercial work for tv, and was later heavily involved with his Ohio State University research center) he returned to high-level artistic creation at the end of the 1980s. Csuri now focussed on algorithmic works generated from digital modifications of his own scanned drawings and paintings. He would subject the drawings to special effects using a three-dimensional graphics rendering package.

This amounted to a 'wrapping' of two-dimensional painterly effects around virtual three-dimensional polyhedral forms. In order to achieve this, Csuri collaborated with programmers to create customized algorithms including 'tools' (i.e. algorithmic functions) for fragmentation, colormix, and ribboning. The fragmentation tool involves the creation of alternative possible positions for objects and variations of magnitude in terms of how they are made present in space. Colormix opens color spaces in which objects can be placed or through which they can be moved. The ribbon tool engenders calligraphic lines reflecting light and casting shadow (an effect of the greatest importance in Csuri's more recent works).

Csuri observes further that

> I often use the same tools and simply change the parameter settings. In some respects functions are related to my signature as an artist. When I am working on an image, I write and define simple functions. I also make changes to the relationships between complex functions. Especially important is that the AL language can be used to generate new functions. My software environment is continually being upgraded. ... The library of functions represents many of my ideosyncrasies [sic].[13]

Let us consider a few examples. A remarkable work is *Gossip* of 1990 (Figure 4.3). To create this image, Csuri scanned a painting of striped colors, and then mapped it on to virtual three-dimensional models. A fragmentation function was used to break the figure into pieces, cluster the fragments, control the range of their displacement, and rotate them. Interestingly, the center section is – in terms of the substance of its parts – the same as the two adjoining sections. However, the constituent elements are more radically displaced, having been repeatedly shifted and rotated by Csuri in order to satisfy his compositional sense.

The term 'gossip' throws interesting light upon the work. Gossip involves an exchange of knowledge and opinions between at least two parties – often with a playful 'for its own sake' intent rather than for the genuine furtherance of knowledge about the topic discussed. However, whilst the content of gossip can be light, the conditions that enable it to be carried out often involve deeper truths. In the case of Csuri's work, both these dimensions are involved. Formally speaking, we have two striped horizontal structures – *almost* like columns of gaming chips, but which (like, indeed, one's fortunes in games of chance) seem, at best, precarious and, at worst, mere illusion. The central area has forms disjoining in a visual rhythm, dominated by a downwards-left momentum of transference from one column to the other.

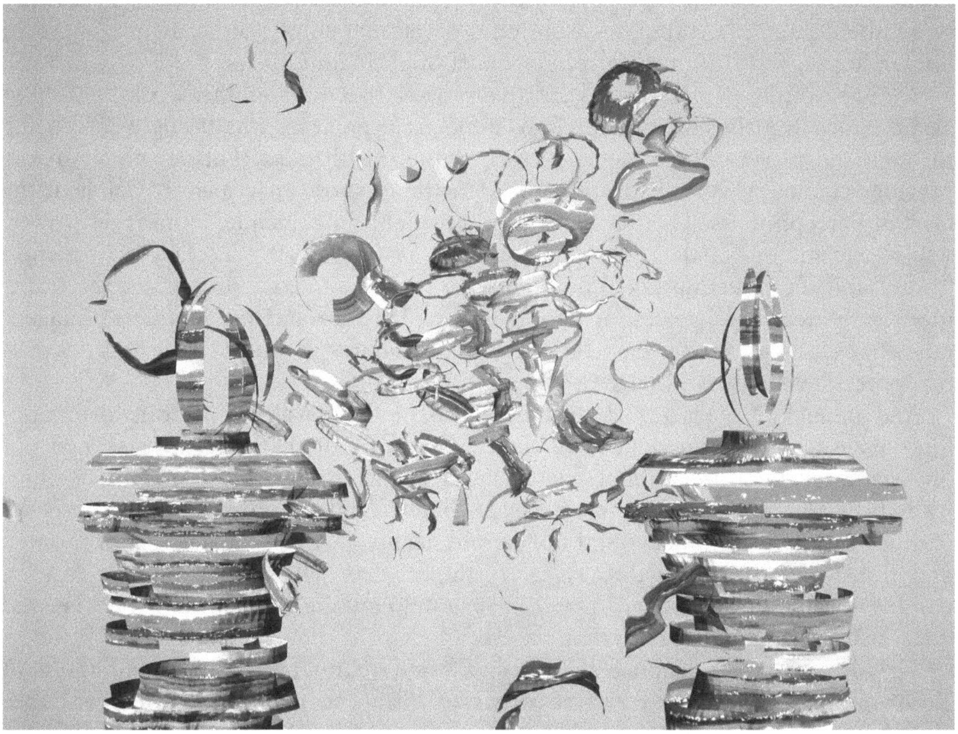

Figure 4.3 Charles Csuri, *Gossip*, 1990, cibachrome print, 60 × 40 inches.

Of course, one might well regard this as one moment in a gossipy formal exchange concerning possibilities of visual configuration. It is, indeed, in this sense, an aesthetically playful structure to behold. However, one must take account, also, of the deeper conditions enabling this play. In this respect, it is interesting that whilst the columns may suggest solid gaming chips, on closer inspection we see that they are only bands of color. This involves a tantalizing perceptual hovering – between seeing the configuration as if it were a solid three-dimensional form, and seeing it as a structure built only from colored tapes or ribbons, or even composed of no more than simple narrow areas of color, as such. Such hovering may be playful, but it is not trivial. The artist's compositional skill has located us in an area of imaginative switching from one zone of spatial being to another. This involves a perceptual freedom that releases us from the more routine patterns of visual recognition at work in everyday life.

The point can be taken further. As noted earlier, the visual transference rhythms between the two columns may seem 'light' and spontaneous, but they are the outcome of repeated trial and experiment by Csuri. When properly appreciated, the achieved playful aesthetic effect points towards a deeper level of artistic originality. And again, playfulness aside, *Gossip* explores the boundaries of figuration and abstraction in a probing way – not only through the three-dimensional virtual physicality of lines and colors, but in the way these structures appear to be both coming apart, yet also, perhaps being drawn together again. *Gossip* embodies a fascinating dialectic of visual becoming and passing away that touches symbolically on the being and finite destiny of all things – from piles of gaming chips, to the slight ribbons of human hopes, and the ultimate coming apart of all spatial things.

We must recall also the actual creative process that enabled this work. It is often aesthetically inspiring to consider how some great painting was brought into being through the marking of a plane surface with brushstrokes. But, as noted in the previous chapter, this transformation is something whose enactment is visible at the level of perception itself – it is something we might, in principle, witness. However, whilst one might watch a digital artist such as Csuri using his favorite function 'tools,' and see something of this activity on the monitor, we do not see the transition from electronic process to visual image. This is what makes digital imagery quasi-magical – no matter how rational the procedures involved. We cannot *see* the real process whereby the image becomes.

And in much of Csuri's work, including *Gossip*, the quasi-magical transformation-into-image has an extra dimension. For, we will recall that this work started out physically as a two dimensional marked surface. Such things can, of course, be physically bent and joined so as to create three-dimensional structures, but here, it is the painting's very appearance – and not its physicality – which has been appropriated and transformed. One might say, accordingly, that when the computer turns a painted surface into a virtual three-dimensional configuration, then we go beyond quasi-magic towards an *aesthetic alchemy*.

The alchemy is just as much at work in Csuri's treatments of the human figure. In *Root of Evil* (1998) (Plate 9) a sequence of instanced male human figures dance away in single file from the viewer, eventually turning abruptly right towards the horizon. Their progress is monitored by an oversized equestrian figure – whose horse and lower torso are rendered in those shape defining and space-enclosing ribbons that are so much a part of Csuri's style. Another such signature characteristic is that of swarming elements – in this case what appear to be flocks of birds distributed across the entire horizontal extent of the upper picture. Here it seems that both man and creature are paying homage to the equestrian figure (whom Csuri playfully suggests may be Bill Gates).[14] Especially striking is the dream-like effect created by the multi-colored shadows in relation to the off-key ground of pink/orange. This effect is amplified further. Several ghostly streams of pale violet insinuate themselves between foreground and background, and hover below the swarm. All in all, the image embodies an aesthetic of dark luminosity. It discloses – in visually seductive terms – how the status of the great individual can beguile the many.

An image of this kind looks, of course, to figures such as de Chirico and Dali for its inspiration. However, as indicated above the image has features that very much define the work as 'in the style of Csuri' rather than that of the other two artists just mentioned. Indeed, whilst a surrealist painter might, in principle, have done such a composition, its particular appearance suggests a work that has been conceived and executed through digital means. The intense precision of both the forms and – ironically – the color density point towards an electronically mediated embodiment. It is interesting that Csuri's compositional strategies often achieve their aesthetic alchemy through very economic means.

A case in point is *Where do we Look?* of 1997 (Figure 4.4). Of this work, Csuri remarks that

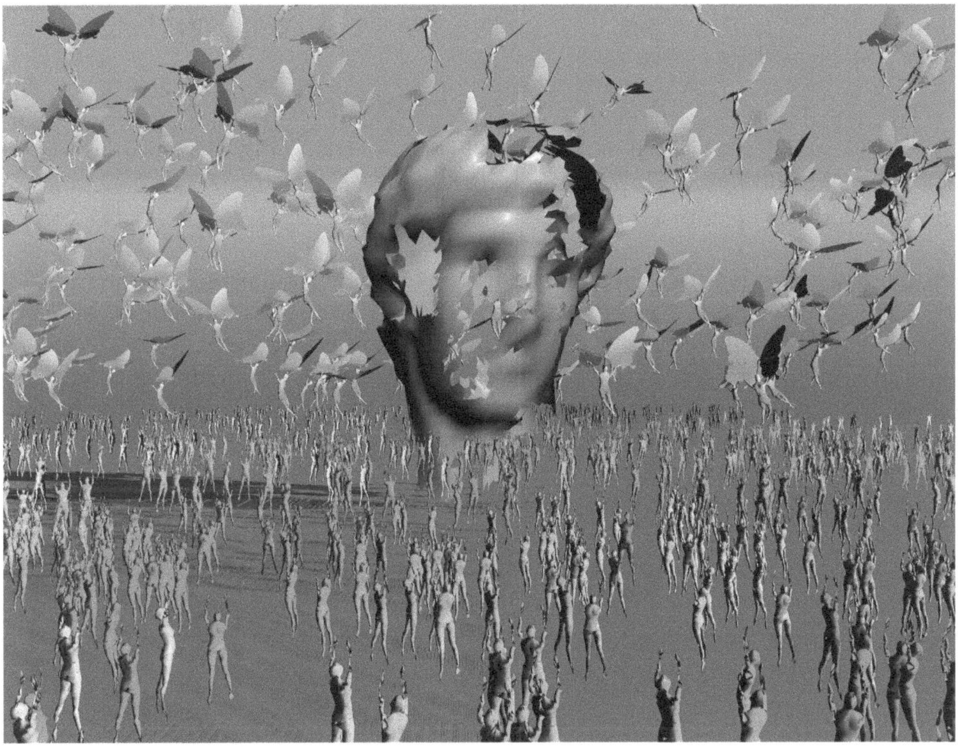

Figure 4.4 Charles Csuri, *Where Do We Look?* (aka *Believers*), 1997, inkjet on canvas, 60 × 40 inches.

> Besides the head, the scene has only two basic figures. I made copies of each of them and there are 2050 figures in the scene. Their representations are at different levels of detail. A decimate function reduced the polygon count and yet preserved the basic geometry of the figure. The lighting was especially difficult to set because there was so much data.[15]

Here, in other words, a simple quantitative device of multiplication leads – through special effects – to important qualitative visual transformation.

Csuri's work, then, constellates around a single creative idea – that the three-dimensional world, as represented in two dimensions, involves visual processes than can be digitally transformed for artistic ends. The other important artist to run with a similar idea – albeit a few years after Csuri, and with very different digital means – is Harold Cohen. It is to his work we now turn.

Two

Cohen first considered the possibilities of computing for artistic practice after a graduate student in music taught him some basic programming in 1968. This was during Cohen's tenure of a Visiting Professorship at the University of California, San

Diego. (Cohen stayed on to become a tenured Professor at that institution.) His introduction to programming seems to have stimulated an idea already formulated some years earlier. In Cohen's words,

> there had to be ways to make art that didn't require continuous invention, painting by painting; that it should be possible to shift the act of invention up a level, where I could formulate procedures that would generate their own inventions in the individual paintings.[16]

As we saw in the previous chapter, Manfred Mohr had formulated a similar idea in the early 1960s, but whereas he looked to a Bensian mathematical aesthetic for guidance, Cohen took an altogether different route. In particular, his desire to create art was influenced by a more general interest concerning the minimum conditions whereby something might count as an image. This meant that Cohen's approach to computer art attempted initially to explore ways in which programming might incorporate features of human image-creation.

In 1973 he took up a position as Guest Scholar in the artificial intelligence laboratory at Stanford University. This equipped him with the practical computing skills to develop the experimental programs that eventually became AARON – the single, continuously extended and diversified program that was the main focus of Cohen's subsequent artistic career. By 1973, his experiments already began to show great potential. He was able

> to model some very general features of cognition and the way they influenced what one did in making images: the ability to distinguish between closed forms and open forms, for example, and between figure and ground. And in implementing those abilities I chose also to adopt the feedback strategies that are characteristic of so much human behavior, modeling freehand drawing as a stepwise procedure for getting from one place to another place, rather than using the mathematical curve-producing functions that were already becoming the signature of early computer art.[17]

The relation at the heart of the factors described in these remarks is a single key relation, namely how a sense of a work's progress so far is implicated in decisions concerning where to place marks. Cohen worked with a program using sophisticated feedback based on progress-to-date. In his words,

> to draw each new line the program needs only to know which of many possible destinations may be reached without crossing an existing line, and, of them, which is the nearest and which the furthest away. But the program is structured in such a way that more particularized decisions may now be reached on the basis of more extended information requiring more complex feedback – which of the possible destinations will result in the straightest lines? Which is closest to the center of the picture? Which is in the densest part of the picture, and so on: with even greater variety of output than we have at the moment.[18]

Cohen's interests here can be illustrated by three works from the Victoria and Albert Museum Collection. In *Drawing* of 1971, Cohen's early program issues in a relatively self-contained image where the joining, separation, and straightening of lines is the compositional basis. Specifically, this involves the forms cohering as a unified open figure. In *Drawing* of 1972, Cohen's early program has gone beyond this to create six recognizable linear groups. These cohere individually in relatively open structures with a potential representational loading – consisting of veined lines suggestive of leaf-like shapes. This individualization means, of course, that the figures are not simply unities but ones that also begin to appear thing-like.

In the *Amsterdam Suite* of 1977 (created by AARON), this is taken much further. Shape, and textures (created from densely packed clusters of small lines and/or perpendiculars), take on a thing-like visual life of their own. None of them form a recognizable example of any specific kind of thing, but the spatial relations between them, and, in some cases, the relation of shape and textures suggest an allusive narrative of contiguous developments.

Cohen's work in the 1970s suggested that the way forward should involve programs based on a 'total system' of machine autonomy – where higher-level decision procedures are integrated with lower-level records (of progress-so-far) on the basis of flexible/adaptive feedback structures. Gradually, however, he became aware that the cognitive basis of human image-making involved negotiation with the 'external' world in a way that rendered its structures far more dense than he had at first imagined. Despite this, after much study of childrens' drawings, he had, by the mid-1980s, worked out a basic creative strategy for AARON. In his words,

> I became convinced that the range of forms AARON could generate would be greatly enhanced if its steering strategy could be made to find its way around a pre-existing 'core figure,' the equivalent of the way the child's initial scribble evidently determines, though not fully determines, the path it traces to enclose it. This conviction proved, in due course, to be justified, to a much greater degree than I could possibly have predicted. The construction of simple core-figures, plus a simple strategy for tracing a path around them, yielded forms of a complexity I could not have generated, if indeed I could have generated them at all, without substantially greater cost. This two-step strategy became AARON's standard mode for generating closed forms.[19]

One effect of this, was the impression that AARON was producing more thing-like forms, on the basis of 'visual experience.' The two step representational strategy allowed the human figure to be presented as a construction from connected parts and postural rules concerning how these parts were articulated. Each element was represented as an array of points, beginning at the juncture with next part. The core figure would be generated by connecting these points by line in a closed form, and so on, the image discursively accumulating the parts for a complete body.

The upshot of all this is that, by the mid-1980s, Cohen had enabled AARON to develop a 'two and a half-dimensional' pictorial space – i.e. a space symbolic of the three-dimensional but not fully realized in such terms. AARON

> knew about perspective, to the degree that it could place figures into a spatial setting with things overlapping each other as they should. But the figures themselves were like cut-outs placed into this space, representations generated in two-dimensional terms directly.[20]

To illustrate this, we might consider *Drawing* of 1985 (Victoria and Albert Museum) (Figure 4.5). Here a group of schematically rendered human figures are linked in ways that present recognizable relations of in front and behind. This strategy contains enough visual cues to suggest a three-dimensional virtual space, but it does not present that space as a space. Rather it is one constituted mainly from the forms within it. Interestingly, in a series based on Picasso's circus pictures (1985–1986) such as the *Drawing* (Figure 4.6) AARON creates figures that are more unified in terms of the cohesion of their parts, but this is to the exclusion of any real sense of active integration with the surrounding space.[21]

In all these works, basic core shapes act as bearers for more specific three-dimensional entities. These entities become individuated – as heads and torsi, or whatever – through particularities vis-à-vis their connection with one another, and through the relation of individual outline shapes to their internal textural details.

It must be emphasized that Cohen did not regard this 'two and a half-dimensional' space as a limitation. He understood western culture to be dominated by visual imagery derived ultimately from photography. Such images deal in abstractions – referring us to information beyond that of their own visual constitution. But AARON's two and a half-dimensional pictorial illusion does not simply refer to that which it is an image of. It invites the viewer to dwell upon the aesthetic richness of how *this* particular visual content is manifest in *this* kind of visual space.

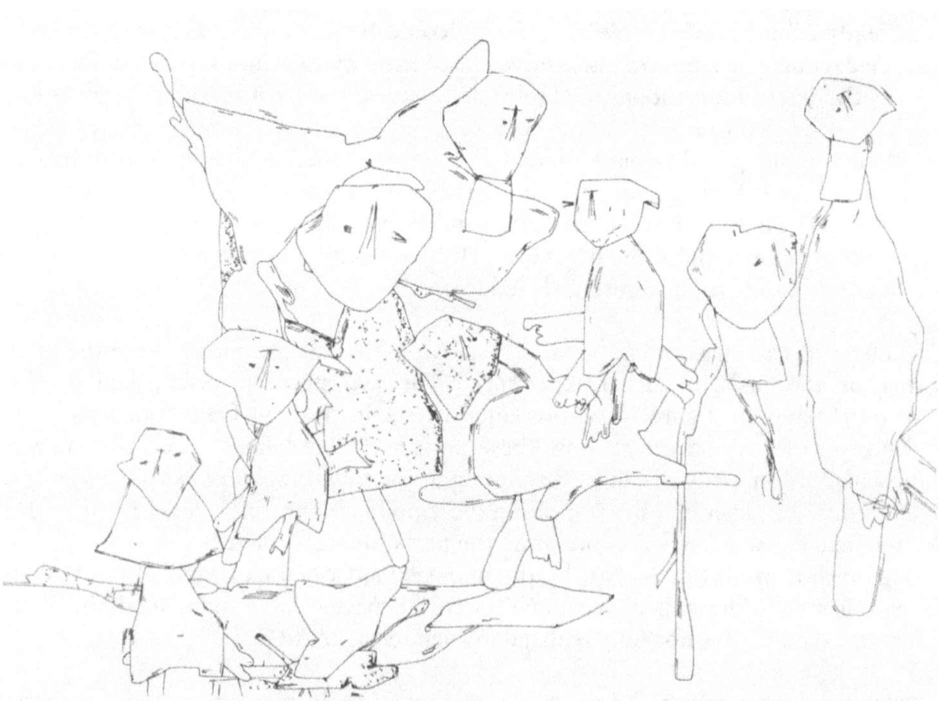

Figure 4.5 Harold Cohen, *Drawing*, 1985, computer-generated drawing on paper, 56.2×76cm.
Source: © Victoria and Albert Museum.

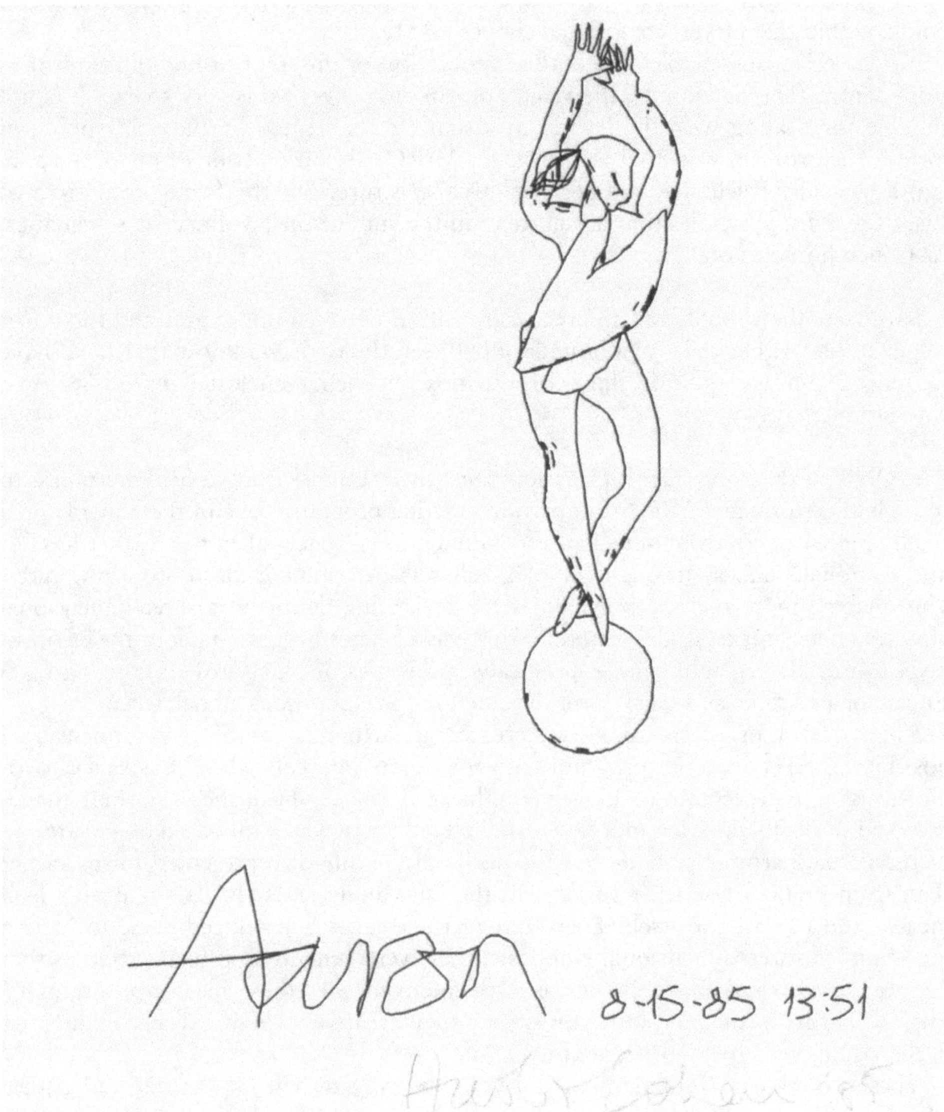

Figure 4.6 Harold Cohen, *Drawing*, 1985, computer-generated drawing on paper, 28 × 2.7 cm.
Source: © Victoria and Albert Museum.

That being said, however, Cohen understood that, in order for AARON to be developed further, there would have to be some steps towards a more complete three-dimensional illusion. For example, an issue arose from the enclosing lines around the core figures in AARON's representational strategy. As we have seen, this enabled illusionistic effects arising from the different distances between points being joined up by lines. These lines link points within, but *not upon*, the surface of their figures. By joining them together, the illusion of bare schematic volume, as such, is created. These volumes take on a more specific identity through their relation to other volumes with which they are adjacent or proximal, and through the joining of points within them to create internal shapes and textures.

Now, whilst this enables the outline-generation of different profiles and postures from contrasting viewpoints, the visual information involved is very sparse. It is not suitable for dealing with the particular visual effects created by the overlapping of forms. The problem was, that at this stage, AARON's construction of pictorial space had a basically discursive and accumulative structure. But the forms in an area of space form visual wholes that are more than the sum of their volumetric schematics. As Cohen himself noted,

> we view the shoulder as an area of transition between upper arm and torso, for example, rather than as a boundary between the two. We know that faces have noses, but we do not think of the nose as being enclosed within its own outline.[22]

AARON's next major stage of development, then, centered on Cohen's response to this. He transformed AARON into two interacting programs; one of them involving a small number of control points in a three-dimensional space taken to a higher level of informational richness through complex rule-sets determining the posture of figures. This enabled more realistic possibilities for presenting figures in a three-dimensional physical environment. A key feature of this was Cohen's programming of the environment to include vegetal forms – specifically, principles of plant growth, ranging from something as simple as a daisy-form to something as complex as an oak tree.

This control program, in effect, created a virtual space of three-dimensional possibilities. The second program allowed it to be realized in a specific two-dimensional representation. Cohen emphasized that, whilst the resulting images involved AARON creating more 'realistic' effects, they were still based on generating pictorial space from points *within* the notional volume of represented forms rather than from points *upon* their surface. In the final analysis, AARON's realism was a means, and not an end itself. Even though the images it produced came to have a more unified three-dimensional emphasis, they were generated in final products that declare the 'two and a half-dimensional' distinctiveness of these specific programmed origins. Through this link, indeed, Cohen's own creative style of expressive interests in the visual were given insistent affirmation.

These points can be illustrated through *Drawing* of 1987 (Victoria and Albert Museum) (Figure 4.7). Here, human figures are immersed in the surrounding vegetation of lush foliage, and giant flower shapes. What were vaguely three-dimensional blobs in earlier works are now arranged in a way that presents them as stones or rocks – leading into the main body of forms within the picture. Most interesting of all is how the human figures are related to the vegetation. The figures seem animated and moving through the foliage – obviously retaining features derived from the Picasso circus figures. However, in this vegetal context, their movement appears not so much as motion as participation in a process of formal growth. There is a deep morphological kinship of figure and foliage that makes the former expressive of the latter as well as being contained within it.

These foliage effects and their absorption of human form within a two and a half-dimensional whole gives Cohen's imagery a highly distinctive character thereafter.

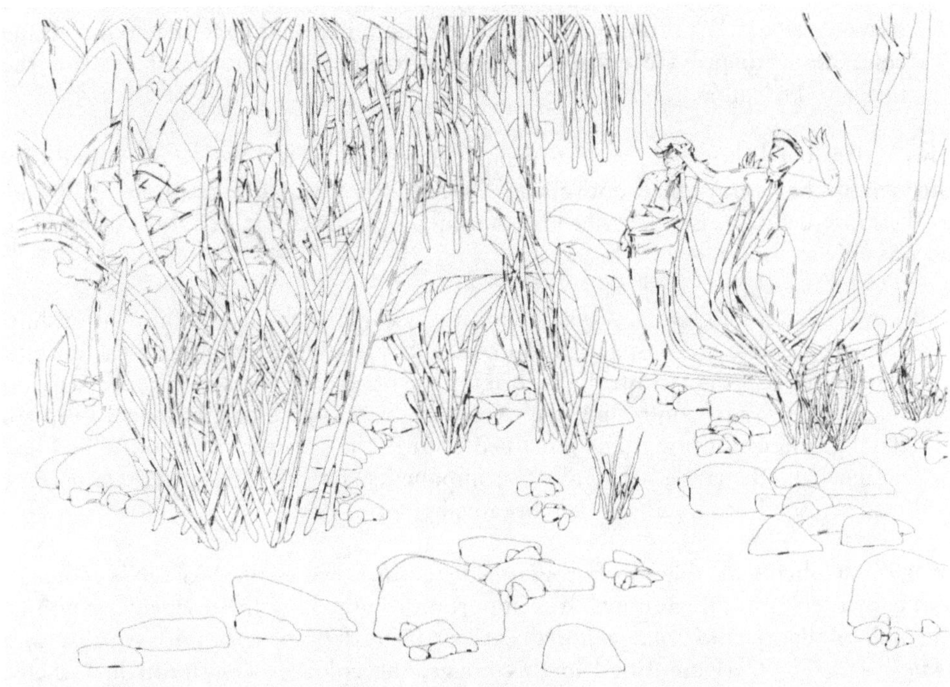

Figure 4.7 Harold Cohen, *Drawing*, 1987, computer generated drawing on paper, 56.2 × 76.4 cm.

Source: © Victoria and Albert Museum.

It is, of course, supremely paradoxical insofar as a computer-generated image becomes overloaded with a creative formal floridity that sometimes hovers on the kitsch without descending into it. This floridity becomes especially important vis-à-vis the next major technical problem that faced Cohen.

He had often colored in AARON's images by hand, but felt the need to find a way of coloring to be incorporated into the program itself. In the course of dealing with this, Cohen also found ways for AARON to produce more three-dimensionally robust configurations. These centered on procedures for the articulation of particular body parts, as well as for producing workable possible variations of proportion and posture – but without losing the stylistic distinctiveness of two and a half-dimensionality.

An important starting point for Cohen's treatment of color was the invention of a robot-arm painting machine – in use by 1990. However, this did not yield satisfactory results. It was not until around 2001 that he was able to achieve authentic digital coloring rather than the mere filling in of outlines. In turning to digital color, Cohen's thinking was prompted also by his understanding of a more general cognitive issue – namely, how we perceive visual material. Specifically, his major clue was an idea that had already guided his teaching for many years – that brightness is more important than hue in the perception of color, and is of particular importance in defining the edges of objects. In adapting AARON to color, this required accordingly, a significant transformation.

> I wanted color to become the primary organizing principle of the image. Since that was the role already occupied by the outline drawing, then the outline drawing would have to go; and then the program would have the goal of using color alone to provide enough differentiation at the edges of objects for the image to be legible.[23]

This task proved, however, very difficult. Cohen moved towards it only gradually through, in the first instance, converting AARON from the C-programming language to the more flexible Lisp. The need for outlines was not eliminated, but, using Lisp, he was able to devise

> a notion of color chords, ways of choosing colors in various spatial relationships from the entire color space, and AARON was able to construct these color chords, rather than control the brightness of more-or-less randomly selected hues, as a way of controlling the overall color structure of the image. Even so, the importance of brightness remained central; the structure of a chord, as I had designed it, demanded that all its components, however selected, retain some required level of vivacity as they became lighter or darker.[24]

By 1993, Cohen was able to photograph the color schemes on AARON's monitor, and copy them into oil paintings. It is important to note how these schemes continue the link of figure and foliage noted earlier. Consider, for example, *Mother and Daughter* of 1997 (Plate 10).[25] In this image, the color process (even in Cohen's hand-made copy) does not involve tonal modelling but simply colors of contrasting brightness deployed in different sized and shaped masses. The observational basis of human color perception is here replaced by a synthetic version based on the contrasts just described.

'Synthetic' in this context has no adverse implications. This is because it signifies the computer's use as an instrument for performing aesthetically creative variations on the normal conditions of visual perception. It assimilates the human form and its settings by adapting them to its own non-human terms. These variations extend, indeed, a development already noted – namely, the close alignment of human figure and vegetal structure. In the examples under consideration, the figures are sometimes represented alongside plants and flowers, but, more significantly, their limbs are configured like stalks with body areas presented as masses compressed into narrow elongated leaves. This strategy can lead to fascinating inconsistencies of relative size (note, for example, the startling disparity between the size of the model's individual hands). Even gestures are sometimes evoked in terms more akin to tendrils than to a momentary disposition of limbs.

A problem remained. AARON's algorithm in these works controlled the path of the brush but not its edge. This meant that some outlines were too small to be covered by the brush, and would be left blank. In his painted copies from the screen image this could be compensated for manually, but to deal with the problem digitally was Cohen's next main challenge. Through dealing with it, he was led to develop a more efficient painting machine, namely

> a large… device that carried a small robot arm on its beam, complete with a simple hand. It could mix its colors from a palette of water-based dyes by having

> the hand open the taps on the dispensers for measured times. And it could pick up and use brushes of different sizes. After making a drawing with waterproof black ink the machine would move a cup from one dispenser to another to mix the required color, deposit the cup where the hand could reach it as it moved around the table, pick up a brush and start filling in the shapes. When it had finished with a color it would empty the cup and wash it out ready for the next color, then wash out the brush and start over again.[26]

This technology of programming and robotic realization was developed even further by Cohen – and, by 2001, he was able to realize his original main goal in devising a color program. Specifically, AARON was able to direct a wide printer via a postscript file, thus creating edges defined entirely by color rather than by the use of drawn outlines. This enabled some startling visual achievements. In particular, the liberation of color from its 'filling in' role allowed the floral elements described earlier to become major recurrent motifs in AARON's images. The exclusive use of colors in combination allows the creation of complex structures that would probably end as a mess, if the colors had to fill-in pre-drawn black outline shapes. In the floral works drawing and painting are not distinguished. Some of the strongest of these works involve a related feature (noted earlier). Consider, for example, *0305–08*, of 2002 (Plate 11). Here flowers and foliage are presented in a sophisticated formal structure. The colors have a kind of atonal, deadpan, flat quality akin to those used in comic books. However, the real interest is how such colors function aesthetically. Their intrinsically bland quality stabilizes the image, but relationally speaking – as shapes and masses – they contribute to a high level of visual animation. For example, whilst the pink flower on the left formally dominates the work, it is challenged by the play of shapes (varieties of green and yellow) that *squirm* around it. In some cases, the petals and leaves are almost *posturing*. They suggest undifferentiated shapes of active biomorphic matter and, at some points, even hint at those human forms that Cohen derived from Picasso's circus figures. This cross-fertilization of vegetal and biomorphic/human shapes gives the floral works a unique Bacchanalian quality – vis-à-vis the interplay of color, shape, and line.

This points directly towards the more general importance of Cohen's work with AARON. The project brings together technology, the science of visual cognition, and detailed consideration of the philosophy of image-making – thus exemplifying the very cross-disciplinary orientation that, as we saw previously, is a central feature of Postmodern culture. However, there is more involved. Even if one knew nothing about the origins of AARON's images, they have the *look* of technological production about them. Yet, at the same time, their appearance involves a reciprocity of the technological and the natural – by dint of the Bacchanalian whirl just described. There is a case for saying this extends beyond questions of appearance. Cohen himself observed that

> The day may or may not come when machines have a sense of self. If it doesn't, it means that machines will never be creative in the same sense that humans are creative. But even if that day never comes, it doesn't mean that machines have no part to play with respect to creativity. Had I not met my first computer in 1968, had I not found this particular way of expressing my own needs with respect to art-making, my life and work surely would have followed a very different vector for the past forty years.[27]

These remarks make a point that is generally important enough to call it *Cohen's principle*. It is that *unless computers acquire self-consciousness, their creativity will always be of a different order from that of humans, but this very difference is such that it can actually be used to extend the scope of human creativity*. The 'two and a half-dimensionality' of AARON's images, and their alignments of human and vegetal form, are examples of this creative difference. Human artists can, of course, create similar images, but AARON's images retain a kind of *gaucheness* of construction – even in the Bacchanalian works – that indicate digital origins.

This construction has an odd effect. It makes the human figure look awkward and fragile in how it occupies the world of spatial things. The particular visual character of AARON's synthetic version of the body, in its very appearance, hints at the destiny of the finite embodied subject. Our limbs and organs are not self-contained by the present moment. Presented through a momentary aspect involving wrong proportions, over-sized limbs, and tendril-like gestures, and the like, we sense that they will some day fall apart.

But – it might be objected – surely the products of an algorithmic process cannot be meaningful in such terms. AARON cannot *really* hint at such things. However, we know also that these images were not created by pure mechanical chance; they follow programs designed by an artist. The program produces works whose individual configuration cannot be determined in advance, but what we see is, nevertheless, known to be the outcome of the artist's creative intention. Indeed, Cohen's (and indeed any digital) works embody – like all art – an invitation to 'see it like this.' Cohen himself may not have created AARON with a view to create images with the meaning described above, but, as Gadamer often emphasized, every artwork has an excess of meaning that is unknown to its creator.[28] Intended or not what he or she does will feed into a broader cultural stock of associations and attitudes, often in complex ways. (This, of course, is the *iconological* dimension of meaning.) In designing AARON to produce likenesses, Cohen's act of creation invites us to consider what is so produced in relation to human expectations and fulfilments. The digital work's very digitality, and all that it implies, can lead us to see many things in a new way, and to reflect on the broader significance of humanity's aesthetic relation to technology.

Three

Csuri's and Cohen's idioms of digital figuration involve creative experiment from the ground up, determining means for the very generation of imagery. Since the 1980s and the paintbox era, there has been a burgeoning of further digital figuration of a technically and aesthetically sophisticated kind. In order to complete this account of the emergence of such figuration, we consider an artist whose work is emblematic of this sophistication, namely Gerhard Mantz.

As we saw in the previous chapter, Mantz was an already established sculptor before turning to the computer. At the time his 'virtual objects' were created in the late 1990s he was already considering the medium's figurative possibilities – with a view to exploring the ambivalent relation between nature and artificiality. This led him to focus on both landscapes and abstraction; and some fascinating overlaps between them. We will emphasize the landscapes.

It should be noted at the outset that Mantz's notion of 'landscape' really means the physical environment in all its key aspects. The category 'landscape' on his website, for example, includes sub-categories of 'air,' 'forest,' 'swamps,' 'brushwood,' 'ground,' 'wasteland,' 'mountains,' 'ocean,' and 'architecture.' He invests these with a complex psychological significance. In his words,

> The landscape subject is not so much about a geographical locale, but more a metaphor for a psychological state. It evokes feelings and moods so that the viewer enters an environment with immediate emotional responses. At first glance it appears realistic, in some cases even photographic, with inviting naturalistic details that lure and seduce. But, upon closer inspection the seemingly realistic details shift to reveal a strange virtual world associated more with an interior 'reality' than an exterior one. [Indeed] My starting point is never a landscape seen in reality, but an abstraction, a constructed calculation of archetypal space. This construct is then transformed step-by-step through simulated light, atmosphere, water, terrain, flora and fauna to conjure memories that translate as complex emotions rather than a specificity of place.[29]

Mantz's criterion of 'archetypal' in these remarks is quite definite. It is a perceptual state of affairs which gives rise to intense psychological connotations, bound up with our awareness of different aspects of finitude. He describes a range of such spaces, of which the following are most relevant to the works by him that will be considered here.

> *The End of the World*
>
> Imagine a place where space ends and time stands still. On every island there is a stretch of coast where the land slips into a haze. The sun does not give warmth. It is barren at earth's far end. Gazing out in this direction all paradise, all happiness lies at your back. A vortex draws you into emptiness.
>
> *The Last Part of the Trail*
>
> An obstruction blocks the view of the trail ahead. But, just one last turn leads through the gloom. Just run, faster, and faster ... then out of breath! ...
>
> *The Cities*
>
> One can wander through these cubic structures and colored patterns to view them from different angles, much like moving through spaces and mazes in the urban environment. Purged of architectural embellishment and pared to essential 3-D form, these abstract spaces remain rich vessels for associative memories of streets and skylines we have known.[30]

These archetypes center, in effect, on a perceptual coming to a halt and the beholding of a spatial configuration that suggests continuation whilst, at the same time, emptying it of positive meaning, or suspending the means of accessing it; or which simply evokes memories of how this position was reached.

The idea of the landscape having a symbolic meaning is, of course, a familiar one. In German art itself, Caspar David Friedrich amongst others, linked quite specific features such as mountains ranges and the sea to infinity, and vegetal features to the finite and earthbound. The possibility of salvation in the face of such overwhelming phenomena was symbolized by devices such as the crescent moon, or overt religious features such as crosses or churches situated at key points in the landscape.[31]

Now it is clear that Mantz's archetypes do not have such redemptive symbolic loadings How, then, is the viewer to find fulfilment in the beholding of existentially barren spaces? The answer lies, perhaps, in the artist's own description of key aspects of his creative process. We are told that

> My programs work with regulated commands but also open a window to the unexpected. They are programmed to create possibilities for surprisingly stunning artworks without my intervention. Evaluating is something the programs are still not capable, I have to do that. Once it comes to complex structures like landscape models with plants, the process is hybrid. One part plays the program with its random factors and the other part is my personal help to bring things together. I always start with a basic structure in mind like a spatial situation. i.e. water in the foreground, a slope in the middle ground and a dense forest hill in the background. Now I set a probability map for the plants I chose to have in the model and let the program propose variations. While tweaking the parameters along from variation to variation I drive the model closer and closer to an expression I like. Until the image starts talking to me.[32]

These remarks emphasize a factor that has been of decisive significance throughout our discussions of digital art, namely the formalized reciprocity of the creative process. The artist does not simply design a program, but lets it create possibilities which he or she can accept or reject, or modify. In Mantz's case, the key point is when the image starts 'talking' to him, i.e. persuading him that it can stand alone as an aesthetic object of *enduring* worth. The importance of this is its relation to the digital *imprimatur* – the sheer look of being digitally originated. We *know* that this look does not simply happen. It is the result of the specific form of creative reciprocity just described. It is aesthetic testimony to the vision of the artist.

Let us now develop this point in relation to examples of Mantz's work. Consider first, *Heimtückische Hoffnung* (*Treacherous Hope*) of 1997 (Figure 4.8). This represents a hilly approach to a sea in the distance. The sea is visible only as a narrow line between the hillocks, but they – and the combination of extended clumps of vegetation with intervening sand – create a dynamic that both points towards it and hurries the viewer in its direction. This dynamic is as much psychological as it is visual. It is as though the viewer is not so much moving towards the sea in a human way, as rapidly *spreading* towards it – through the distribution of clumps and sand. This sense of spreading carries also a sense of exhaustion, of one's substance being dissipated before the shore is reached.

At the heart of this effect is the way the green clumps change their character when viewed closely. They (and the sand spaces between them) visibly *congeal* – changing from illusory organic formations to the artificial reality of *manifestly* digital forms. The passage to the virtual sea is trapped by the revelation of virtuality. This *anomie* is accentuated by the ambiguity of the viewer's own position – which is close to the ground but above ground-level. The panorama is not being viewed from an airborne vehicle, but neither is it the body's normal orientation. It is like moving through the landscape as in a dream.

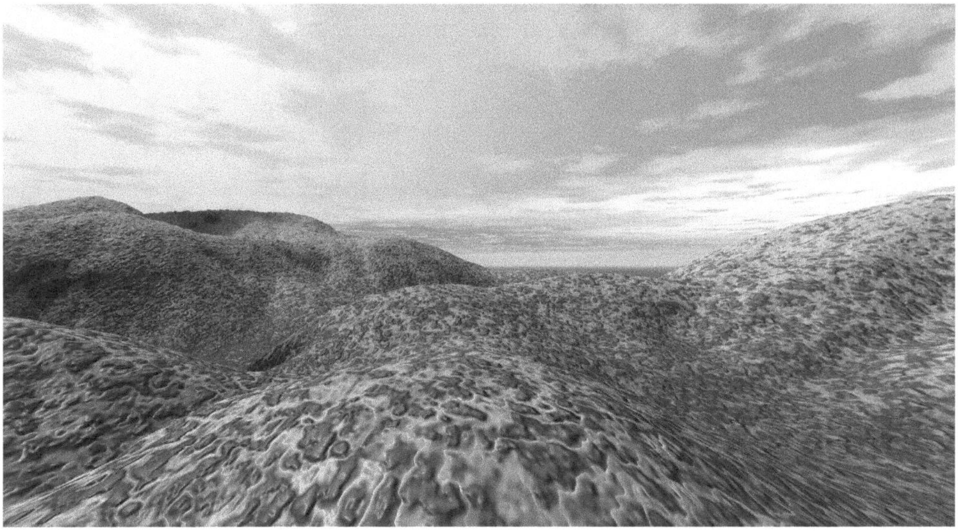

Figure 4.8 Gerhard Mantz, *Heimtückische Hoffnung* (*Treacherous Hope*), 1997, Cibachrome, Diasec, 110 × 205 cm.

A severe viewing ambiguity is operative also in *Landohne Heimat* (*Land without Home*) of 1999 (Figure 4.9). To understand it, however, we must first consider some specific details. Here, the viewer arrives at the sea at but the point of arrival is dislocated by a profusion of giant boulders – some in the sky, and others spread out individually at sea level in the distance. There is a suggestion that they continue beyond the limits of the image – but in meaningless accumulation rather than as indicators of infinity.

This effect is accentuated by the way the boulders hover in the sky and perch upon the sea. This is done in a way makes them more suggestive of the prosaic rather than of the miraculous (the latter effect, for example, being a feature of some boulder-in-the-sky works by Magritte). Two such rocks are near the viewer, tipped at oblique angles that visibly suggest threat, whilst at the same time seeming wholly inert and locked into position. This *stasis* arises through a lack of visual clues as to whether the boulders are in motion, or perpetually stationary, or have come to a halt after being in motion.

The great power of this work also lies (again) in the character of the vegetation and its spatial positioning in relation to the viewer. In one reading, the vegetation seems as it might appear if viewed from far above the earth's surface, but this effect is simultaneously deflated by the way some of the boulders are in the sea or almost at ground level with it. An especially curious role is played by a horizontal structure to the lower left of center that has patterned features indicative of construction. In some respects, it appears to have been built on the ground, in other respects it may seem to have crashed there.

This ambiguity of ground and altitude is again complicated in a disconcerting way by the green vegetation. Whilst in terms of the the work's spatial organization, it cooperates in the general recessional effects, it also has a manifestly digital character

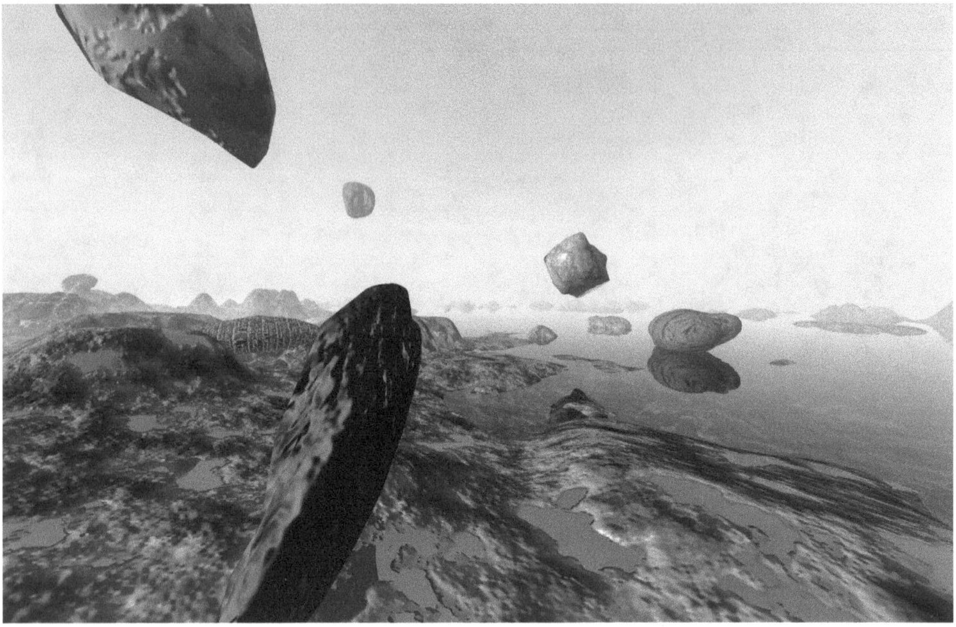

Figure 4.9 Gerhard Mantz, *Land ohne Heimat* (*Land without Home*) Nr. 23, 2003, inkjet on canvas, 100 × 170 cm.

whose optical effect (especially in the left center) involves the green shades beginning to disembody themselves *towards* the frontal plane. Indeed, the configuration of the green ground masses and surrounding water in the lower right quadrant involves a curious stretching effect – wherein virtual elasticity subverts the natural appearance. In all these cases, whilst the distance solicits the viewer, its contents deny it.

One of the most important recurrent motifs in Mantz's works is that of extended greenery – in the form of forests, swamps, or other verdant ground phenomena.

Let us consider two contrasting examples of this, *Macht des Schicksals* (*The Power of Fate*) of 2008 (Figure 4.10), and *Einleitende Begrüßung* (*Introductory Address of Welcome*) of 2005 (Plate 12). The former presents a horizontal line of trees with rows of others arranged recessionally behind them. Sunlight breaks through behind the trees. This occupies the top half of the work. The lower half is constituted by an expanse of water whose center is dominated by a confined burst of reflected sunlight. Equally striking is the reflection of the trees – which are inverted but otherwise exact vertical continuations of the casting bodies.

These vertical forms and their visual rhythms are rich in associations. On the one hand, the sunlight breaking through the central trees invites the viewer to continue his or her journey. But, on the other hand, their insistent horizontal distribution is not so enticing. It is suggestive of a barrier or limit. Indeed, this effect is amplified by bushes and undergrowth gathered in clumps (almost boulder-like) and distributed across the entire horizontal extent of the treeline, in a way that seems to block out the gaps between individual trees. There is a sense of menace, of hidden forces waiting to pounce.

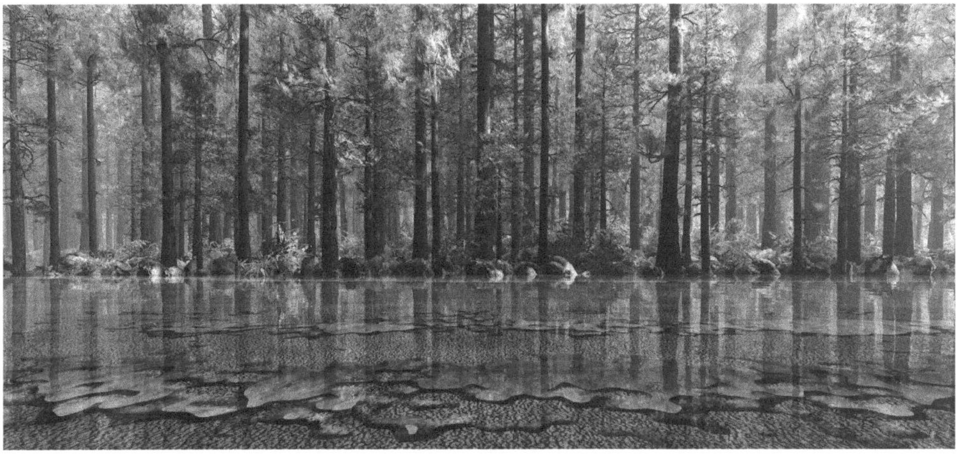

Figure 4.10 Gerhard Mantz, *Die Macht des Schicksals* (*The Power of Fate*), 2008, inkjet on canvas, 100 × 220 cm.

Most striking of all in this respect are the vegetal growths distributed in two broad horizontal bands beneath the surface of the water. The nearer one involves grey bodies with black edging; the further one is a placid brown-orange color. Whilst the colors are subdued the vegetal forms appear primed with predatory malevolence – a cross between stingray and poisonous fungi, their substance spread in masses that may actually be in motion. They hover or even dart rather than float beneath the surface of the water and do nothing to clarify its true depth. Literally, the viewer does not know what he or she would be walking into.

All this being said, there is a haunting concordance between the rows of verticals and the underwater expanses, mediated by the play of sunlight across both. Despite the promise of eventual sunlit openness, there is a hypnotic rhythm that locks the viewer into the present moment of beholding – distributing it to-and-fro across the field. The image hovers on the edge of seeming like a photograph. However, the curious exactness of distribution amongst the verticals (and the intervals between them) suggests an element of artifice, of digital *imprimatur*. This is reinforced by the strange 'not quite right' intersection of the vegetal forms beneath the water with the reflections cast upon the surface, and, most important, the ambiguity as to whether these forms are floating, hovering, or darting beneath the surface.

Einleitende Begrüßung has a very different formal structure. It presents an untroubled place standing in or at the edge of an expanse of water. The vegetation extends in lengthy stems with a regular (but not dense) distribution of leaves. The stems appear to be growing through space in a rightwards motion, obliquely to the picture plane. Their formal motion is interrupted by a leftwards intrusion from three bright poppy-colored flowers of roughly circular shape with red stems. One flower is half-shadowed, one is half-submerged, and one visually rules the right upper center of the image.

The tranquillity of this scene is subverted by several – easy to overlook – insidious features and one that is rather obvious. The obvious one is the sharp projectile-like rod which penetrates and emerges from the main red form. Another such rod glides beneath the water in the lower left. A further subverting feature is the character of the leaves and red flowers. On close inspection there seems something odd about the leaves – as though they are cut-outs. Similar considerations apply to the red flowers. Their irregular undulating surfaces are paper-thin – suggesting that they may not be flowers at all, but rather some transient decorations which may have been blown to this watery locale. The viewer is invited to question what is at issue visually here, through the way the penetrating rod draws attention to the slight physicality of the flower's surface.

The main subverting factor is again a study in green. The stems and leaves are one thing, but they do not seem wholly congruent with their reflections in the water – if, indeed, these forms are reflections at all. It could be that they are, indeed, cast by foliage hanging above and outside the image. But we have no way of knowing this. And, whatever the case, the 'reflections' – irrespective of their source – seem to curl up beneath the water, taking on a tendril-like character and apparent momentum of their own. Again, there is a psychological pressure here, suggesting that it might be wise to stay rooted to the spot or go back, rather than move forwards.

We turn, now, to Mantz's so called architectural subjects. Let us consider *Southport Avenue* of 2004 (Figure 4.11), and *Latent Tolerance* of 2006 (Plate 13). The former work is formally of extreme tranquillity. Its placid sky and the horizontally pitched shapes below are fully at ease with one another. Likewise the scheme of colors – embodied block-like in regular solids, with a balance that might aesthetically pacify any restless vision.

But why would aesthetic pacification even arise as an issue here? The answer is that, whilst Mantz's image represents a street, in another sense it does not – it is an extremely active intervention on that which it represents. The day to day life of the

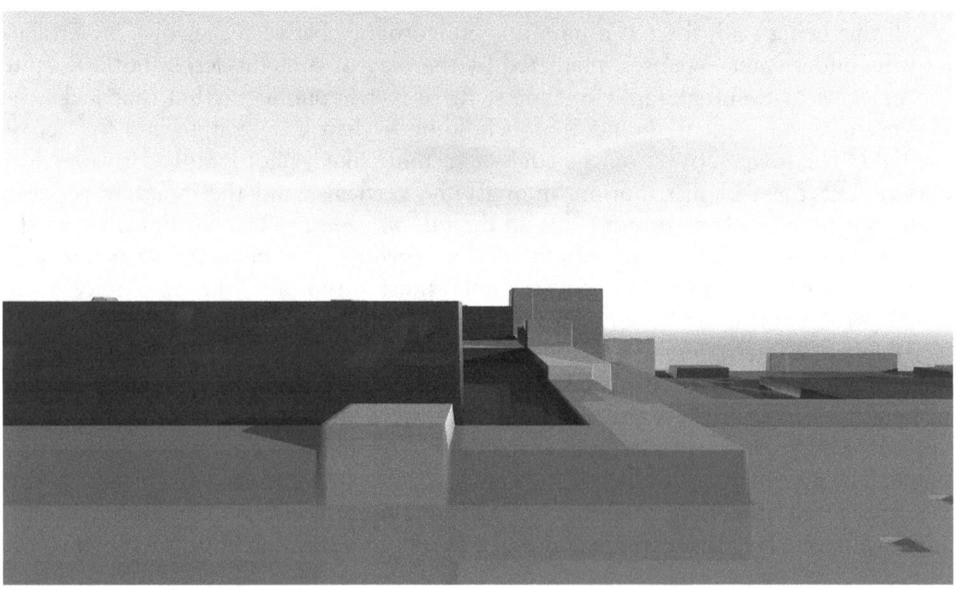

Figure 4.11 Gerhard Mantz, *Southport Avenue*, 2004, inkjet on canvas, 100 × 180 cm.

city – its noises and smells, and the dense fabric of physical events and personal interactions from which they arise – are all erased by the image. In real life, even if the city were hit by a neutron bomb the infinitely rich textures of building surfaces and interior spaces would be left untouched. But here the textures have been eliminated, and the inner spaces have been absorbed into uniform solid blocks.

This is actually a deep response to the problem of finitude in the context of social space and, especially, its physical settings. One lives in a city but the rich features described above can sometimes amount to a tumult from which we need release. Equally significant, one never steps in the same city twice. It is not only that there is a constantly changing stream of events minute after minute, hour after hour, day after day, year after year, etc., but, in the course, of this, *the city itself changes fundamentally qua city*. Buildings are refronted, many get demolished, new buildings and streets take their place. The city that one loved in one's youth has gone forever.

Southport Avenue responds to this. It presents the city through an aesthetic schema where the formal reduction of buildings and streets compensates for existential loss. This is because the shapes and forms remain familiar and can still be tied by imagination to the places we have known and loved. However, the stability of shape and color in the image creates structures which evoke the originals but allow us to possess them in imagination rather than in the dictatorial terms of the original's physical vicissitudes. Indeed, the security of this is enhanced by the kinship between architectural structure and the plain building bricks of childhood play. The redemptive power of the image, here, is not just a purity, but the form of purification itself (in almost a Platonic sense). We find aesthetic compensation for a fullness that can never be preserved or brought back once it has gone.

Latent Tolerance presents contrasts with all this, but also has key underlying affinities. It is interesting that Mantz himself treats it as one of his architectural works rather than a complex work of abstraction. In it, a building or other construction is resolved into basically planar bodies, planks, or poles of varying thickness, their masses each uniformly colored. The space is extremely crowded. Indeed, the planes, planks, and poles disconnect from their usual space-enclosing function to disperse in different directions and angles. Through this they create regional spaces, each with its own episodic identity. There are no defined clearly defined boundaries between these spaces, though many of their key forms radiate at different angles outwards from a broad central area. (This constellates loosely around the cross effect created by the conjunction of the white plane and the vertical sand-colored plank.)

If *Southport Avenue* purifies space-occupancy, *Latent Tolerance* performs a similar function for the sheer *power of space-enclosure*. This power is not a dry fact concerning the linkage of particular volumes, proportion, and materials, it involves a sense of aesthetic shaping, fitting, and constructing. Of course, builders plans and models express this power, as do photographs of the exteriors and interiors of buildings. But these are tied to quite particular edifices. To evoke the power of space enclosure *as such*, however, requires a dynamic of aesthetic construction that is not tied to any specific edifice, nor to any one technique of enclosure. And to introduce details of texture would also make the strategy too specific. Mantz's planes, planks, and poles, and the open spaces they create are able to express this formative power through the sheer purity of their shape, bulk, and color. We possess the formative power through an evocation prompting our own imaginative associations.

Both *Southport Avenue* and *Latent Tolerance* embody the relation between loss and aesthetic compensation that is basic to Mantz's psychological archetypes. This is, in existential terms the position of *the hoverer on the brink*. In the previous examples considered, the beholder is brought to a position which promises fulfilment in the distance but, at the same time, has contents that threaten or enervate this promise. We are caught between wanting to go forward and staying where we are. In the case of Mantz's architectural subjects, we behold the city and want to enjoy the things that make it uniquely special, its rhythms of life and particular streets and special places, but these – and the city itself – are transient phenomena tied to existents which change and decay irrespective of our will. Mantz's image takes us to the city, or to the power of space enclosure, but leaves us with a timeless schematic rather than a representation of the real thing.

It is clear that Mantz's landscapes (other than the architectural ones) present a specific risk. For whilst he wishes to declare the image's emergence from both nature and artificial reality, in many of his works the nature is far more manifest than the artifice. The images end up looking like wonderful photographs rather than creations based on programming. However, that being said, if we know that the image is wholly digital and not derived from an existing scene of photograph, then this goes some way towards overcoming the risks just noted. Indeed, in many of Mantz's works the digital *imprimatur* is actually intrinsic to the appearance of the image itself.

In this respect, let us take stock of the examples we have discussed. Mantz's green-expanses-with-water scenes all incorporate features whose visual congealing or stretching, or artificial contours, or strangely exact distribution of form, are intrinsically suggestive of the digital. In the architectural works the digital factor is manifest through the intense purification of particular scenes into solids and monochrome color. Such schemata have profound visual richness of their own and count as aesthetic purifications.

It is by reference to the digital *imprimatur* that the hoverer on the brink's dilemma in Mantz's works is resolved. If the beholder simply follows the illusionistic logic of the work, then an impasse is arrived at. But when this beholding centers on the relation between what the work projects and the digital artifice of projection, then the image's character as humanly created possibility takes over.

The psychological dilemma of hovering on the brink is something we have all faced at some time or another. By embodying it in digital images, Mantz allows it to be experienced it in a way that shows how another human has achieved unusual insight into the scope of it, and which allows us to empathize with that insight at the level of perception. To enjoy an illusion of the hoverer on the brink in terms of digital projection may not be a liberation, but it is at least an *aesthetic release*. The confinements of subjectivity are transcended.

Four

Finally, we must attend to the other dimension of figurative art – sculpture. There has been much interesting three-dimensional digital work – some of it purely virtual, and in other cases, using technologically driven three-dimensional physical material. In this context, sculptural figuration quickly overlaps with installation and interactivity factors. We shall focus on an artist whose work tends to have these factors strongly directed by a central figurative element.

The artist is Kenneth Feingold. He attended Antioch College, and graduated with Bachelors and Masters Fine Art degrees from California Institute of the Arts. He was at various times a studio assistant to John Baldessari and Vito Acconci. After success with video installations, he produced his first interactive artwork – *The Surprising Spiral*, in 1991 (which will be discussed in detail in the next chapter). However, by the late 1990s he was taking advantage of the rapid development of new technologies to combine visual and auditory dimensions in the most striking way.

A key example of this is Feingold's use of 'animatronic' sculpture. For example *Head* of 1999–2000 (Kiasma Museum of Contemporary Art, Helsinki) is a realistic looking elderly male head placed upon a small table. It peers into space and blinks its eyes as if conscious. Its most remarkable feature, however, is a capacity to understand and respond to spoken English. Its responses allow a conversation to develop with the viewer who addresses it – albeit with strange inflections, determined by the idiosyncratic 'personality' that is generated by the program. A small extract from such a conversation is as follows.

VISITOR: Hi
HEAD: Hello
VISITOR: How are you?
HEAD: I am so offended. I can't tell if everyone would prod her to the left or not.
VISITOR: Who offended you?
HEAD: The delicious conditions delay disturbed daredevils.
VISITOR: Which daredevils are disturbed?[33]

Another key work by Feingold is *Self Portrait as the Center of the Universe* (1998–2001). The installation centers on a life-sized head (cast from the artist himself), an 'audience' of puppets, and the head's alter ego, projected on a screen in front of the group. The screen also projects landscape scenes, and other figures generated through real-time three-dimensional computer generation. These reconfigure in correlation with how the conversation develops.

Feingold himself describes this as follows

> The self-portrait animatronic head has open-ended, improvisational conversations with its alter ego, a virtual head that appears as the central figure in the projection. ... [T]he conversations between these two figures do not include the audience; rather, they interact only with each other. Their conversations are generated in real time, utilizing speech recognition, natural language processing, conversation/personality algorithms, and text-to-speech software. The physical side of the conversation is performed by an animatronic figure (a speaking silicone cast of my head) and the central subjects of their conversations revolve around, on one side – generalization and distance; and on the other – questions and memories of himself.[34]

Obviously, there is a profoundly narcissistic element to this work, but it is a narcissicism that ranges beyond self-indulgence. In effect, the artist asks important questions about what the artist's own role actually is in the creative process. In making things for an audience, is it not the artist himself or herself who occupies center stage in this? And, of course, whatever happens in the course of the creative process, will come back ultimately, to how the artist has experienced things, and how he or she continues a self-dialog about the meaning of everything.

This existential factor is also deeply implicated in *If/Then* of 2001 (Figure 4.12). The work involves two identical androgynous heads, sculpted in clay and cast in silicone, with an underlying skeleton of fiberglass, and customized software. They project from a crate and are surrounded by polystyrene packaging material. The impression is that they are factory-made 'spares' for some android type, newly taken from the assembly line, and awaiting final despatch. The two converse with one another in real-time on the basis of software (incorporating speech-recognition, natural language processing, conversation/personality algorithms, and a text-to-speech program).

In this work, the dialog between the two heads is neither scripted nor random, but is rather more thematically focused than the vocalizing of some of Feingold's other animatronic heads. They discuss the nature of their own 'self-awareness,' and whether their way of existing can ever be understood. Again, here a sample extract from such a 'conversation':

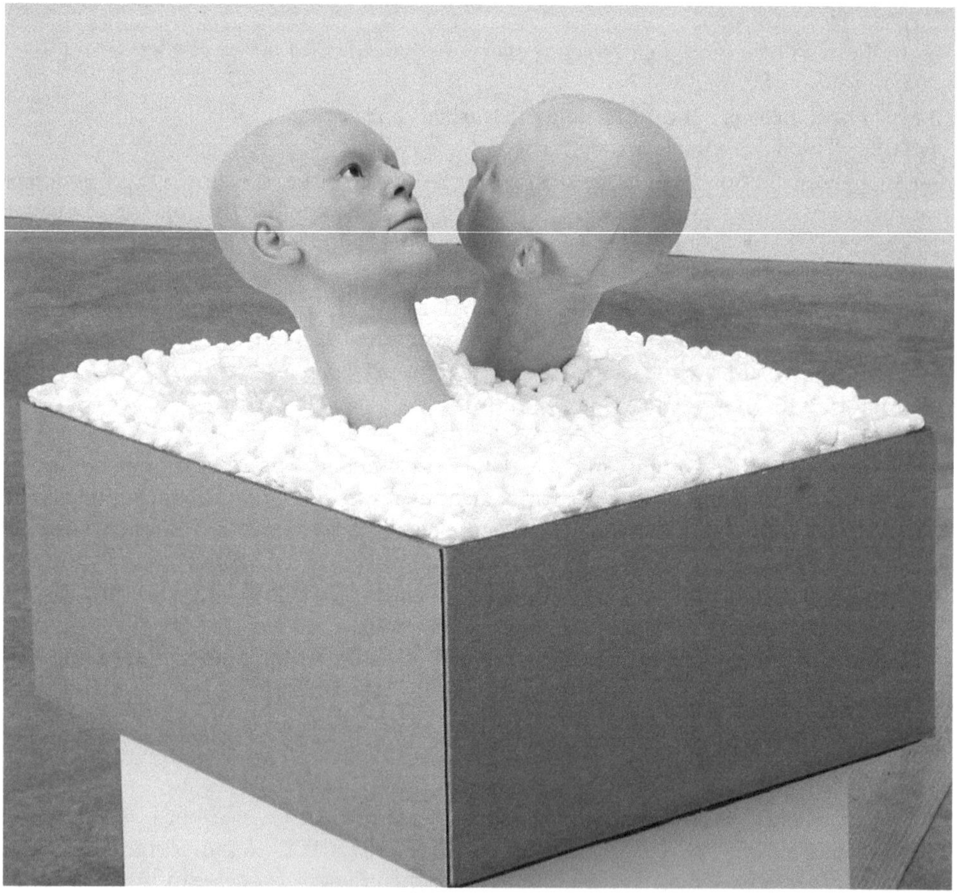

Figure 4.12 Kenneth Feingold, *If/Then*, 2001, silicone casts (from clay model), fiberglass skeleton, and customized software, 24 × 28 × 24 inches. Photo: Ken Feingold.

I think we are exactly alike.
You roof moonlight.
Is this life?
Imagine being me.
Do you see things clearly?
How do you feel?
Sometimes I feel very confused.
Can I control my feelings?
I feel like I exist.
I feel like I am inside my head.
What does it feel like to be inside your head?
Inside my mind I can sense that there is an I that is something that's not the one who is sensing.
Why?
Why do you look just like me?
No, I don't look just like you – I am accidental.
I'm not sure how to take that.
Why are you not sure how to take that?
I don't know...[35]

The digital *imprimatur* of these two heads is especially uncanny. There is a simultaneous strength from appearing to be a factory-made structure, and yet also a vulnerability through seeming to be a sentient that questions its own being. Existentially, Heidegger says of the human that 'in its very Being, that Being is an *issue* for it.'[36] But here, of course, this defining feature is encountered also in a simulacrum. This creates many associations. There is perhaps a hint that one day androids with artificial intelligence will exist, but – if their self-awareness reaches the highest level – they too will be caught in the same existential perplexities that beset human beings.

Another association is symbolic. Whether created by God, or mechanistically evolved, humans are responsible for their own passage through life. But interpreting the meaning of that which is, takes us to a limit. We cannot know the Ultimate; neither can we ever experience just what it is like to be another person. In the final analysis we are as helpless and forlorn as the two heads – asking one another questions with no definitive answer.

Conclusion

In this chapter, then, we have considered the main origins of figuration in the genesis of digital art. Since the 1990s its potential has been developed in many different and impressive ways but the innovations of Burson, Csuri, Cohen, and Mantz, and Feingold, in particular, have been of the most decisive significance.

Burson establishes morphing as a key creative possibility even for static visual images. Csuri's work from the beginning was orientated towards the conditions of artistic modifications of the subject-matter and ways in which digital techniques might be used to develop a distinctive artistic style. Cohen's work was more exploratory in a theoretical sense – considering the minimum conditions for something to be an image, and how the image was perceived – and adapting programming and support technology to negotiate and clarify such issues. Mantz's work has refined the scope of figuration to an extraordinarily high degree – always foregrounding the decisive issue, namely the digital image's mediation between three-dimensional environmental structures (of one sort or another) and the artificiality of digital programming and projection. Feingold has brought visual innovation in three-dimensional digital art into an integrated harmony with audio material, and developments in AI development.

The outcomes of Burson's, Csuri's, Cohen's, Mantz's, and Feingold's work are quite individual styles – recognizable as theirs at a glance. It may be that the next great stage in the development of digital figuration will be through programs which allow the computer to draw, paint, or sculpt images directly from life – as in Patrick Tresset's work with the drawing machines 'Paul' and the painting machine 'e-David' (developed in collaboration with Oliver Deussen).[37] If this 'life-drawing' were developed further, it might mean that the computer would be able to work at the level of 'sketch' and 'finish' programs. However, whilst this might make digital art more akin to traditional artistic practice, it might be at the risk of diminishing the distinctively digital contribution. Perhaps one of the keys to future artistic development will be in combining these.

Notes

1 The best source for information on these developments is A. Michael Noll's 'First Hand: Early Digital Computer Art at Bell Telephone Laboratories, Incorporated,' *Leonardo*, Vol. 49, No. 1 (2016), pp. 55–65. Lillian Schwartz's website shows her extraordinary range of talents, http://lillian.com (accessed September 21, 2017). An interesting survey of Schwartz's and other women's roles in computer art is Grant D. Taylor's '"Up for Grabs": Agency, Praxis, and the Politics of Early Digital Art,' included in *Lateral*, No. 2, *Journal of the Cultural Studies Association*, http://csalateral.org/issue2/theory/taylor (accessed September 21, 2017).
2 Paul Christiane, *Digital Art*, 2015. Burson's website is http://nancyburson.com/# (accessed August 17, 2017).
3 See Margit Rosen, 'A Record of Decisions: Envisioning Computer Art,' included in Janice M. Glowski (ed.), *Charles A. Csuri: Beyond Boundaries, 1963 to the Present*, 2006, pp. 25–46. For the Csuri-Bense relation, see pp. 36–37.
4 For more on this, see Rosen, op. cit., p. 32.
5 Csuri, quoted at www.siggraph.org/artdesign/profile/csuri.
6 The drawings can be seen at http://csuriproject.osu.edu/index.php/Detail/objects/757.
7 The Charles Csuri Project at Ohio State University (see note 6) gives the date 1965 for this work.
8 See, for example, the discussion at http://csuriproject.osu.edu/index.php/Detail/objects/761 (accessed April 23, 2017).
9 The structure of Cubism is analyzed at some length in the present author's 'Interpreting Cubist Space: From Kant to Phenomenology,' Chapter Five of *The Phenomenology of Modern Art: Exploding Deleuze, Illuminating Style*, 2012, pp. 132–171.
10 See http://csuriproject.osu.edu/index.php/Detail/objects/775 (accessed January 23, 2017).
11 Charles Csuri, IEEE (Institute of Electrical and Electronics Engineers) Proceedings, 1974. Quoted from www.siggraph.org/artdesign/profile/csuri (accessed April 23, 2017).
12 See Ruth Leavitt (ed.), *Artist and Computer*, 1976, available online at www.atariarchives.org/artist/index.php. Mezei's contribution is accompanied by reproductions of some of his own work; the article is also available at www.atariarchives.org/artist/sec7.php (accessed April 23, 2017).
13 Quoted from www.siggraph.org/artdesign/profile/csuri.
14 At www.siggraph.org/artdesign/profile/csuri.
15 Quoted from http://siggrapharts.hosting.acm.org/wp/charles-csuri/artworks/algorithmic-paintings (accessed September 21, 2017).

16 Quoted from the artist's website, www.aaronshome.com/aaron/publications/tate-final.doc.
17 'A Sorcerer's Apprentice,' Talk at the Tate Modern, 2004, www.aaronshome.com/aaron/publications/tate-final.doc.
18 'Parallel to Perception: Some Notes on the Problem of Machine-Generated Art,' 1973, www.aaronshome.com/aaron/aaron/publications/paralleltoperception.pdf.
19 'the further exploits of AARON, Painter,' 1995, http://web.stanford.edu/group/SHR/4-2/text/cohen.html.
20 Ibid.
21 For more on this, see Pamela McCorduck, *AARON'S CODE: Meta-Art, Artificial Intelligence, and the Work of Harold Cohen*, p. 105.
22 Quoted from 'the further exploits of AARON, Painter'.
23 Quoted from 'A Sorcerer's Apprentice.'
24 Quoted from 'the further exploits of AARON, Painter.'
25 See 'Decoupling Art and Affluence,' 2001, http://aaronshome.com/aaron/aaron/publications/index.html.
26 Ibid.
27 Harold Cohen, 'Driving the Creative Machine,' Orcas Center, Crossroads Lecture Series, September 2010, p. 5, www.aaronshome.com/aaron/publications/orcastalk2s.pdf .
28 See, for example, Hans-Georg Gadamer, *Philosophical Hermeneutics*, trans. David E. Linge, 1977, p. 102.
29 Quoted at www.gerhard-mantz.de/wp/text/landscape (accessed April 18, 2017).
30 *Gerhard Mantz, Berlin 1998 and New York* 2004. Translation by *Jay Judge,* ibid. (accessed April 18, 2017).
31 The degree to which Friedrich understood the landscape in terms of symbolism is controversial. A classic reading which emphasizes the possible symbolic meanings is Helmut Borsch-Supan's *Caspar David Friedrich*, trans. Sarah Twohig, 1974.
32 Personal email correspondence with present author, August 23, 2016.
33 The sculpture can be seen 'in action' at www.youtube.com/watch?v=EK-7w56jN0E.
34 Quoted from www.kenfeingold.com/SelfL2.html.
35 See www.kenfeingold.com/IfThen1.html.
36 Martin Heidegger, *Being and Time*, trans. John Macquarrie and Edward Robinson, 1967, p. 32.
37 Tresset's website is at http://patricktresset.com/new. For a detailed discussion of Tresset's and Deussen's work, see the present author's 'Conditions of Creativity: Drawing and Painting with Computers,' Chapter 7 of *What Drawing and Painting Really Mean: The Phenomenology of Image and Gesture*, 2017.

5 Computer-Assisted Hybrids

The art considered so far has been mainly work designed on computers and then printed electronically on to paper or some other appropriate medium. Drawings executed through plotters exemplify this. In such cases, the computer physically creates the work on screen or on an external surface, as well as playing an essential role in its design. Now, in different fields of computer art, there are often interesting hybrids. Some works, for example, are computer-designed but not physically created through plotters. Their physical execution involves, rather, robotic or autographic painting or sculpture. In other cases, the final physical work is a Conceptual form of some kind, which the computer assists in delivering. In this chapter we shall consider some interesting examples of both these strategies as developed in the Postmodern era.

We start with the work of Joseph Nechvatal. His computer-assisted paintings date from 1986. They derive from his interest in ideological issues raised by art media, an interest arising from studies in philosophy and Walter Benjamin's theories about art and mass-production. As Nechvatal puts it,

> My interest in the ideology of media led me to using the possibilities of computer-robotics as a timely alternative art tool, a new way to make conceptual paintings that addressed issues of distribution through excess. There were no PCs then, of course, this was 1986. But the studio I was working with in Midtown had access to a big computer painting machine that had been developed in Japan. So I started making computer-robotic assisted paintings like *The Informed Man*.[1]

The Informed Man (Figure 5.1) is physically embodied on a large scale – 82×116 inches. It used the Scanamural process to create an image from acrylic paint on canvas. This was done by computer-driven robotic arms. The arms were fitted with airbrush guns, and directed electronically on the basis of degraded information patterns extracted from a small scanned image.[2]

Nechvatal's rationale in creating the work was set forth in a theoretical document that accompanied the Documenta exhibition of 1987 in Amsterdam, where it was first exhibited. In this text Nechvatal argues that computers are attractive to users because of the apparent total control they offer. However, he also emphasizes that this comes at a price, insofar as computer technology places constraints on what can be expressed and transmitted. It standardizes patterns of knowledge and communication within a general managerialist ideology. The problem then is the finding of

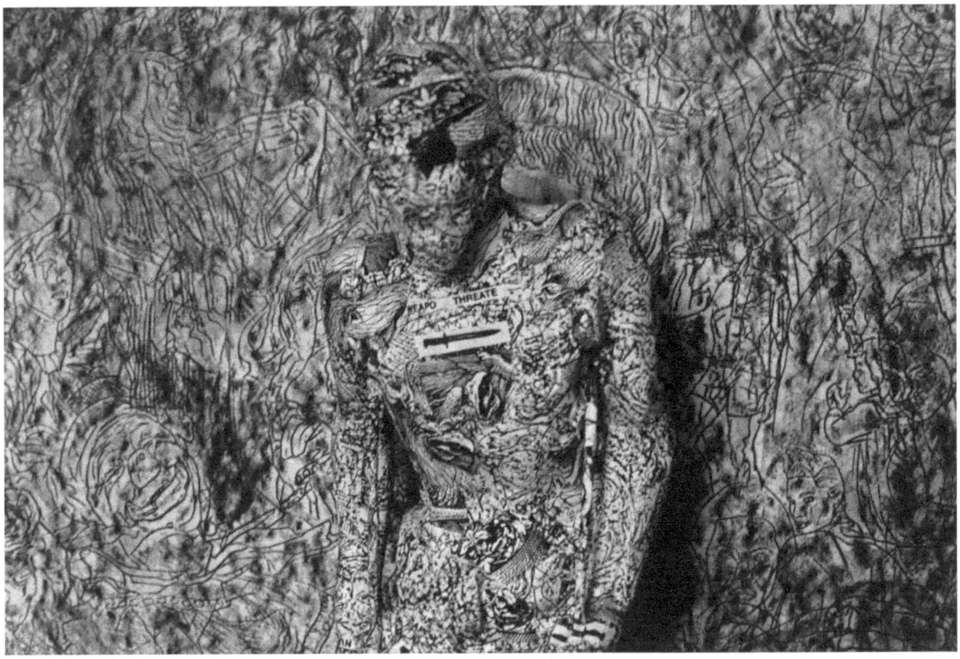

Figure 5.1 Joseph Nechvatal, *Informed Man*, 1986, 82×116 inches, computer-robotic assisted acrylic on canvas.

> an answering response, of an indeterminate kind in order to allow for participation in the creative act. ... Creators must place themselves above the level of the mechanical through the integration of art and technics – resist the quantifying of life in the interests of power, prestige and profit – resist the fashion of idealizing mechanical forces.[3]

For Nechvatal, accordingly,

> The computer-robotic paintings symbolize a society that has freed itself from total rational utilitarianism through the symbolism of poetry in technology; and by linking the primordial horrors to the technology of today. They are in great measure a reaction against the organizational harness of post-industrial society, the technocratic mind view.[4]

The Informed Man performs an immediate aesthetic disclocation through its size. Computer technology since the silicon chip transformations of the 1980s is usually associated with compact hardware and software whose creative energy operates in largely imperceptible terms. Nechvatal's painting, in contrast, presents the realm of computer activity through a physical space where it has to be reflected upon.

The central figure in *The Informed Man* is a human form that is both embedded in, and emergent from networks of surrounding visual substance. The substance seems primordial like the rock of a cave, but its materiality also appears consistent with the physicality of the figure itself. This consistency is accentuated by patterns that animate the surface of both figure and context. On closer inspection, the patterns show themselves to contain other figurative elements such as faces, and human profiles and gestures. They are a combination of realistic and caricature schemata. However, these loose their individual identity within the manic linear energy arising from their conjunction.

This impacts directly on how we read the main figure. Unlike the other elements it is manifestly – almost heavily – three-dimensional. Its lumbering physicality is rendered through both the shadows it casts, and the concentration of forms that compose its 'flesh.' The figure gives the impression of emergence – but with weariness, and/or hesitancy – a sense of Heidegger's 'The Dreadful has already happened.' In this case, however, what has happened is not a realization of our being-towards-death, but that knowledge has become a plethora of information which we inhabit and which inhabits us. This is not a benign reciprocity, it is one which threatens ultimate annihilation.

But at least, Nechvatal's painting does not present this as inevitable. The inevitability is subverted by four manifestly recognizable visual features – the truncated words 'weapo' and 'threate'; the picture of a dagger (or bayonet), and the figure's eye-patch. It is the relation between these and image's other elements that is important. The suggestion of randomness involved in the latter is contradicted by the realistic artifice of the former. This sets up a reflective position for the viewer wherein he or she can understand how information enables and disables simultaneously, carrying the threat of destruction. And, most decisive of all, is understanding that the creative strategy in the image – combining chance and decomposition as well as deliberate choice – has turned computer technology into a means of critical *aesthetic* reflection. *The Informed Man* does not document Nechvatal's understanding of the ideology of IT, rather, it makes it emerge through the particularity of the image – where specifics and uncertainties weave in and out of one another in an interpretative unity available only to aesthetic perception.

In Nechvatal's subsequent works, this takes on a sharper edge, as a response to the HIV/AIDS epidemic – wherein the artist suffered distressing personal loss. This led him to the creative use of computer viruses. In his words,

> In 1990, my Computer Virus Project's initial goal was to produce physical paintings by using algorithms implementing 'viral' processes. It's based on a simulation tool which allowed me to virtually introduce artificial organisms into a digitized reproduction of an earlier artwork, the host, and let them transform and destroy that original image. During these 'attacks' a new still image can be extracted and painted on canvas, which is a way to realize them—to bring back the virtual into the real. [Indeed] The negative connotations of the HIV virus as a vector of disease is reflected in the principle of degradation of the image. But here, the virus is also the basis of a creative process, producing newness in reference to the major influence of the virus on evolution in biological systems.[5]

To carry out this process, Nechvatal sends his files over the net to a remote computer-driven machine which paints the work robotically. It is a product of *telepresence*. A key work in this respect is *the birth Of the viractual* (2001) (Figure 5.2).

In this work (as Christiane Paul describes it)

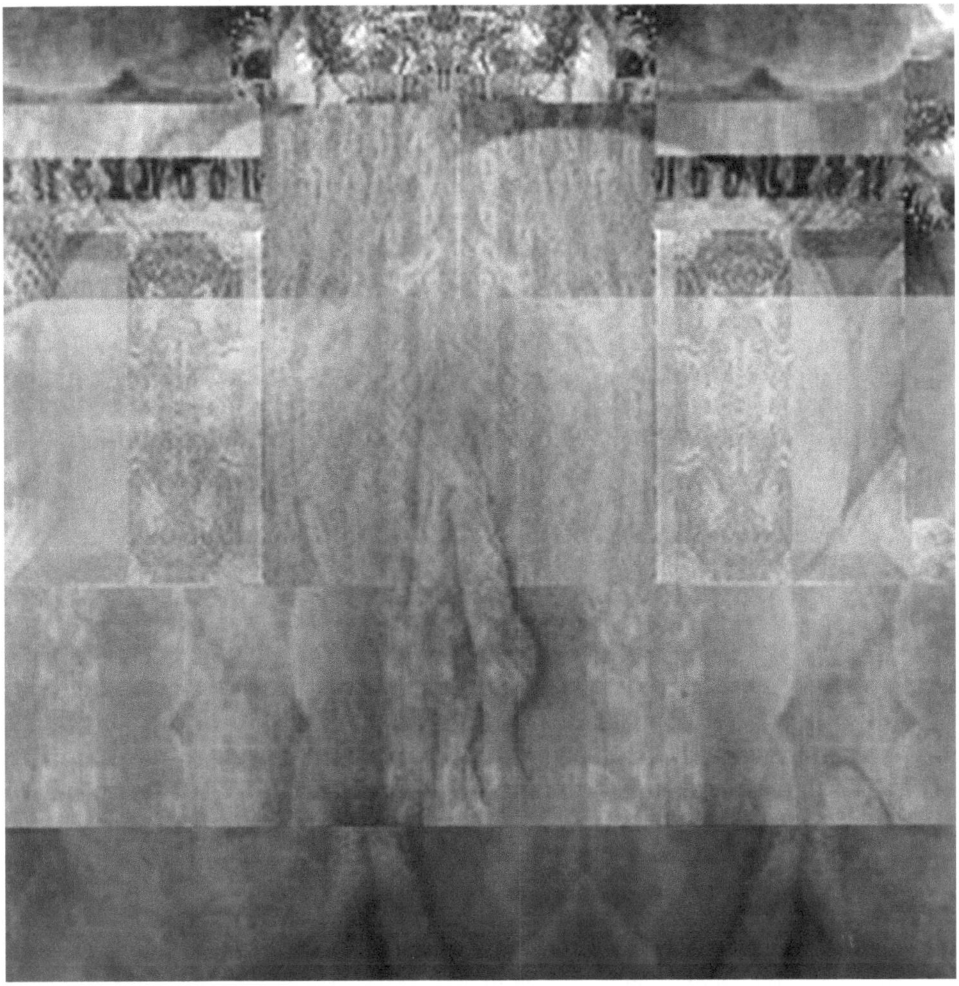

Figure 5.2 Joseph Nechvatal, *the birth Of the viractual*, 2001, 70 × 70 inches, computer-robotic assisted acrylic on canvas.

> parts of the intimate human body are intermixed with flower or fruit ornaments into a virally created collage. The hybrid image suggests an androgyny that Nechvatal traces to the Roman poet Ovid's Metamorphoses, which depicts transmutation as a universal principle driving the nature of the world.[6]

In these remarks Paul, in effect, identifies Nechvatal's major creative insight – an intuitive feeling of a monism at the heart of visual and other transformations. This monism finds unity even within potentially destructive conflicts. Whatever formulaic distinctions shape our experience of the world, these only work through cognitive linking – that embraces recognition, memory, and imagination. There is a primal unity wherein the stuff of the world and ways of giving it form are in harmonious reciprocity. This is not only ontological it is also aesthetic.

Nechvatal's notion of the viractual gives this a specific expression.

> *Viractuality* is a theory that strives to see, understand, and create interfaces between the technological and the biological. The basis of the viractual conception is that virtual producing computer technology has become a noteworthy means for making and understanding contemporary life (and thus art). And that this virtual production – a digital production that has been going on for a long time now – brings artists to a place of paradox where one finds increasingly the emerging of the computed (the virtual) with the uncomputed corporeal (the actual).[7]

In this theory Nechvatal perfectly exemplifies the way in which art gives expression to the techno-habitat of Postmodern culture. Indeed, in the viractual's mutual absorption of the real and the virtual we find also a an expression of those post-digital values wherein electronic media and non-electronic phenomena blend in the creation of new behavioral patterns. However, it is also important to bear in mind the way in which some of these interactions – in the form of social media – are bringing about a truncation of thought processes into simplistic forms of the kind that enabled Donald Trump to be elected. This suggests that viractuality needs to be developed in more sustained critical terms, and to be more sharply focussed in how it is applied.

A very different mode of computer assisted painting was developed by Chris Finley in the 1990s. He is of special interest insofar as his artistic development is closely correlated with the widespread adoption of computer technology for personal use in the 1990s. Indeed, whilst a student at the Art Center College of Design in Pasadena California he took a basic computer design course as an elective. Despite the course not providing Finley with many relevant skills, it did leave him with an interest in electronic files stored within other such files, and the navigation interfaces for these. He observes that

> At the time, I was searching for a new way to conceptualize sculptural space influenced by technological developments. I began making sculptures out of Tupperware that mimicked the process of opening computer files. Layers of sculptural information were stacked inside each other. Viewers of the sculpture had to deconstruct the sculptures to discover hidden elements.[8]

An extraordinary contingency intervened on Finley's approach. An exhibition of his work entitled 'Double-Click' at Santa Monica in 1994 was damaged during an earthquake, and its contents jumbled up. Finley sent diagrams using the Aldus Freehand program on his recently acquired Apple computer to assist the gallery staff reassemble the works. This experience inspired him (a few years later) to use the same program to create full color digital images as studies for his paintings. The paintings were influenced by video game imagery, with their hard-edge shapes constructed with a mouse – one click at a time. In relation to this, Finley observes

> I felt that the click of the mouse was a kind of ironic gesture of our time in contrast to the heroic gesture of action painting. I associate action painting like that made by Jackson Pollock, as a kind of overtly macho action that involves the

> whole body to perform, while constructing a painting from the clicks of a mouse is a passive, tiny physical gesture that is slightly pathetic in comparison and only takes place in the tips of the fingers.[9]

Indeed, whilst Finley's subsequent paintings are done autographically, they are designed on a Macintosh computer.

> 'I'm constantly clicking on the screen, zooming in to look at the details,' Finley says. 'The computer even can tell me what percentage of what pigment makes the color I'm going to paint on the painting. I can click on a certain color and it can tell me the percentage of red and blue and yellow to mix.'[10]

The upshot of all this is a 'fun' hedonistic form of painting. Noteworthy in this respect is the *Goo Goo Pow Wow* series done in 2001, and exhibited at the Rena Bransten Gallery in San Francisco. The title's conjunction of baby talk, and allusion to a Native American ceremony is derived from the fact of Finley having become a father, and his sustained listening to the Robbie Robertson album, *Music For The Native Americans*. During this time, he longed also to go camping in the great outdoors.

Finley's method method of creating the *Goo Goo Pow Wow* paintings can be related to this through the intricacy of his creative strategy. In his words,

> I made a series of sculptures that combined baby related objects with camping gear that borrowed a generic Native American aesthetic. I photographed that work and dropped the images in Adobe Illustrator. I used the auto trace feature to vectorize the images and distorted them by dragging, rotating and flipping elements of the image. I projected the outlines of the illustrator files onto canvas and painted them with my signature sign enamel style.[11]

Consider the first *Goo Goo Pow Wow* work Goo Goo Pow Wow of 2001 (Plate 14). This appears to be a three-dimensional environment that has been rearranged and/or disrupted. The occupants of its pictorial space appear to be linked as things in space might be, but their individual thing-like identities and relations appear distorted. There is the suggestion of a playroom with a bunk, with the forms' outlines and elongations giving the impression of having originated as toys, before their transformation.

The key structural players in all this are the plain enamel colors. They are presented with no tonal gradation, the depth effects arising, rather, from their juxtapositions. They are presented through forms with tilted and oblique planar emphases that (in concert with the character of the shapes) create three-dimensional effects through optical push/pull. In this way, the forms are rendered palpable – full of tactile promise even though they are physically flat.

The richness of the composition captures something of the intensity of early childhood experiences. In particular, the raggedness of outlines and edges, and the insistency of color seem to track a child's manic attention to toys – where interest can shift from one object and back in a few moments. This sets up a related association. The pictorial scene of *Goo Goo Pow Wow* creates a impressional whole that seems familiar, but has arisen from a highly episodic sequences of original encounters (as in childhood) that prevent it being recalled as anything other than the impression of a scene.

One of the most interesting visual features of this painting can be brought out through a contrast with *Mallardbride* of 2002 (another painting by Finley).[12]

It contains a maroon floor and pale mauve wall that meet to form a well-defined horizon. However, this relation's pictorial function is mainly as a setting for the large group of forms in the center of the work. Now, *Goo Goo Pow Wow* contains this very same horizonal configuration of maroon and pale mauve, but with the horizon significantly more extended, and much less cluttered with forms. These differences allow this horizonal relation to evoke the confluence of two different spaces – that of the impressional playroom, and also that of a possible 'great beyond' – a peaceful open space to compensate for the chaotic immediacy of the nursery. Of course, the magic of this is that, in Finley's pictorial space, these are not alternatives, they are both complementary factors in the same aesthetic unity. The actual, and the imaginary with which we surround it, are brought into unity.

The palpability of forms in Finley's works retain their vigor even in the more monochrome pieces, post 2001 (such as *Director* of 2007). Indeed, the quasi-Tupperware disaster of the 1992 exhibition seems to have left a lasting mark on how Finley constructs pictorial space. His approach centers on digital deconstruction, compression, and re-extension of images into quasi-ceramic and wire-like forms. The computer program is a means of distending and rearranging the physicality of the actual to make it amenable to the artist's own sense of painting. There is, of course, something hedonistic and wish-fulfilling about this, but it also has a deeper (more Faustian significance) as an alchemical transformation of the three-dimensional world-substance into something controlled by the artist's two-dimensional will-to-form. In this way, the physical slightness of moving the computer mouse gives rise to much profounder aesthetic ramifications.

I turn now, to computer-assisted sculpture. Interestingly, the first example of it dates from as far back as 1968, with the late Robert Mallary's *Quad II* (Figure 5.3).[13] Mallary was a profoundly underestimated artist whose work ranged over many aspects of sculpture, as well as drawing and painting. His computer-assisted work was only a small part of this output, but remains, nevertheless, profoundly significant.

Mallary developed interests in new materials for use in painting in the late 1930s, and in the late 1940s did research on technical means for three-dimensional projection. Around the same time, he formulated an approach to 3-D image formation based on sequential contour projection. In 1967 he once more re-addressed these early art-and-technology interests through first experiments with computer sculpture. This involved Mallary updating his earlier work on sequential contour projection in cooperation with computer specialists. On the basis of these collaborations, he developed an approach to computer-assisted sculpture known as TRAN2. On the artist's site, it is summarized as follows.

> TRAN2 is a computer graphics program with twenty sub-routines to generate sculpture. The program presupposes a means of compiling form description data for use by the computer. This is done by breaking down the solid into a regular series of parallel cross sections, or contour 'slices,' which are then graphed and digitized as X, Y and Z coordinates and transferred to punch cards. A sequence

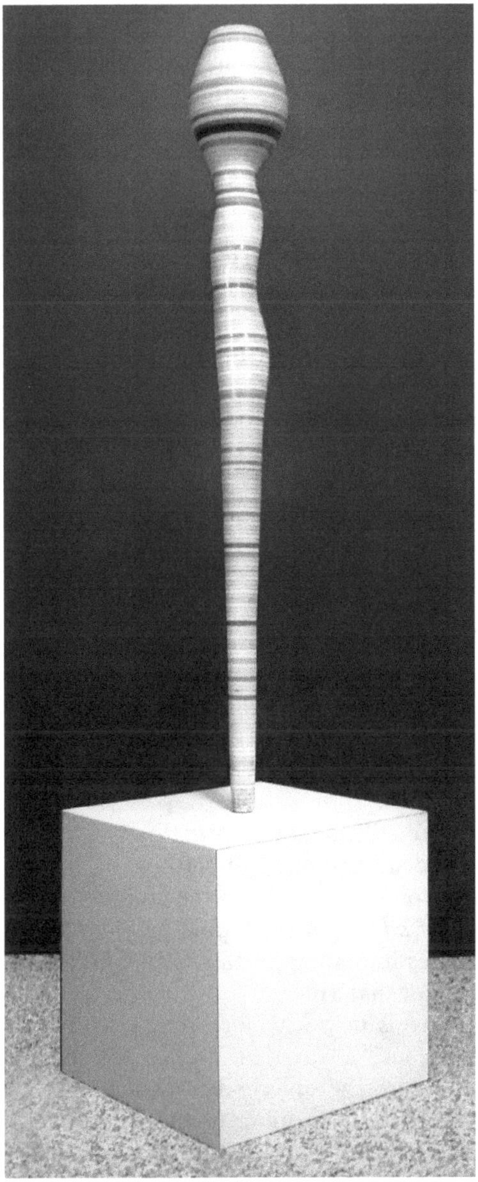

Figure 5.3 Robert Mallary, *Quad II*, 1968, 71½×11 inches, computer designed sculpture in laminated veneer.

of mathematical transformation procedures is brought to bear on the contour sections whereby the computer, in effect, models and reshapes the contour sections into an original sculpture. The computer plotter reproduces a series of perspective views of the generated form together with a complete set of the transformed contour sections. These are used as patterns to complete the sculpture in some appropriate material.[14]

In *Quad II*, using an input of four profiles and segments derived from four ellipses, the computer filled out each of the forty-eight contour 'slices' involved in this, and composed them along a common vertical axis. Through an additional series of transformation procedures this input was varied in three different ways. This design was then physically realized in three dimensions in laminated veneer (an engineered wood, created from thin layers bound together with adhesive).

The work's visual effect is quite striking. It has an upright 'posture,' with this uprightness acted upon by the character of the horizontal 'slices' assembled one on top of the other. There is a vertical axis around which the different sized slices appear to rotate. The strict concentricity of these individual slices, their even thickness, and the insistency of their vertical arrangement, suggest also, a mechanical principle of organization.

However, this effect is mediated further. The different diameters of the slices mean that their perimeters are at different distances from the axis. But these differences are graduated rather than abrupt. They combine to create a smoothly animated appearance (something like the clay on a potter's wheel as it is gradually given shape). This animation invests the work with a 'wobble' – suggesting mechanism geared not towards functionality, but towards the creation of aesthetic form for its own sake. This is an early manifestation of what, earlier in this book, we called the *digital imprimatur*.

Since Mallory's abstract innovations, computer-designed sculpture has been taken to some extraordinary levels vis-à-vis figuration. A key figure in this respect is Robert Lazzarini. His sculptures are created in physically three-dimensional material using materials that are physically akin to the subject represented. *Skulls* of 2000, for example, are constructed from ground bone, resin, and pigment. However, the key digital contribution to his work is in its transformations of the object–space relation in terms of both optical and haptic dimensions.[15]

This gives Lazzarini's work a highly distinctive digital *imprimatur*. His sculptures are derived from images mathematically distorted through the use of algorithmic programs. This extends far beyond anamorphic distortion (of the kind made familiar through the skull in Holbein's *The Ambassadors*). Anamorphic projects involve an angle of viewing wherein the object resolves into an appearance consistent with our normal cognitive expectations of an object of that kind.

However, in Lazzarini's sculptures, there is no such 'normative' viewpoint. The space-occupancy of the object is skewed in such a way that it will not resolve into a familiar perceptual viewpoint. This is because the objects are reconfigured on the basis of both planar and sine wave distortions. The former involve skews and scale shifts, and the use of accelerated and de-accelerated perspectival effects. The sine-wave transformations are composed from compound projections of intersecting sine waves. In the case of the planar distortions, in particular, the relevant geometries involve perspectival constructions in two dimensions. This yields no single vantage point where the sculpture conforms to the aspectual constancies that constitute the object's 'normal' three-dimensional appearance. The planar and the wave distortions, in other words, turn the normal appearance into something alien. Hence, when presented with a Lazzarini object, visual and haptic perception cannot settle down to their usual correlated routine.[16]

To see what is at issue here, we need to remark upon the nature of perceptual routine. It extends far beyond mere constancy in variations of appearance. Normally, the objects in our surroundings – both natural and everyday functional artifacts – are weighed down with associations based on their intrinsic character or use-value. Functional artifacts, in particular, are things we never think twice about, even whilst using them. They take their place unremarked upon in the day to day visual-haptic continuum of our engagement with the world.

However, it is precisely this mundane facticity that Lazzarini's sculptures intervene upon. On the one hand, by suspending the usual patterns of perceptual constancy, the unfamiliar that so often lurks within the familiar is made into a startling alternative aesthetic *entrée* to the object; on the other hand, the particular character of the distortions in Lazzarini's sculptural objects engage also with the routine of existential associations noted above.

In respect of this latter point, consider *payphone* of 2000 (Figure 5.4). The work is made from anodized aluminium, stainless steel, plexiglass, and silk-screened graphics. These materials allow its distorted substance to seem real in terms of

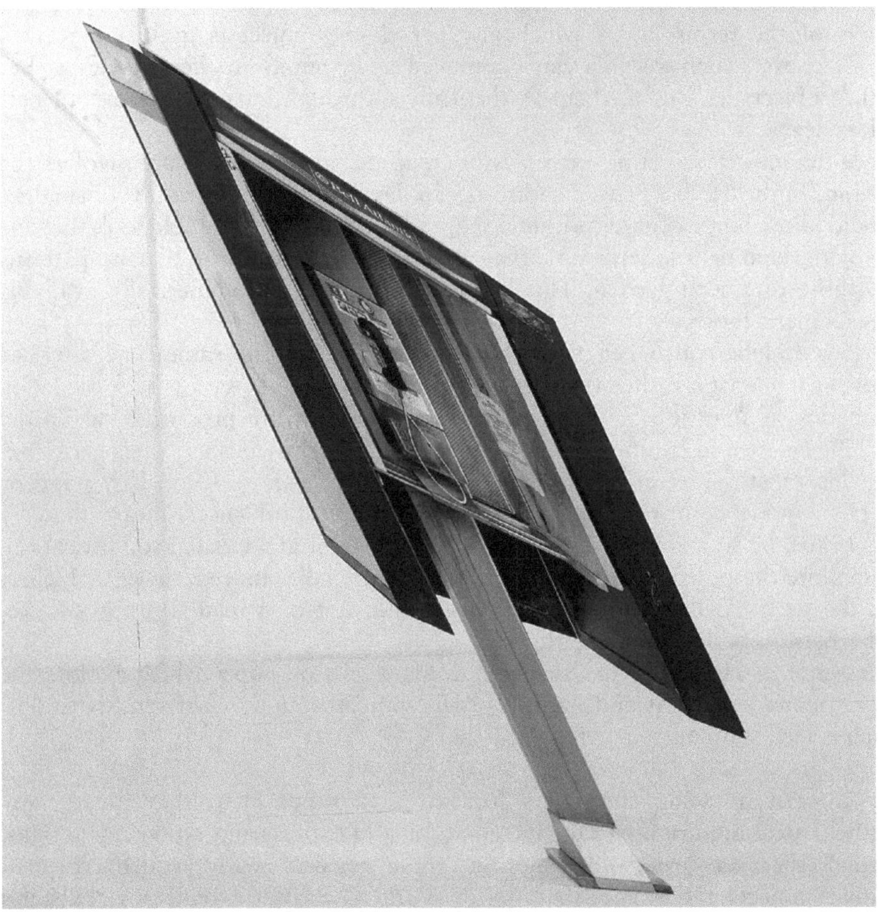

Figure 5.4 Robert Lazzarini, *payphone*, 2000. Anodized aluminium, stainless steel, Plexiglas, silk-screened graphics, 108 × 84 × 56 inches.

Source: Image courtesy of Robert Lazzarini Studio.

physical substance. However, the distortions wrought upon the nominally mundane artifact suggest that it is clue to some catastrophic event or crime or combination of both. In some more recent works, indeed, such as *Motel Door* of 2012, the object bears explicit evidence of violence through having been kicked-in, and bearing residual blood stains.[17]

There are two ramifications to this. First, this connotation of criminal context allows the general unnoticed meaningfulness of mundane objects to be thematized in an interesting way. But second, it also brings out the deeper ontology of the object as something which we share space with, and which bears witness to the things we do, as well as being a resource for us. Merleau-Ponty – following artists such as Klee – emphasized how, sometimes, the object seems to be peering back at one.[18] In the case of objects that figure in crime scenes, this is especially the case. For – instead of their usual mundane function – *they have a story to tell.*

The importance of this is that to imagine our gaze being returned by inanimate things such as the objects in a crime scene helps habituate us to the unlimited reversibility of viewing positions in the horizon of perceptual space. It helps focus our awareness of the terms under which any perceiving subject is itself a perceived *object.* Of course, such insights can be arrived at in purely intellectual terms, but Lazzarini's objects lead us to them aesthetically – through intricate avenues of perceptual intricacy.

One of the most fascinating examples of computer-assisted sculpture involves the use of sand. In the 1990s, Bruce Shapiro began developing motion control machines that would allow him to cut algorithmic shapes in wood and metal. He took this one further by developing a kinetic table that would allow the creation of sand-patterns akin to those of a Zen garden. This has led him to make commercially available 'Sisyphus' kinetic tables.[19]

Jean-Pierre Hébert also began working in this field at the same time, but has focussed on its artistic rather than its commercial potential. As far back as 1959, Hébert had a summer job at IBM, where he learned Fortran programming. In the early 1970s he created computer-designed pen and ink drawings as a means of augmenting his artistic interests in natural patterns such as those formed by wind or water. His experience in this medium, and technological advances, meant that, by the late 1980s, he was able to create plotter drawings of great visual sophistication, and to explore the potential of computers in related media. Indeed, in 1995, Hébert devised the term 'Algorist' for his own work and that of a related group of like-minded artists, notably Roman Verostvo.[20]

The essence of Hébert's work is found in his works on paper which explore the interfaces of mathematical and natural order with profound visual sensitivity. His approach is well summarized as follows.

> My interest in using computers for art is twofold. First, they answer my mathematical inquiries, free my imagination, and express and evolve my designs. Second, they set devices into motion in the physical world, which create or animate objects and images that are my work. The latter extends my skills and thus empowered my mind can ask what my hands alone could not do.[21]

Hébert's approach has been extended beyond the medium of paper. One key aspect of this is *Ulysses*, an installation that he first built and displayed at the Siggraph'99

Art Exhibition (Los Angeles, 1999) (Figure 5.5). *Ulysses* centers on a computer-driven magnet rolling a ball across a sand table, to create mathematically inspired designs. The original installation itself has a strong physical presence insofar as the plate containing the sand is supported by a broad sculpted base (comprising three tiers of walnut). This, in turn, carries a mechanical table with a magnet, driven by two motors that connect to the computer through a serial cable.

Of decisive importance, of course, is how the computer is programmed. Hébert's original sand designs employ the Mathematica language and the *Ulysses* installation was coded using the Python language. However, sand tracing is a difficult medium. It requires that standard visualization tools are mediated by the artist's own sense of light and compositional possibilities. Hébert describes the workings of the installation as follows.

> The ... motors have their own command language and interpreter. A driver translates the tracings geometry into motor instructions, polls the motors' feedback, controls communications and provides a graphical user interface. ... A digital camera is connected to the computer to survey the sand on demand and can be set to interact with the process. As the ball moves through the sand from the magnet pull, it rolls and does not slide. Its speed fluctuates as periodically

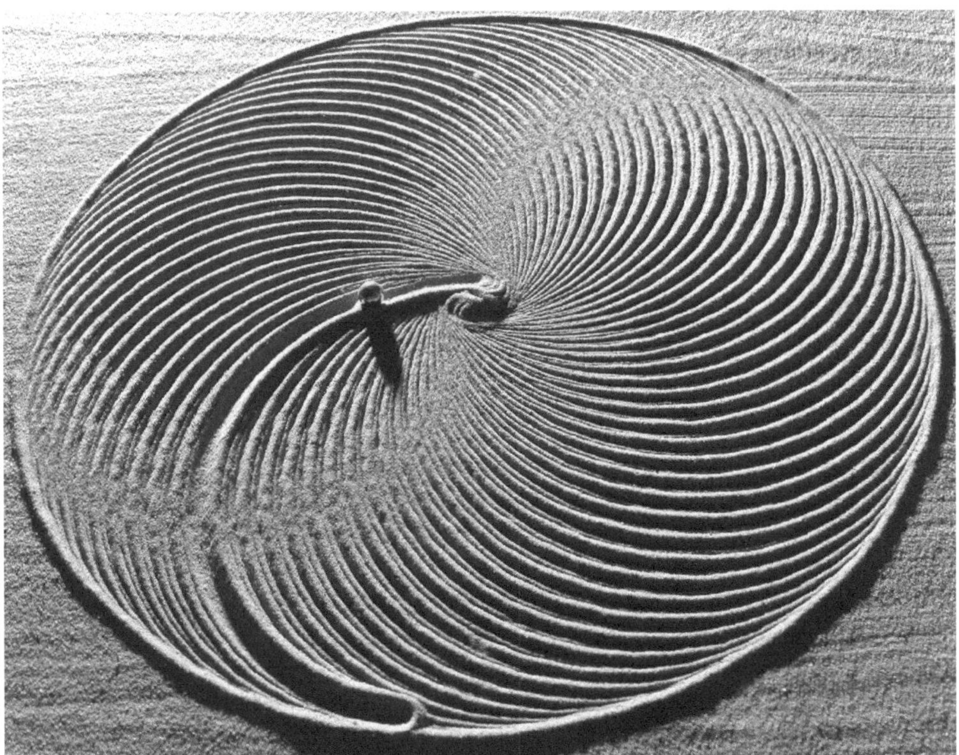

Figure 5.5 Jean-Pierre Hébert, *Ulysses*, computer directed installation, 1999.
Source: Photo © Jean-Pierre Hébert.

> the sand is first compressed and then gives in, freeing the ball to jump ahead. ... The piece foreseen must be thought as one line: the ball can backtrack but not levitate off the sand ... yet. The inspiration for it can come from all the walks of life, art or mathematics.[22]

After each digital image has been taken, Hébert combs the sand back – edge to edge – to form regular patterns. On occasion, he uses a fine-haired wide brush to disperse the sand into a blank surface. Over and above the digital photographic records, each created pattern is stored as an algorithm in the computer's memory. Through such storage, Hébert accumulates a complex repertoire of – in effect – geometric strategies which can be used in the creation of subsequent compositions.

Interestingly, the artist himself emphasizes that the photographic record is of limited use in appreciating *Ulysses*. Its real importance is as a *live installation*, wherein both artist and audience can observe the temporal progression of the emerging sand pattern. As Hébert notes

> One can interact by direct sketching, wandering through mazes, playing with algorithms, choosing patterns from a library, placing rocks, setting lights. Following the progress of a tracing for a full performance, or now and then observing a tracing from different angles, and coming back for the surprise of a new design ... makes the Ulysses experience.[23]

For the general audience, the experience of *Ulysses* can be equally rich – involving (as Hébert goes on to say) such things as 'the surprise, the expectations, the feelings elicited by the motion, the activity of the ball, the plasticity of the sand, the exacting development of the tracing.' All in all, Hébert's general creative strategy is summarized as follows

> I have a taste for quietness and beauty, for simplicity and depth, for rich effects of lights and matters enjoyable from a wide range of distances and angles. I find that mathematics can create the motifs, the compositions and the multiple depths of texture that allow these criteria to be met. ... helped by natural elements like sand, water, light, shadow, wood, and stone, our eyes and brain can be stimulated and satisfied to the extent of their capacity, without the dryness and the bandwidth constraints of the digital world closing in on us. ... Nature contributes to the work as it multiplies the effects of the simple instructions provided to the ball for its movement.[24]

The aesthetics of Hébert's *Ulysses* – like all his digital work – is both simple and complex in terms that are complementary. He himself emphasizes its origins in his interest in Zen gardens and aesthetics. Perhaps one can add to this. Mathematics allows the measurement of extension, intensive magnitude, and the velocity and positioning of material bodies. It is integral to our experience of physical presence and changes thereof. However, it is not just a means of measurement. For the very fact that physical processes are amenable to measurement suggests that mathematical relations are an aspect of the formative metaphysical processes of Being, per se.

However, the ultimate nature of metaphysical process is not something the individual human mind can fully comprehend. Our conception of the universe is a centered one – we describe it as it appears from the viewpoint of a specific kind of sentient being. However, the universe as it as a whole exceeds any such species-specific viewpoint. In particular, the distinction between the microcosmic and macrocosmic does not apply, since this is determined by the relative sizes of specific kinds of individual entities.

Now, Hébert's *Ulysses* installation intervenes on this in interesting different ways. Whenever we watch someone doing a calculation, or listen to the unobtrusive noises of a computer working, then we get a sense of mathematical relations as a part of a living formative process. But in the workings of *Ulysses*, this takes place in a revelatory manner. The simple movement of the ball through the sand is, in effect, a highly focused revelation of mathematical structure/being created and working as an engine of creation. The simple furrows and the linear forms they constitute when viewed from above take on a representational meaning. We can see the suggested forms of ridges, hills, valleys, mountains, dried channels, and even human edifices such as constructed canals and urban layouts. Just as important is the physicality of the grains of sand themselves – suggesting countless possible past and future configurations. And, in all this, the placing of rocks, and the combing of the sand at the end of each creative act as symbolic visual punctuation.

The message so punctuated is metaphysical. It says that what is immediately present is subtended by vastnesses beyond it, and within it. We cannot comprehend the whole of nature and the integral role of mathematics, but *Ulysses* offers symbolic visions of the powers that are at issue here. Indeed, they offer an especially poignant perspective. For whilst human beings cannot comprehend the reality of nature's formative process, yet, at the same time, without recognition from rational beings, this process is blind, mechanical, and without meaning. *It is only the individual's finite path that allows nature as a formative principle to be revealed. Ulysses*'s single ball – making and marking a path through the sand – is an astonishingly stark revelation of this. But in its starkness it is also an aesthetic redemption. The lights and shades of the pattern, and the intricacy of its lines present beauty as an economy – wherein the many levels of nature work together, creating a 'fit' with those beings who inhabit it.

Hébert's *Ulysses* is, as we have seen, an installation. However, whereas the outcome of this is computer-assisted sculpture, other such assisted installations have a more Conceptual orientation. Again, the precedents for this go back as far as the 1960s. An important example of this idiom is from 1969, when Vladimir Bonačić set up the installation *DIN. PR18* on the facade of the NAMA department store at Kvaternik Square in Zagreb. Similar installations were set up by him in 1971 on the NAMA at Ilica Street in Zagreb and on the façade of the Museum of Contemporary Art in Belgrade. These works involved lights flashing in a sequence programmed by a computer, and the novelty of this innovation served, in effect, to make the computer-driven visual rhythms of the lights into part of their meaning.[25]

The computer-directness of Bonačić's strategy has been repeated many times since then, and in many different ways. Erwin Redl's work (discussed earlier in this book) is an example that remains close to Bonačić. In other computer-assisted installations, the Conceptualist dimension is given more direct emphasis. Jenny Holzer's *Protect Me From What I Want* of 1986, for example, an electronic spectacolor billboard projected its eponymous title over Times Square.[26] Here, of course, the positioning of the work in this locale is of political importance, insofar as Times Square is the psychological center of New York city's consumer universe. There is no apparent reason for the declaration to be there. All the other hoardings and billboards in the area served some recognizable informational or sales-related persuasive function. This means that the work has an existentially dislocating effect – one, indeed that is heightened by the no-frills, deadpan visual delivery of the message with its monochrome upper-case text.

Holzer's *Laments* of 1989 continues this electronic presentation of text for critical ends. As Margot Lovejoy succinctly puts it

> In *Laments*, words pass up and down via vertical columns of light emitting diode (LED) displays, and fragmentary first-person confessions of pain, fear, greed, flying by in the the dark in glowing reds, greens, and yellows. Occasionally, the spectacle stops, the room goes black and the columns glow in pure color before starting up in motion again. In an adjoining room, the same texts were etched into stone sarcophogi.[27]

Some computer-assisted public art can assume spectacular proportions. A good example is the work of Raphael Lozano-Hemmer. His creations specialize in projections of light effects in ways that transform physical environments, mediated by specific informational contexts. A good example of this is his *Displaced Emperors (Relational Architecture # 2)* of 1997 – done in cooperation with Will Bauer and Susie Ramsay. This installation used an "architact" interface that transformed how aspects of the Habsburg Castle in Linz appeared. Wireless 3D sensors calculated points on the façade pointed to by visitors, in order to project a large moving hand there. As the visitors thus 'caressed' the building, they could also create projections of the interiors of the Habsburg residence of Emperor Maximilian in Mexico City. By making a payment, a 'Moctezuma button' could be switched on so as to trigger a temporary 'post-colonial' superimposed image of an Aztec head-dress followed by a sequence of images showing jewels from the Austrian-Hungarian Empire, to the accompaniment of music by Toña la Negra.[28] According to Lozano-Hemmer, 'As an architectural mise-en-abîme, the project supports the idea of perpetration of culture instead of calls for its vampiric preservation.'[29]

This presents an interesting interpretative ambiguity, for the building itself, and what is projected upon it create an aesthetic configuration that is more than the sum of the two parts. The configuration tends to transcend the ideological components stressed by the designer, and creates, in effect, a visual spectacle wherein the formal elements actually displace the historical meanings that are supposed to be drawn attention to. This can be regarded as politically retrograde; but equally, it can be regarded as expressive of the truth of what computers enable so effectively, namely the conjoining of appearances from radically different sources. Even as the spectacle focusses attention on its immediate selected space, we know that this is also a blending of visual spaces physically far distant from one another.

In looking at Holzer's and Lorenzo's works we are already crossing the boundaries boundaries of computer-assisted work to questions of interactivity. It is to this question we now turn.

Notes

1 Interview with Joseph Nechvatal, *Brooklyn Rail*, December 9, 2015, https://brooklynrail.org/2015/12/art/joseph-nechvatal-with-thyrza-nichols-goodeve.
2 For a discussion of this work, see Margot Lovejoy's *digital currents: art in the electronic age*, 2007, p. 154.
3 See Nechvatal's 'Theoretical Statement Concerning Computer-Robotic Paintings' that accompanied *The Informed Man* in the Documenta VIII exhibition (Amsterdam, 1987). This is conveniently republished online at www.nictoglobe.com/new/articles/jn.html.
4 Ibid.
5 'Interview with Joseph Nechvatal,' *Brooklyn Rail.*
6 Christiane Paul, *Digital Art*, 2015, pp. 57–58.
7 Joseph Nechvatal, 'Emergence of the New Paradigm: Viractuality,' Talk/demo delivered at the École Supérieure d'AudioVisuel, Université de Toulouse le Mirail, November 3, 2010, Toulouse, France, www.eyewithwings.net/nechvatal/Viractuality/Viractualism.html.
8 Email message to the author, December 28, 2017.
9 Email message to the author, December 28, 2017.
10 'Hide and SECA': a review of an exhibition by Finley from 1999. See www.metroactive.com/papers/sonoma/01.21.99/seca-9903.html.
11 Email message to the author, January 3, 2018.
12 An image of *Mallardbride* is available online at www.invaluable.com/auction-lot/chris-finley-mallardbride-2002-137-c-vshweps8dg.
13 For a brief but insightful discussion of Mallary, see Lovejoy, op. cit., p. 170.
14 See Mallary's website at www.robertmallary.com/Art/Art.htm.
15 See the artist's website at www.robertlazzarini.com/skulls (accessed January 3, 2018).
16 See the feature on the artist at www.museomagazine.com/ROBERT-LAZZARINI.
17 See the artist's website at www.robertlazzarini.com/motel-door.
18 See, for example, the reference in the essay 'Eye and Mind,' included in *The Merleau-Ponty Aesthetics Reader: Philosophy and Painting*, ed. Galen A. Johnson, 1993, p. 129.
19 See Shapiro's company website, www.sisyphus-industries.com.
20 See the artist's website, http://jeanpierreHébert.com/17s.html.
21 See Hébert's '*Ulysses*: Sand As Medium,' in *The Mathematica Journal*, Graphics Gallery, Volume 7, Issue 3, 1999; www.mathematica-journal.com/issue/v7i3/graphics. See also Nick Lambert's substantial discussion at http://computer-arts-society.com/static/cas/computerartsthesis/index.html%3Fpage_id=322.html (accessed January 1, 2018).
22 Hébert, 'Ulysses: Sand As Medium.'
23 Ibid.
24 Ibid.
25 For a discussion of Bonačić, see Jonathan Benthall, *Science and Technology in Art Today*, 1972, pp. 62–63.
26 The work does not seem to be included on the artist's own website. For a visual, see https://artaspoliticalvoice.weebly.com/jenny-holzer.html.
27 For a useful discussion, see Lovejoy, op. cit., p. 185.
28 The work is described on Lozano-Hemmer's website, www.lozano-hemmer.com/displaced_emperors.php.
29 See ibid.

6 Interactivities

One of the key features of digital art is its interactive aspects, wherein, in effect, digital space is extended into the real spaces of the Postmodern techno-habitat. Tendencies such as Dadaism, Happenings, Performance Art, and Conceptual Art have often involved physical interactions with the audience as a key feature of their meaning, but these were mainly tied to the time and place of the interaction and, in many cases, to the identities of the participants. Digital art, in contrast, involves interactions based on programs wherein the computer acts upon some physically given input, sometimes changing its appearance into a new visual form and, in other cases, eliciting specific responses from the participants. Hence, whilst the design of the program is tied to the imaginative creativity of the artist, its subsequent deployments do not require the physical involvement of the artist – though, of course, on many occasions, the artist may be present at the interaction.

Earlier in this book, an emphasis was placed on digital graphics as still-images, in the development of digital art. This emphasis is warranted insofar as interactive modes developed later, and whatever their mode of interactivity is, this will always to some degree, depend on the character of the basic graphics involved. Indeed, it was also argued at length, that the still-image has an aesthetic and ontological uniqueness that is not available from interactive works that are based on linear temporal presentation of their content.

However, it is vital to reiterate that this is a question of ontological difference, not artistic hierarchy. Many interactional works have temporally based aesthetic qualities that still-images cannot have. Indeed, some of the most profound digital artworks of all are interactive through-and-through. In this chapter, we attend to key examples of these.

It must be emphasized that, whereas in previous chapters, it was possible to trace the development of individual artists' work in some detail, here, in order to do justice to the sheer diversity of interactivities, it is necessary to survey a much broader field, and to focus on key examples rather than individual artists (though of course, in a few important cases, we will consider more than one work by the same artist).

The origins of interactive digital art go back to the 1960s.[1] There are two main aspects: first, the development of technology causally responsive to presence and/or movement and, second, visually relevant modes of direct physical interaction with computers. In terms of the first of these, the development of computer technology causally responsive to presence and movement owes much to Myron Krueger. His work from the late 1960s explores the scope of electronically mediated interactions between persons and environments. From 1974, onwards, he developed VIDEOPLACE based on rooms that can be placed anywhere, at any distance from one another. Each room contains a video monitor, wherein anyone entering such a room can see their own image and those of persons in the connected rooms projected on the monitor. By moving around their respective rooms, the participants can interact with the images of others, and see their own image transform in correlation with their movements. Other operations – such as coloring the images, and interacting with other virtual objects, are also available.

In terms of visually relevant modes of interacting with computers, Ivan Sutherland of the University of Utah worked on early versions of head-mounted displays from the late 1960s onwards. The display was worn like a pair glasses based on two monitors, each enabling a stereoscopical view for the user. Movements of the head were registered through computer-driven sensors, enabling the viewer to experience perspectival effects, and the possibility of virtual movement within the image.

Krueger's and Sutherland's innovations, set out, in effect, the basic vectors along which interactive computer art developed in the late 1980s and in the 1990s, before the advent of the internet. In what follows, we shall identify the main idioms of interactivity, and some key examples which are important for its origins and/or developments after the advent of the net.

One

The first main variety of interactivity is the *detectional* mode. Here the computer is programmed to transmit signals or to generate responses on the basis of detected causal impacts from motion, vibrations, sound, optical phenomena, or, of course, combinations of any or all of these. These impacts can be registered automatically, when any relevant stimulus comes within the detectional field, or they may involve the program being activated manually when appropriate kinds of stimuli are within range.

An early, very basic example of this is Kit Galloway's and Sherrie Rabinowicz's *Hole In Space: A Public Communication Sculpture* of 1980.[2] For three days in November 1980, the artists set up a satellite link between the Lincoln Center for Performing Arts in New York City and The Broadway department store in Los Angeles. Cameras and mikes, and screens positioned behind the windows, allowed life-size images from both venues to be registered, projected onscreen, and transmitted via satellite, thus enabling passers-by at one location to see and hear those at the other, in real-time.

No informational devices were provided to explain what was going on, or the reasons behind it. People simply found themselves, without warning, able to see and talk with people at the other side of the country. In the absence of guidance, these interpersonal engagements were, in effect, a case of *found* encounters, with digital satellite technology acting as a passive transmitter of interactivity.

Subsequent detectional interactivity has, of course, given the digital dimension a more direct *generative* role. For example, Jim Campbell's *Interactive Hallucination* of 1988 (Figure 6.1), is an important transitional work. It is an installation consisting of a couch, a table, chairs, plants, a television, and other familiar living-room type objects.[3] A video camera next to the television detects the viewer's image. When the image is projected on the tv screen, customized electronics make the viewer

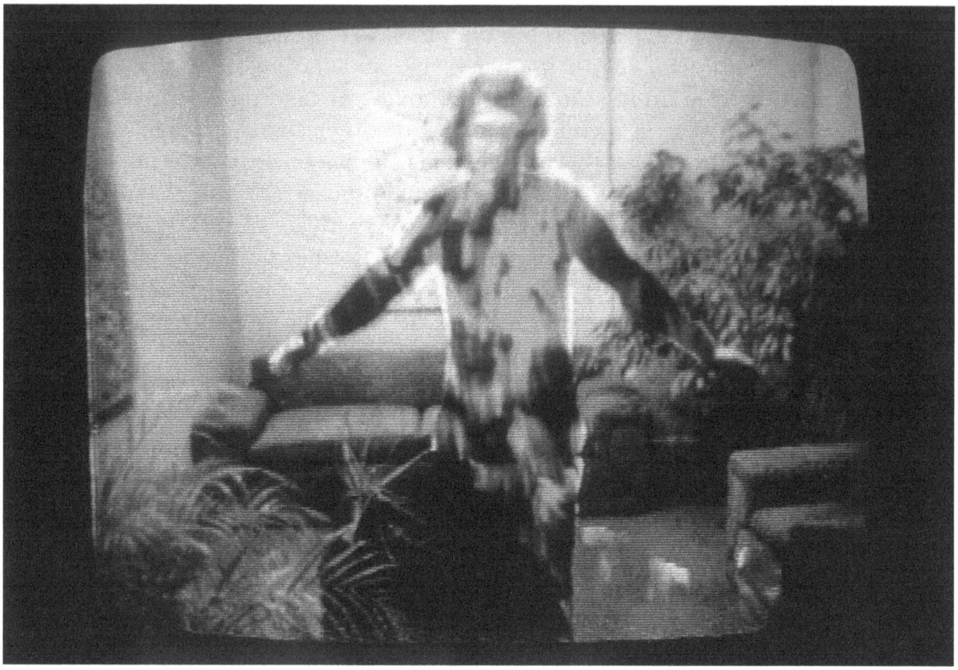

Figure 6.1 Jim Campbell, *Interactive Hallucination*, 1988. Custom electronics, black and white video camera, television, VCR. Dimensions variable.

appear to be on fire (with accompanying sound-effects). This effect occurs when the viewer enters the installation space. It is automatic rather than voluntary.

The digital *imprimatur* of *Interactive Hallucination* is one which combines an aesthetic of threat – horror, even, but also relief in that we know the effect has been staged digitally. Indeed, the work's particular aesthetic quasi-magic consists not so much of the body seeming to spontaneously combust, as the fact that the flames stick only to its shape and mass and the immediate wake of its movements. There is, in other words, a digital transformation of how the physical reality of combustion should appear. This confinement of flame to the body and its motion is actually a powerful symbolic device. It creates associations with the pain and anguish – the 'burning up inside' – that people may experience *psychologically*, even in the most seemingly benign environments.

A work where the voluntary aspect is to the fore is David Rokeby's *Very Nervous System* (1982–1990). The work is an installation that can be assembled indoors or outdoors. It involves video cameras, image processors, computers, synthesizers, and a sound system. The artist or other user occupies a space wherein his or her movements are detected by the techno-sensory array, and are then re-expressed through music and other sound effects. Of special visual interest is the feedback between program and body that develops through the ongoing interaction. For, as the viewer moves and the music is generated, he or she can develop a repetoire of visual gestures that will elicit corresponding sounds. There is an audio-visual reciprocity involved based on the body, and it is this which is the real subject of the work. Rokeby himself observes that

> The computer as a medium is strongly biased. And so my impulse while using the computer was to work solidly against these biases. Because the computer is purely logical, the language of interaction should strive to be intuitive. Because the computer removes you from your body, the body should be strongly engaged. Because the computer's activity takes place on the tiny playing fields of integrated circuits, the encounter with the computer should take place in human-scaled physical space. Because the computer is objective and disinterested, the experience should be intimate.[4]

In these remarks, Rokeby is focussing on an aspect of what, in this book, has been described as the naturalization of technology. His point is that that this does not have to involve submission to the mechanical aspects of technology, rather this aspect can be used to create effects at the experiential level that cannot be achieved without technology. This focus on reciprocity shows that a balance is possible. Instead of the human sensorium being trained – and thence colonized – by technology, computer art can open up some extraordinary new possibilities for bodily expression itself. Through this, we are immersed even more closely in the Postmodern techno-habitat.

A rather more prosaic but influential work is Scott Snibbe's *Boundary Functions* of 1998. This involves a set of lines projected from an overhead camera and projector. The lines track movements on the installation floor through a customized software program that processes the video image. In response to such movement, the floor is marked out into areas dividing occupants from one another.

One person on the floor elicits no response from the computer. As soon as two or more are present, a single line appears and bisects the floor. The line changes in correlation with the participants' changes of position. As soon as more than two people become present, the line divides the floor into cells, wherein the space within any such cell is closer to its occupant than to any of the other participants.

This cellular structure is a 'Voronoi diagram.' Such diagrams are analytic devices based on the partitioning of a plane into regions based on their distance from a set of points that form a specific subset of that plane. Once this subset is specified, it defines a region constituted by all the points closer to it than to other such subsets. These are Voronoi 'cells.' Diagrams of this kind describe a mathematical structure of spatial relations that is ubiquitous in both physical and biological nature, including, of course, the spatial expression of human behavior. According to Snibbe,

> By projecting the diagram, the invisible relationships between individuals and the space between them become visible and dynamic. The intangible notion of personal space and the line that always exists between you and another becomes concrete. The installation doesn't function at all with one person, as it requires a physical relationship to someone else. In this way Boundary Functions is a reversal of the lonely self-reflection of virtual reality, or the frustration of virtual communities: here is a virtual space that can only exist with more than one person, in physical space.[5]

The *Boundary Functions* title is taken from the doctoral thesis of the 'Unabomber' Theodore Kaczynski, an individual, of course, who was in manifest conflict with surrounding society. By using a title with these associations, Snibbe underlines that his digital strategy is meant to express the realm of psycho-social relations consequent upon spatial proximity and distance between people. The Voronoi diagram, in other words, here evokes a kind of living mathematics based on how humans populate physical and social space.

A second major idiom of interactivity is *active interfacing*, where the audience has to physically engage with the computer rather than simply be scanned by it. This can involve both *local and non-local modes of interface*. An interesting – and pioneering – example of the former is Kenneth Feingold's *The Surprising Spiral* of 1991. The artist describes it thus:

> *The Surprising Spiral* is an interactive artwork, utilizing a computer controlled videodisc, computer graphics, digitized sounds and texts, and synthesized voices, embedded within sculptures. The work responds to the form of the viewer/participant's engagement. ... In a cut out in the center of the cover is embedded a transparent touch screen, which appears to be the glass 'cover' of the book. On this touch screen are fingerprints. ... When a viewer touches any of the fingerprints, various things can happen: there are always sound responses to these touches, usually speech; the video can change to another location in the world, or an animated text might be evoked. ... The work has a complex cause and effect structure, and a touch that the viewer makes might have an immediate visual response, happen a short time later, or much later. I wanted these to mirror our daily cause and effect experiences.[6]

In these remarks, Feingold emphasizes that our daily activities sometimes have immediate and sometimes delayed effects. But, to appreciate the full significance of this work, one must add that the effects in question are not usually remarked upon – they are simply part of the ebb and flow of our everyday activities. When encountered in the context of *The Surprising Spiral*, however, these effects are made available in explicit terms. Indeed, the fact that they arise from specific interactive choices rather than immersion in a network of general cognitive activity, gives them an aesthetic focus that sets them apart from everydayness. There is also a second important aesthetic factor. For whilst engagement with technology is often the stuff of routine, *The Surprising Spiral* shows the pleasantly surprising outcomes that can also be involved in this. The naturalization of technology described earlier in this book, in other words, is here shown to have possibilities beyond merely training the human sensorium.

This naturalization of technology, indeed, has become a familiar thematic in much active interface art. An especially impressive example is David Small's and Tom White's *Stream of Consciousness/Interactive Poetic Garden* of 1998. This installation involved a six foot square garden (inspired by ancient Persian formal designs) divided recursively into a series of smaller squares. A computer-driven video projector is used to create the illusion of words floating on the surface of water as it flows through the garden. The flow begins at the back of the garden and cascades through a series of pools until it reaches a large square one. This is lined with crushed white coral, and the water moves through it slowly. Words appear to tumble down over the rocks, carried by the water into the shallow pool, afterwards reappearing at the top of the stream. As the creators observe,

> The words mimic the physical behavior of objects floating in a real fountain. The person sitting at the bench can interact with the words through a special hand interface letting her stop the word flow, push and pull words, and over time change the content of the words themselves. These physically modeled words are projected from above onto the rocks and coral. The computer computes the word image as well as managing the camera based input device, which lets the person control the word flow.[7]

The viewer's interaction involves some extraordinary effects that are worth describing further. As the creators continue,

> Through the hand interface, a person can reach into the pool of words and create a blue aura behind them. The words are repelled by the hand, making it easier to create blockages in the flow. But if the person presses directly onto a word so that the glow is directly behind it, it begins to swell larger than the other words. Eventually it bursts into two words, the original along with a related word. If the hand is not moved, more related words will continue to be generated from the seed word. As the pool circulates, old words are removed, so that over time the words in the water are the words that have been chosen as interesting.[8]

This work is extraordinarily powerful at different cognitive levels. The flowing of water is itself a potent symbol – of the coming to be and passing away of life, and of the continuity of episodes within this process. The role of the projected words is especially potent. The stream of consciousness, as such, is composed of words and the experiences they articulate, but because we inhabit language so closely, it is an uncanny experience to see words functioning like detritus carried away in the stream of time.

Of course, whilst we exist *in* language, the generation of thought is not entirely volitional – we think of one thing, and find that it gives rise to another through association rather than choice on our part. Indeed, the particular way that words feature in this installation is even more poignant. They are generated by touching the water. Touch is the most concrete and physical sense, but, in this context, it takes on a quasi-magical power through making words appear and undergo transformation at the level of objective phenomena. Many of our deepest words try to make sense of the flow of time. We say things like 'I can't find the words for it…' etc. And when we engage in associational thought, the words and thoughts that come up divide again into component words/ideas, or linked ones – sometimes as the outcome of volition, but many times not.

The words in the pool itself allude to the nature of individual and cultural personality. This is because frequently made word choices mean that the selected words persist, creating an enduring identity, whilst the others are washed away in the waters of oblivion. The way the installation is framed – with a square border of pebbles – ensures that the elemental power of earth is evoked as the ultimate ground of all this.

Another major innovator in active interfacing is Jeffrey Shaw. In *The Legible City* of 1988–1991 (created in cooperation with Dirk Groeneveld) (Figure 6.2), the viewer rides a stationary bicycle in front of a representation of a city projected on a

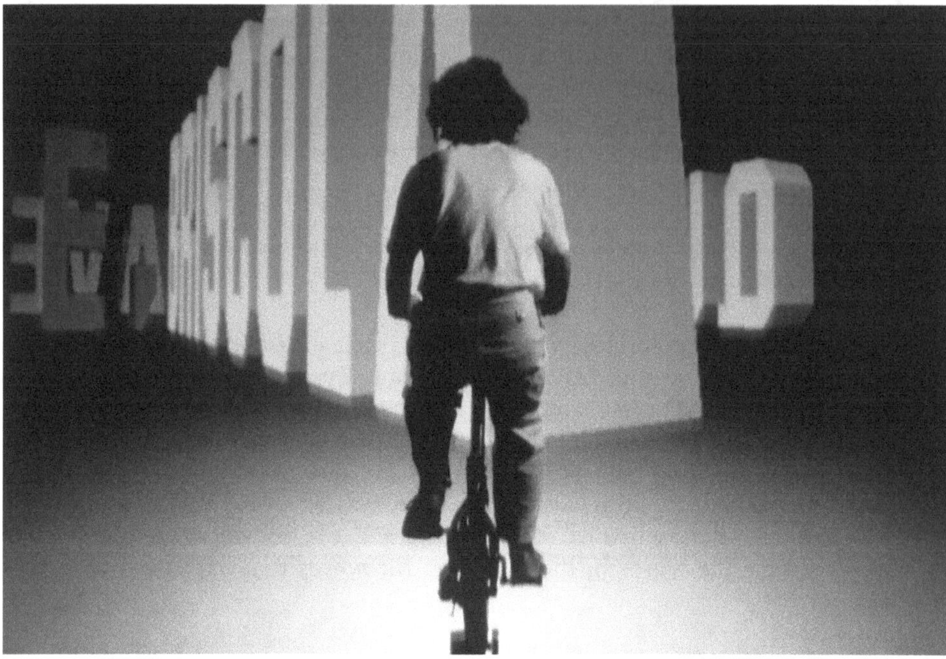

Figure 6.2 Jeffrey Shaw, *The Legible City*, installation.
Source: Photograph courtesy of Jeffrey Shaw.

large screen immediately before him or her.[9] The city 'streets' are composed entirely of computer-generated letters of the alphabet arranged in words and sentences. The layout of this visual/linguistic material is actually based on street maps and architecture from the Manhattan area of New York, Amsterdam, and Karlsruhe. A monitor in front of the cyclist shows his or her position within the relevant city; and he or she can choose which direction to follow (using controls on the handlebars), and how fast to travel. On the basis of this, the on-screen letters change to create the effect of cycling through the 'streets' so presented. Indeed, there is a close and intended correlation between the physical character of the letters, and that of the specific city streets which they represent.

In this work the curious relation of subjective space, physical space, and linguistic descriptions of location, undergoes metamorphosis. Letters and words are *types* of which the individual instances are tokens. This means that, in the context of ordinary linguistic communication, the only visual information that is relevant in the token is the minimum we need to recognize which letter or word-type is being presented. Such things as color, or surface texture are not involved in this, but in Shaw's virtual cities, the communicative function is modified by an overload of visual information, and a displacement of the context of encounter. Specifically, attention focusses on how the letters exist as individual phenomenal configurations as well as on their communicative function as tokens of types. And the individuality in question here involves both the physical appearance of the letters and their spatial isomorphism with the streets they delineate.

The fact that particularity is made a focus of attention in a context where it is usually inert, makes recognition of the letters and texts into an aesthetic experience. A similar aesthetic reorientation arises through the spatial isomorphism between real streets and those of *The Legible City*. The cyclist's journey is determined here by choices in how the text of streets is read and, in that respect, makes something that is normally involved in all our movement through space, into something manifest. This is the fact that directionality is not just instinctual, it is based on how we interpret or 'read' the meaning of spatial layout. Hence the populating of space with isomorphically distributed letters and texts gives this normally subconscious feature an aesthetic presentation.

This interchange between words and spatiality in *The Legible City* is, of course, a special case of that aesthetics of quasi-magic that we have associated with digital art in general. But here the magic is double-coded. For as well as Shaw's virtual cities having the characteristic digital *imprimatur*, the very switching of language from the realm of spoken and written, to the palpability of virtual architecture is itself something magical. It is as if the mischievous digital magician says: 'Humans *live* in their language, you say? Well here's living proof of it!'

Interestingly, in 1998, Shaw created a new version of the work entitled *The Distributed Legible City*.[10] It involved the same basic features as the original work, but with an extra dimension of interactivity. The program was changed to allow two or more cyclists at different interface locations to occupy the same virtual environment, at the same time. In their navigations they can encounter one another as avatars, and even verbally communicate.

Hence the experience of the letter and text space becomes a focus for interpersonal communication as well as private exploration. (We shall return to work involving net-access, a little further on.)

One of the most ambitious examples of active interfacing is Maurice Benayoun's *The Tunnel Under the Atlantic* (Figure 6.3).[11] This was an art installation that, from September 19 to 24, 1995, established a simultaneous *televirtual* link between the Museum of Contemporary Art in Montreal and the Centre Georges Pompidou in Paris. Televirtuality is a mode of communicating at a distance using computer generated 'virtual' imagery. *The Tunnel Under the Atlantic*, specifically, was enabled by Tristan Lorach's, '3D Digging Engine.' This allowed the user to 'dig' into the surface of 3D virtual space material, gradually creating/uncovering new pathways and caves (with their own surfaces) to form a unique network.

The 'entry' point to the tunnel at both venues was a metal tube, 2 metres in diameter, and extending physically into the ground. However, the actual 'entrance' to both structures (at the front of the tubes) was purely virtual – a circular monitor projecting recessional depth. Participants at either end of the installation faced the tunnel entrance and had to 'dig' through the virtual material as if it were some kind of obstacle. (This digging action was performed through a control panel allowing movement in any direction.)

At the beginning of the dig, the layers of presented virtual data are just that, a formless mass of visual forms and masses, with a few recognizable figurative elements (representative of the cultures of the connected national locations, and held in the respective host museums). They have the crude appearance of geological strata. However, by navigating the figurative clues on the basis of choices made through information points on the control panel, the data is gradually shaped. Geological

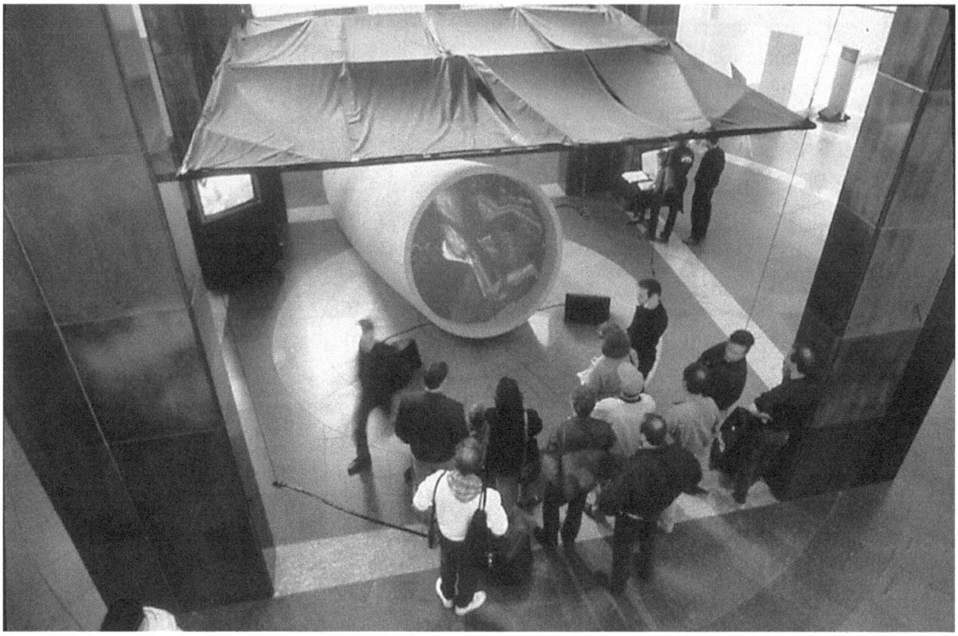

Figure 6.3 Maurice Benayoun, *The Tunnel Under the Atlantic.* Televirtual art installation linking the Museum of Contemporary Art, Montreal, and the Centres Georges Pompidou, Paris, 1995.

strata become iconographical strata. The participants dig thematic tunnels, leading one participant towards the other. In the course of this, the interactive features make suggestions, and guidance is provided, also, by music, sound, and vocal communication with the person currently at the other end of the tunnel. The participants' own activities in the tunnel are recorded on camera, and can be played back during the dig. Eventually – after days of digging (and with different participants coming and going) – the tunnel is complete. There is a virtual audio-visual meeting of the participants at both venues; Montreal and Paris are joined.

The Tunnel Under the Atlantic relates to Galloway's and Rabinowicz's *Hole in Space* work discussed earlier, and allows some instructive contrasts to be made. In the latter work, the digital role is mainly passive – a case of transmitting audio-visual imagery between the two locations. This enabled a host of social interactions between the passers-by and, indeed, enduring relationshsips were formed as a result of this. The whole set of encounters had the poignancy and surprise of unexpected human interactivity. But it was the reality of these contacts which was to the fore. The mediating satellite technology wrought no aesthetic transformation on them, and hence no digital *imprimatur* was involved.

Benayoun's work is the exact opposite. The relationships between the participants is created through digital transformations in virtual space. There is a pervasive digital *imprimatur* whose aesthetics have a liberating significance. Key to this is another contrast, based on understanding both the tunnel itself and the tunnelling activity, metaphorically. The contrast is with the contemporary practice of 'data mining' – where algorithmic programs scour the net, scooping up and processing massive quantities information for marketing, socio-economic research, and surveillance purposes. In this arid cyber landscape there is no real place for personal or social contact between individuals. It is a disembodied space existing only as a flow of information. One might say, indeed, that in terms of the ecology of personal and societal relationships, it is an environmental disaster – a scarring of the existential earth.

The Tunnel under the Atlantic, in contrast, involves exploration rather than exploitation. This begins with the way the installation combines real physicality – in the form of the tubes, with metaphorical physicality in the form of digging tunnels through virtual strata. The digging restores the connection between cyberspace and the grounding in embodiment from whence all our motor, sensory, and cognitive capacities derive. However, the more important point is the goal which orientates all this. It is to make contact with other people from a different place by following mutually significant clues that are uncovered in the course of the process. This is a form of unalienated labor through which all involved achieve self-discovery along the way. Digging the tunnels is an exploration of a space that is as much hermeneutic as it is virtual. And, in this, of course, it creates an echo of our inhabiting of physical space – which is not just an encounter with brute things, but a movement through a field of meaning.

The upshot of all this is a dramatic digital *imprimatur*. In this case, instead of leading into darkened earth, the virtual digging is illuminated throughout by the encounter with clues leading through the labyrinth towards final contact with the Other. There is something of *The Odyssey* about this – an aesthetics of patience, discovery, and homecoming.

Two

By the mid-1990s detectional and active interfacing were often combined. Another work by Jeffrey Shaw – *Golden Calf* of 1994 – is instructive here.[12] This involves a white pedestal with an LCD color monitor connected to computing devices. The viewer is meant to pick the monitor up. It projects a virtual image of the pedestal itself – but this time with a computer-generated golden calf on top. As the monitor is moved around the physical pedestal, the digital devices detect this motion, and correlate it with changes in how it appears on the screen. Through the appropriate movements it can be explored in terms of its three-dimensional virtual aspects. These appearances are rendered more complex by the fact that the calf has a shiny surface with previously digitized photographs of its reflection of the installation location mapped onto its skin. This immaterializing effect is further enhanced by the fact that the viewer's movements in manipulating the monitor are also reflected in the LCD screen itself.

Shaw suggests that

> In *The Golden Calf* the body is no longer a corporeal object but instead the immaterial subject of a specifically physical process of disclosure. When moving the monitor screen up, down and round the pedestal, the viewer performs what looks like a ceremonial dance around a technological pilaster construing an almost tangible phantasm.[13]

In these remarks, Shaw is clearly alluding to the iconography of the Golden Calf – namely, its biblical reference. In Exodus 32:6, the Israelites worship a golden calf idol, fearing that Moses will not return from his absence on Mt. Sinai. Their dancing is evoked by the play of visuals in Shaw's *The Golden Calf*. However, there is also a deeper question at issue. The calf is, of course, presented here as a visual object, whose virtual three-dimensional substance is made perceptually accessible from different viewpoints and under different light effects. This accessibility is, of course, correlated with how the viewer moves the object, and the physical position he or she takes in relation to it. The correlation in question here is one that operates in all our normal visual perception of objects – virtual or otherwise. As Merleau-Ponty observes,

> the thing is correlative with my body and, in more general terms, to my existence, of which my body is merely the stabilized structure. It is constituted in the hold which my body takes upon it; it is not first of all a meaning for the understanding, but a structure accessible to perception by the body ...[14]

The point is that whilst the thing's physical existence is independent of our body, how it discloses that physicality through its different appearances is directly correlated with the range of abilities that are available through human embodiment, and the particular way we deploy these in our interactions with things. This correlation is so basic to visual perception that we scarcely notice it. Shaw's *The Golden Calf* evokes this iconologically – by making the correlation between the virtual object's conditions of appearance and the subject's viewing position into something aesthetically enjoyable, and more available to explicit recognition.

A more complex combination of detectionality and active-interfacing is a work by David Rokeby – *The Giver of Names* (Figure 6.4).[15] This is an installation that has been a major ongoing project for Rokeby since 1990. The installation involves an empty pedestal, a video camera, a computer system, and a video projection screen. The visitor chooses an object or set of objects from a number that are present in the gallery space, or which he or she might happen to have with them. The object is then placed on the pedestal and an image of it is 'grabbed' by the computer. This inaugurates a complex image-processing involving such features as analysis of outline, division into separate objects or parts, color and texture analysis.

These various processes are visible on the life-size video projection screen and, through them, the object is transformed from its initial appearance into different sets of abstract relations. The results of these processes are then 'radiated' through a database of known objects, ideas, sensations, involving metaphorical and/or associative links. The results of these links show up in the background of the computer screen, evoking what Rokeby regards as a 'state of mind.' Then, on the basis of those words and ideas that have the closest affinity with the original object, the computer proceeds to construct a linguistically correct phrase or sentence in English, and speaks it aloud. This phrase is not a literal description of the object, but neither is it randomly generated. In effect, it reflects the computer's 'experience' of the object as enabled by its programming and the character of the installation.

Of course, this experience is not founded on human embodiment and its physical travails. But, interestingly, if *The Giver of Names*' activities are observed over a period of time, it presents enough idiosyncracies and patterns of connection and expression to form a coherent style of its own – something of a dialect.

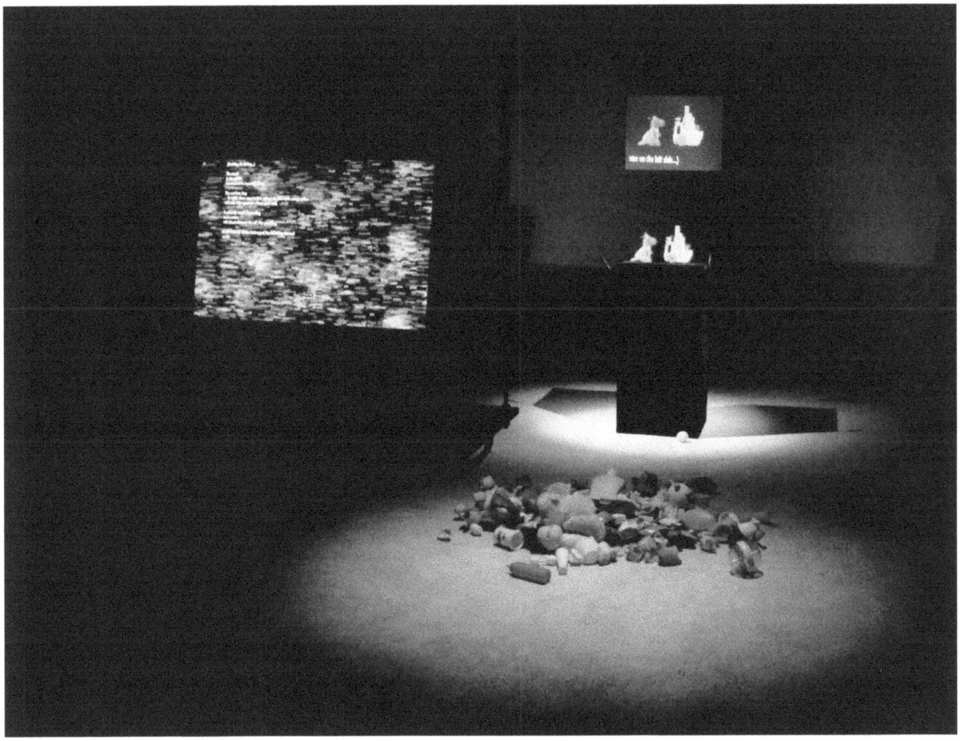

Figure 6.4 David Rokeby, *The Giver of Names*, installation, 1995.
Source: Photograph by David Rokeby.

Rokeby observes that

> My intent as an artist is that sufficient tension exist between the object and the name given to challenge the viewers' preconceptions of the objects, and draw them into speculative exploration. The names will have something of the quality of titles that artists give artworks: something a little out of left field, representing a re-interpretation, or alternate interpretation of the visual image of the object. One aim is to highlight the tight conspiracy between perception and language, bringing into focus the assumptions that make perception viable, but also biased and fallible, and the way language inhibits (or alternately enhances) our ability to see.[16]

Here, Rokeby is offering a nominally deconstructive approach to how we understand the perception-language relation. But actually the work has a deeper significance. *The Giver of Names* evokes an associational dimension that is essential to perception and self-consciousness, but is not usually noticed, let alone understood. Nothing we experience is simply present as raw sensory data. Neither is it recognized through simply applying a concept to it. Its recognition involves, rather, a relation between conceptualization *and* a latent *contextual space* of background knowledge based on factual memory steeped in imaginative and emotional associations. This contextual space includes details of the object and the background field that are present but not explicitly noticed, anticipations and exclusions of possibilities in relation to the object's potential behavior, and, especially, associations prompted by the cognitive object's personal and/or cultural significance for the subject.

All the individual contents of our perceptual and general cognitive life are given their character by how their particular features are positioned in relation to this. *The Giver of Names* explores this positioning symbolically, insofar as it moves from the presence of an object, to a characterization of what the object means in relation to the computer's 'personal' database. In this way, it digitally interprets the contextual field that subtends all cognitive experience.

The most complete combination of detectional and active interfacing is provided by immersive programs. Char Davies' *Osmose* of 1995 (Figure 6.5 and Plate 15) is a key early example of this.[17] In the artist's words, *Osmose* is

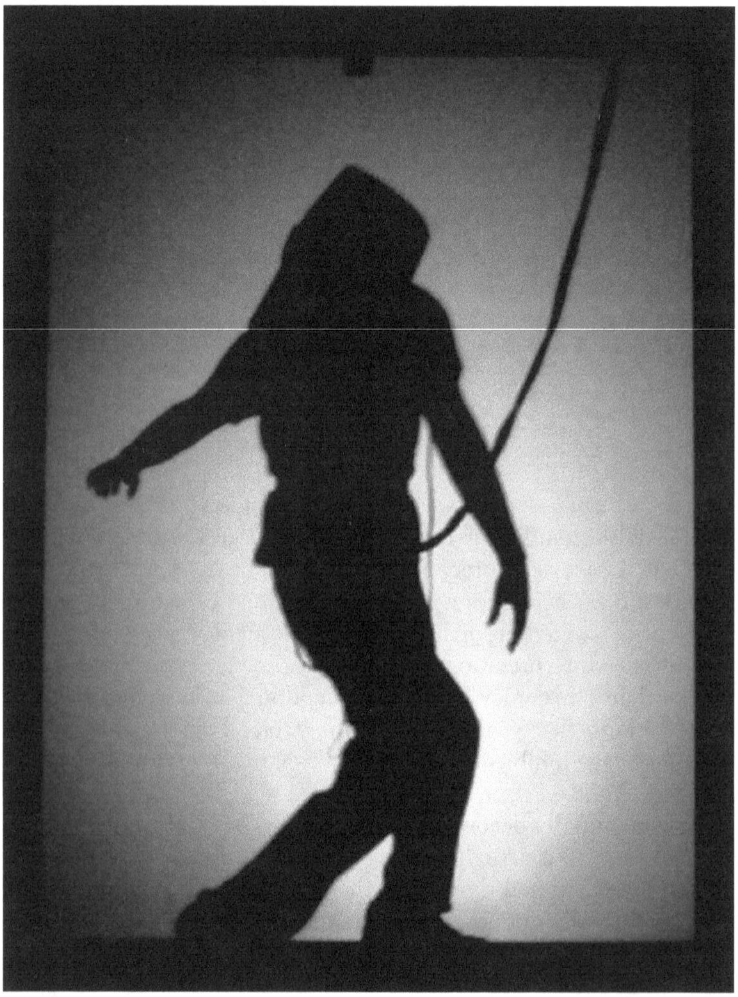

Figure 6.5 Char Davies, Immersant performing in the immersive virtual environment *Osmose*, at the Australian Centre for the Moving Image, 2003.

> an immersive interactive virtual-reality environment installation with 3D computer graphics and interactive 3D sound, a head-mounted display and real-time motion tracking based on breathing and balance. *Osmose* is a space for exploring the perceptual interplay between self and world, i.e., a place for facilitating awareness of one's own self as consciousness embodied in enveloping space.[18]

The immersion process begins with wearing a stereoscopic head-mounted display and motion-tracking vest. This allows full-body immersion in a 360 degree spherical, enveloping space. The space is navigated through breathing and balance. By breathing in, the immersant floats upward, and, by breathing out, falls downwards (a method inspired by scuba diving techniques). Altering the body's center of balance enables the immersant to change direction.

A first – orientating – level of virtual space is provided by a three-dimensional Cartesian Grid. The immersant's breathing leads the grid to transform into a forest clearing. There are twelve virtual world-spaces available in *Osmose*, mainly centered on metaphorically significant aspects of nature. These include Clearing, Forest, Tree, Leaf, Cloud, Pond, Subterranean Earth, and Abyss. By using their own breathing and balance, immersants are able to move anywhere within these virtual worlds as well as linger in the ambiguous zones between them.

Osmose contrasts keenly with the kind of digital hard-edged effects that we have discussed in previous chapters. In the artist's words,

> the visual aesthetic of *Osmose* is semi-representational/semi-abstract and translucent, consisting of semi-transparent textures and flowing particles. Figure/ground relationships are spatially ambiguous, and transitions between worlds are subtle and slow. This mode of representation serves to 'evoke' rather than illustrate. ... The sounds within *Osmose* are spatially multi-dimensional and have been designed to respond to changes in the immersant's location, direction and speed: the source of their complexity is a sampling of a male and female voice.[19]

The immersant's initial experience involves a perceptual reorientation – usually achieved within ten minutes – wherein the normal human urge for control and action is substituted by a sense of free-falling. Spatial envelopment rather than directionality becomes the main basis of perceptual orientation and, correlated with this, floating becomes the dominant idiom of movement. These environmental experiences are contextualized by a Code 'substratum' and Text 'superstatum' which act as 'conceptual parentheses' around the virtual worlds. The former consists of material that includes much of the software used in creating the immersive effects, and the latter of quotations from the artist and selected texts on environmental philosophy and on the body and spatial perception.The immersion experience can be completed in fifteen minutes.

Whilst its focus is obviously on the immersant, *Osmose* is also showable as a public installation. This centers on real-time transmission of audio-visual imagery generated by the immersant's activity – and projected through stereoscopic video and audio. This allows an audience (wearing polarizing glasses) to witness the development of each immersive journey. Indeed, a translucent screen (as large as that used for the video projection) also allows the immersant to be seen by the audience in silhouette form.

Davies' goal in creating *Osmose* is to take the immersant on a profound journey of introspection. However, the installation version ensures that the aesthetics of the work as an achievement of both conception and imagination is also made publically manifest. As is the case with all great artworks it offers new ways of engaging with perceptual reality, on the basis of insights concerning the poetics of embodiment. However, Davies' is also mindful of the work's broader significance. She notes that

> the after-effect of immersion in Osmose can be quite profound. Immersants often feel as if they have rediscovered an aspect of themselves, of being alive in the world, which they had forgotten, an experience which many find surprising, and some very emotional. ... Immersive virtual space, when stripped of its conventions, can provide an intriguing spatio-temporal context in which to explore the self's subjective experience of 'being-in-the-world' – as embodied consciousness in an enveloping space where boundaries between inner/outer, and mind/body dissolve.[20]

The last points here are, perhaps, a little over-stated. Gareth Evans has argued that

> The capacity to think of oneself as located in space, and tracing a continuous path through it, is necessarily involved in the capacity to conceive the phenomena one encounters as independent of one's perception of them – to conceive the world as something one 'comes across'. It follows that the capacity for at least some primitive self-ascriptions – self-ascriptions of position, orientation, and change of position and orientation and hence the conception of oneself as one object amongst others, occupying one place amongst others, are interdependent with thought about the objective world itself.[21]

On these terms, the recognition of objects and the origins of self-consciousness are reciprocally correlated. One can only become aware of oneself by reference to the *enduring* character of objects we engage with. But reciprocally these objects only disclose their objecthood through awareness of them *as* re-encounterable or as transient, in terms of our movements amongst them. Their re-encounterability, of course, is based on such things as constancy of shape, size, mass, number, position, i.e. what are traditionally called 'primary qualities.'

Now the immersant's experience in Osmose is only a transitory one. Its possibility is dependent on the 'real world' correlation of the unity of objects and of subjective experience that Evans describes. However, what *Osmose* invites is a more probing investigation of what the limits of that correlation might be. For example, the human mode of embodiment has breathing and posture as *conditions* of being able to perform its motor and locomotional activities. However, for the immersant these become more than conditions. They become organs of movement. This means that as well as receiving audio-visual stimuli that are more insubstantial and diffuse than those of everyday life, the immersant's cognitive negotiation of them is altered. *It is as though he or she becomes a different form of life.* The primacy of breathing and posture suggests the phenomenology of a form of embodiment that might exist under different gravitational conditions than those on earth. Indeed, the transformations at issue here are correlated with perceptual transformations of the object. In this respect, for example, the semi-transparency of *Osmose*'s forms turn the hard-edged 'objectness' of things into more ambiguous figure/ground relations, and spatial positionings.

This might not dissolve the boundaries between inner/outer and mind/body in the way Davies' suggests, but it would certainly change the relationships involved in these dualities. Could there be a possible world of the *Osmose* sort which was still consistent with Evan's criteria of the correlated unity of subject and object of experience? This is the main philosophical achievement of *Osmose*. It invites new investigation of how the dualities might be embodied under alternative physical conditions.

Osmose is also significant in one final and, perhaps, prophetic respect. Clearly, if art refines and clarifies truths about our sensible experience of the world, and embodies the artist's personal ways of understanding these, then immersant interaction has the most extraordinary future potential. As should have become clear from earlier descriptions, works like *Osmose* involve aesthetic and philosophical experiences. They have a scope that goes far beyond most idioms of visual art.

When *Osmose* was first created from 1994–1995, its technological basis was cumbersome and expensive. Now it can be experienced through consumer-grade technology for less than $5000. Indeed, as the relevant technology is made even smaller and more efficient, then works such as *Osmose* may become may become more widely accessible in their full immersive form – rather than as something accessed audio-visually on a PC or smart phone or whatever. This might turn out to be the single most important development in the history of digital art – taking it to an entirely new experiential as well as technological level.

Four

The next major mode of digital interative art centers on *net-access*. This involves the navigation of an online site or sites, or programs that have been downloaded from the net. The mode of access can sometimes be tightly controlled, as in those cases where the user's choice is restricted to such things as pressing 'Enter,' opening or shrinking windows, or choosing between links, and where no significant creative feedback from the computer is involved. A good example of this in early net art is Olia Lialina's *My boyfriend came back from the war* of 1996 (Figure 6.6).[22] The work starts with grainy black and white images of a man and woman; when clicked on, these lead to several military subjects, and the Twentieth-Century Fox film logo. When clicked on, again, these larger frames divide into smaller ones. These center on simple phrases – apparently of dialog between the man and woman. Having been separated by the man's absence in a war, the two find it hard to reconnect with one another. It emerges that the woman has had an affair with a neighbor, and that the returned soldier wants to marry her.

The narrative is cumulative but non-linear. By clicking on one frame, another opens, but there is no guide as to which one should click on next. There is an enigmatic sadness and melancholy to the process of clicking on one frame after the other without immediate linear direction. The fonts and the sizes of the words, their juxtapositions, the precedents and antecedents between them, and sometimes even their color, all go to suggest different vocal intonations and the facial expressions and gestures that might accompany them. Without the linear orientation, when the frames dwell alongside one another it is as though feelings and resolutions are kept

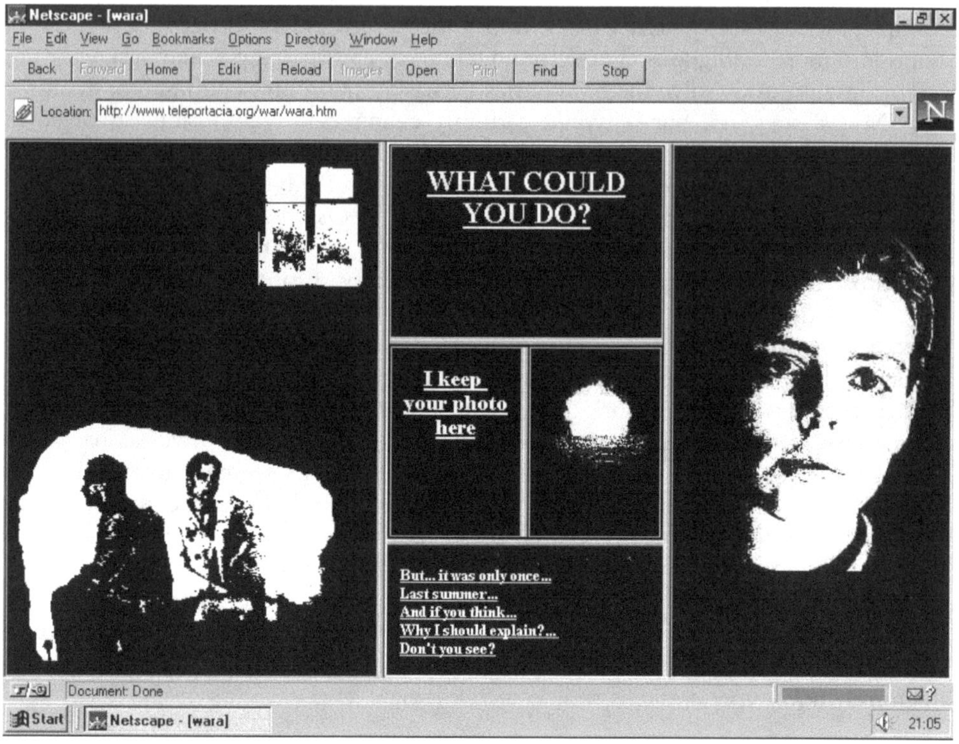

Figure 6.6 Olia Lialina, *My boyfriend came back from the war*, 1996. Screenshot from interactive net artwork.

Source: Image courtesy of the artist.

'in the air' – like the waters from a fountain. The process comes to an end when the screen is full of empty black frames, but this device, in itself, reinforces the overall emotional effect of the navigational process, turning it into a cascade of helpless feeling. The spectator becomes visually stuck in the same kind of impasse that the protagonists appear locked into. This aesthetic effect is not just a personal psychological association. It is created directly by the mode of net navigation that the work involves.

In other examples of net-access interactivity, the program involves more complex patterns of user navigation and computer feedback. Martin Wattenberg's and Marek Walczak's *The Apartment* of 2000–2004 is a good example.[23] Inspired by Cicero's 'Memory Palace' (a mnemonic device based on recollecting rooms with walls on which themes from the Orator's speeches had been noted). *Apartment* is a series of related projects whose modus operandi is to build virtual 2D and (in some versions) 3D 'apartments' online in correlation with what the viewer types on a keyboard. The character of these blueprint-like structures is determined by a semantic analysis of the viewer's words, which are reorganized to evoke underlying themes associated with those words. 'Work,' for example, may lead to the projection of an office; or 'look,' to the projection of a window. The apartments are then grouped into buildings and cities on the basis of their linguistic relationships. In Wattenberg's words,

'Establishing an equivalence between language and space, Apartment connects the written word with different forms of spatial configurations.'[24]

Some works combine net access and active interface with even more complexity. In Eduardo Kac's *Rara Avis* of 1996, for example, the installation consisted of an aviary composed of thirty zebra finches, and a perched macaw, with a pronounced bill and extravagant plumage.[25] The macaw was motionless, except for left to right head movements. This 'bird,' or 'Macowl' as Kac termed it, was actually a telerobot with two CCD (charge-coupled device) cameras for eyes. When visitors put on a headset, by turning their heads left and right they could see the whole aviary from the visual perspective of the Macowl. The real space become a more focussed virtual one. Audio-visual data from the headset was shared in real time on the internet, thus enabling remote participants to share in the experience. Indeed, through the microphones on their PCs, such participants could trigger vocal effects from the Macowl. Its body was, in effect, shared simultaneously at different spatial locations – including some very distant ones.

Kac suggests that

> By enabling the local participant to be both vicariously inside and physically outside the cage, this installation created a metaphor that revealed how new communications technology enables the effacement of boundaries at the same time that it reaffirms them. The installation also addressed issues of identity and alterity, projecting the viewer inside the body of a rare bird who not only was the only one of its kind in the aviary but was also distinctly different from the other birds (in scale, color, and behavior).[26]

This complexity of active interface and net-access is taken to an even more complex level by John Klima's *Earth* of 2001. This is a geo-spatial visualization system, that takes real-time data from the internet and maps it onto a three-dimensional model of the Earth.[27] It has numerous levels of participator involvement. Its final stage was the 'unique' *Earth* projection shown at the Whitney Bienalle in 2002. The installation involved two separate *Earth* user stations and an overview projection.

The bearer of the projection was a translucent latex weather balloon. This allowed a real image of the earth's outer layer to be rendered in virtual terms – with perceptible depth – on a real physical object. The image so realized was rotatable. It also carried Landsat 7 images as viewed from the viewer stations and by users of a Java browser module. In this way, the projection indicated both viewers' positions other than the immediate spectator's own, and also what was being viewed from those positions.

Now the very fact that *Earth* involved real-time images projected on a three-dimensional rather than the usual two-dimensional monitor is in itself an important aesthetic shift from our normal perceptual expectations. This shift is reinforced by the balloon also carrying details of specific aspects of the Earth's appearance as encountered from different human interface positions. Klima himself observes that this provided 'the overview of the complete system, the "Big Brother" in an a benign informational universe, reminding us of the often frightening nature of the techno-informatic landscape developing in the real world, often not for such benign ends.'[28] This optimism has to be carefully measured against the fact that it may represent an aesthetically induced false sense of security – vis-à-vis digital technology's potential misuse by surveillance snoopers of one sort or another. In such matters, it all comes down to the character of the particular work, and the technology it involves.

Another important aspect of net-access digital work has been in the form of games, and interventions upon existing visual material. An interesting example of both is in Vuk Cosič's deconstructive work. He uses the ASCII computing characters (developed as early as 1967, but now outmoded) as a medium through which to filter specific visual material such as music videos, games, porn, and films. Consider, for example, *ASCII Unreal* of 1999 (Plate 16).[29] This is a modified level of the computer game *Unreal*. The deconstruction takes place through a substitution. The illusion of concrete three-dimensional objects with surfaces, is regenerated by Cosič – using letters of the Cyrillic alphabet in ASCII format. The *netzspannung* site summarizes what is at issue here. It

> demonstrates the absurdity of the perfectionism with which three-dimensional reality is represented in most first-person shooter games. At the same time, it confronts current high-end computer graphics with the history of computer screen display: until the nineteen-nineties, standard computers had an interface limited to green letters on a black background.[30]

The interesting thing is that whilst Cosič's work is clearly an instance of techno-conceptualism, it is far more than a mere critical intellectual operation. This is because of the specific visual relation between the original material and the ASCII characters that it creates. At issue in this is a *making strange* – an enigmatic beauty arising from the intrinsic quality of the characters, and their transformation of the original imagery into off-key shades of green and black. Works of this kind manifest the digital *imprimatur* in especially strong terms.

Some game (or related) programs have attracted large-scale public participation, and widely expanded the scope of net-interfacing. Scott Snibbe's *MotionPhone*, for example, was worked on between 1989 and 1996 and eventually developed into a highly advanced interactive network art 'app.'[31] It is now globally accessible through an iPad. The program allows the user to create animated abstractions over a network, with the forms themselves generated through fingertip gestures recorded by the user's device. By connecting with others it is possible to comment and play, as well as visually communicate. *Motion Phone* features include an interactive animated canvas (that can use up to 30,000 animated brushstrokes) and a range of colors, shapes, transparencies, speeds, and zoom capacities. Whatever is so created can be saved, and loaded to Twitter or Facebook, or simply emailed.

Second Life is an online site that offers a virtual alternative world.[32] It was developed by Linden Lab of San Francisco, and launched in 2003. By 2013, it had a million regular users. It facilitates a huge variety of role-playing fantasies based on membership of specific virtual communities based on both present-day America, and scenarios involving other places and times. Users are personally embodied in the space as avatars, and can interact with other avatars, as well as engage in wide range of virtual activities. Most of the platform's content is 3d user-generated (using a modelling tool based on simple geometric shapes, and the Linden in-house Scripting Language).

There are some rather more theoretically searching online sites than *Second Life*. Perhaps the most important of them all is Victoria Vesna's *Bodies INCorporated* – created in 1996 (Figure 6.7), and still accessible. At the time of the project's

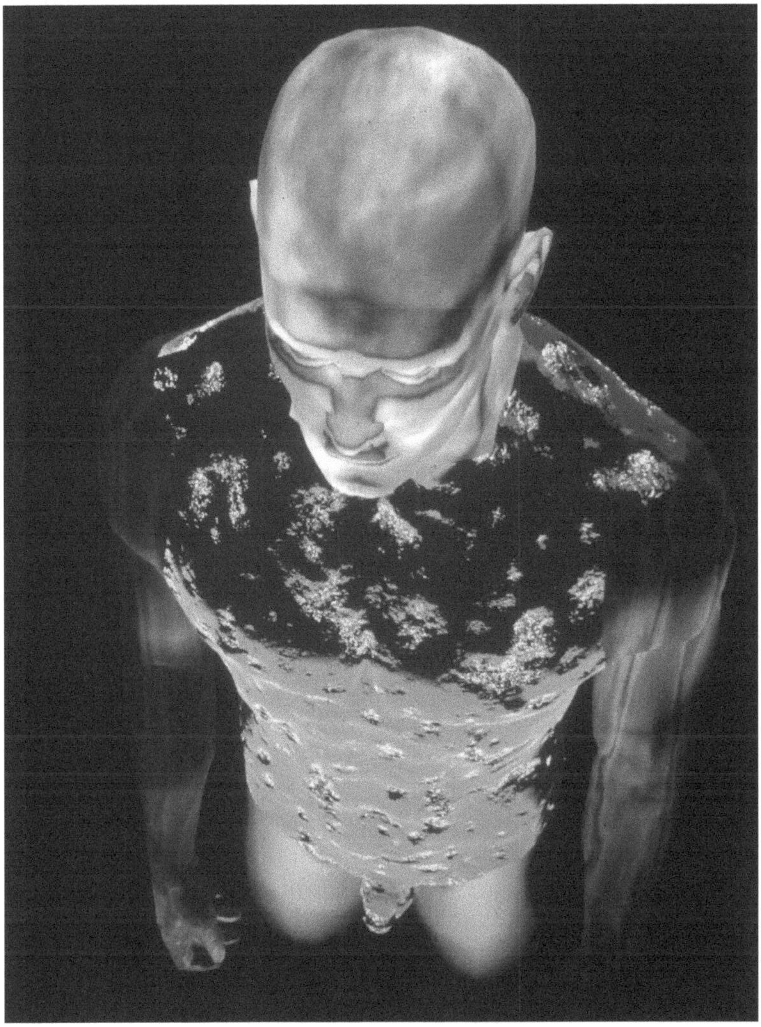

Figure 6.7 Victoria Vesna, *Bodies INCorporated*, 1995. Computer screen image.
Source: Photo courtesy of the artist.

commencement, the linking of the self to digital avatars had become a familiar practice. Vesna felt, however, that the interpretation through an avatar in such practices often followed social stereotypes far too closely. As a critical alternative, she created *Bodies INCorporated.*

In both the gallery and online versions users could use VRML (Virtual Reality Modeling Language) to create their own virtual three-dimensional avatar. It would be constructed from body parts ranging over different genders, sizes, and ages. These ready-made parts were sourced from a commercial company offering CGI bodies for purchase. They were shaped on the basis of existing stereotypes but could, however, be combined to form customized hybrids.

Once their avatars were assembled, users could situate them in a limited range of virtual environments. 'Home,' for example would navigate users to a fully three-dimensional environment; 'Limbo' involved gyrating text cubes linked to texts, and completed order forms for the bodies; and 'Necropolis' consisted of gravestones created by users in memoriam for bodies that they had deleted.

However, there was an important 'catch' to all this. One of Vesna's concerns was how issues of ownership, and/or commercial liability impinge profoundly on the way the body occupies social space in a market economy. One's identity is shaped by positioning in relation to this economy. Hence, in *Bodies INCorporated*, users could only create their avatars after clicking through extensive terms and conditions, wherein they forfeited all rights and ownership. This not only made the customizable body into a kind of commercial asset, it also made the construction process much drawn out through having to negotiate so much 'paperwork.'[33]

In terms of the general site content, we are told that

> 'Initially, the participant is invited to construct a virtual body out of predefined body-parts, textures, and sounds, and gain membership to the larger body-owner community. The main elements of the online site are three constructed environments (subsidiaries of Bodies� INCorporated), within which different sets of activities occur: LIMBO� INCorporated, a gray, rather non-descript zone, where information about inert bodies that have been put on hold – bodies whose owners have abandoned or neglected them – is accessed; NECROPOLIS� INCorporated, a richly textured, baroque atmosphere, where owners can either look at or choose how they wish their bodies to die; and SHOWPLACE!!!� INCorporated,' where members can participate in discussion forums, view star/featured bodies of the week, bet in the deadpools, and enter 'dead' or 'alive' chat sessions.[34]

It is also made clear that there are categories of involvement on the site ranging from Member, to Adept, to Avatar. The criteria determining these are engagingly fuzzy, but it is clear that movement from one category to the other is determined by obtaining 'shares' in *Bodies INCorporated*, through certain forms of input – such as providing quotations from dead philosophers. The process of ascension here is actually described in terms that combine corporation jargon with that of esoteric/eastern religion. For example,

> In the cases of avatars, it is the Will aspect which is brought into play, taking form for a specific purpose. It involves a higher display of creative faculty that is displayed by the Adept in the creation of a Body of manifestation, the Mayavirupa. The Mayavirupa is literally the illusory form; it is the body of temporary manifestation which the Adept creates on occasion of the power of the will. … The terms 'appropriation of a body' or 'construction of a body' must be extended to include all the planes of the corporate system.[35]

The constructed bodies in Vesna's techno-conceptualist site differ markedly from those in *Second Life*. The latter are fully interactive, allowing the users to live vicariously in a virtual world. *Bodies INCorporated*, in contrast, presents the body as static in itself – though manipulable in terms of different angles of presentation, and contextualizable through accompanying documents and environments. The distance between viewer and body involved in this enables a critical orientation to be developed. There is a space for reflection as well as absorption.

For, example, there is a wonderful deconstruction of the pervasive way that documentation and commercial agreements dog every aspect of the things we do – from holidays and entertainment, to workplace regulations, and the purchase of items and services for the domestic environment. Corporations and corporate 'values' impinge on us at every point. Their ubiquity is such that they may seem to have taken on a quasi-religious meaning – the market is now a gospel of redemption as well as an economic structure. And in *Body INCorporated*'s particular critique of this there is 'added value.' For many New Age-type religions operate through heavy marketing strategies and corporation-babble.

But the main focus of *Bodies INCorporated* is, of course, the body and its enmeshing in social practices. One might be reminded of Orlan's 'carnal art' from the 1990s – involving constant transformations of the artist's bodily appearance through plastic surgery. The artist herself noted that

> Carnal Art is self-portraiture in the classical sense, but realised through the possibility of technology. It swings between defiguration and refiguration. Its inscription in the flesh is a function of our age. The body has become a 'modified ready-made', no longer seen as the ideal it once represented; the body is not anymore this ideal ready-made it was satisfaying [sic] to sign.[36]

Vesna's project relates to these neo-Duchampian ideas in a key respect. Like Orlan, she, in effect, treats the body as an assisted 'ready-made' rather than one which is entirely pre-given, and which only needs to be, as it were, signed-off on in order to be lived in it. But Orlan's changes are physical – whatever she becomes is through a contiguous life-process in which the surgical processes play a part. However, *Bodies INCorporated* situates the body in virtual space where the realities of everyday causal process are suspended. It offers a new vicarious body assembled from shopped-for parts. Indeed, whereas personal surgery is a costly thing, and constrained by the physicality of the body, *Bodies INCorporated* turns what Orlan exemplifies in the real world into a realizable fantasy.

Transforming one's body is the ultimate quasi-magic. We often desire to improve our bodies so as to do things that it will not allow at present, but the *Bodies INCorporated* fantasy goes far beyond this. For we must remember that the body is not just the site of desire, it is also the basis of our perceptual relation to the world – both in terms of species characteristics shared with others, and vis-à-vis the origins of personal self-consciousness (as shown in the remarks by Gareth Evans that we mentioned in relation to Char Davies).

The body transformations at Vesna's site intervene upon these factors in a special way. The user constructs the body from a choice of parts, but what makes the digital *imprimatur* of this *so* distinctive is the emphasis given to skin texture. The skin contains and protects vital organs but is equally vital to our bio-social identity. However, the choice of skin textures offered by *Bodies INCorporated* is spectacularly non-natural – at least in respect of human norms. The textures are black rubber, blue plastic, bronze, chocolate, clay, cloudy, concrete, glass, lava, pumice, water, and wood. A body presented in any of these skins suggests identity that is humanly originated, but which has gone beyond it – either through strange evolutionary turns, or from having developed in an extraterrestrial environment. A being with such skin may have human mobility, but its adaption to its environment and to fellow beings will involve different principles. This is not just a question of new identity; it is, in principle, that of a new form of life. The user can, in other words, can enjoy the ultimate aesthetic quasi-magic – creating the appearance of a new, *transhuman* being.

There is one final mode of interactivity to be considered which involves all the aforementioned modes, namely, the *informational environment*. In this respect it will have been noted that at many points in this book we have referred to the Postmodern naturalization of technology as, in effect, a 'techno-habitat.' There are some interactive works which model this – using, detectional, active interfacing, and net-access, to surround the viewer with information.

A key example of such an informational environment is Marco Peljhan's and Carsten Nicolai's collaboration *Polar* of 2000 (with subsequent new versions).[37]

The original version is an installation that strives to create a responsive data-space in a physical environment. The environment is entered by two people at a time, each with a device that registers its physical features, such as images, sounds, temperature, and even the presence of micro-organisms that respond to changing conditions of light and temperature. The data recorded on the devices is transformed into seven keywords that are shown on the two monitors in the environment. By choosing a keyword, the participants trigger a search-mechanism that compiles a network of related concepts from net-based databases and websites. By interacting with this network, users can form more personalized perspectives upon it, within the parameters determined by the base program. The sense of being immersed within a living data matrix is accentuated through real-time projections of wave shapes whose configuration is shaped by the information collected by the users. Through all this, the individual is explicitly situated in the Postmodern techno-habitat.

Conclusion

We end this chapter with a brief consideration of problems and achievements. The problems derive in large part from the net-access works just considered. An important question is raised about the relation between interactive digital art and entertainment. Net-access works are especially problematic. Something like *Second City* seems little more than pure escapism and/or self-indulgence. Aesthetic experiences of art – as we have shown in the greatest detail elsewhere – are not merely modes of enjoyment based on beholding.[38] In the beholding, we engage with the fact that the possibility of experience that we are sharing is one created by another. We can be provoked by it, learn from it, and find our own perspectives on big issues in life are changed. The point is that it takes us far from merely being a consumer of the work. There is a critical edge involved, and this separates aesthetic experience in its deepest sense, from that based exclusively on the enjoyment of formal harmonies and the like.

Now many interactive idioms – especially those involving net-access – involve enormously complex functions that frequently address the nature of digital technology, net-control and conditions of access, or present novel effects, and different levels of information simultaneously. However, if these are to be more than pieces of glorified agit-prop or mere amusement, per se, there must be something about *this* way doing of things digitally that is visually telling in a critical way, *qua* visual. If a work is no more than an exploration of the scope and meaning of some aspect of information technology per se, then there is no reason to think of it as art. Techno-conceptualism of this narrow kind will be of interest mainly to a professional elite of other specialists, curators, and art critics. If it should be claimed that such works challenge accepted notions of art, then, in effect, we reach a dead end – since we know in advance that there are no challenges to 'accepted notions of art.' Since the 1960s it has become established practice that anything that the artist offers as art, must, indeed, be art.

Fortunately, many of the works discussed in this chapter go beyond all this. Of special interest is the different ways that some of them visualize the existence of language, and through this, find poetic expression for its role in consciousness, and, in particular, our experience of finitude. The means of this are uniquely digital. By this we do not simply mean that such strategies are impossible without the aid of digital technology. Something more intimate is at issue.

Throughout this book, the naturalization of technology has been emphasized. In the works by Rokeby, Feingold, Shaw, Davies, Small and White, Cosič, and Vesna that we have considered, this is taken to a different level. It is as though, in their works, the realm of technology is made to behold its own creators – with benign quizzicality. It asks 'How do they understand things? What makes stuff meaningful to them?' In effect, technology is here *so* naturalized as to mechanically 'imagine' processes at issue in the existence of its own creators. Earlier in this book we emphasized the importance of the digital still-image. Here we encounter the astonishing evocative power of its interactive modes. Perhaps of all the achievements of Postmodern art this is the most original one.

Notes

1 A generally good guide to these developments in early interactional digital art is Söke Dinkla, 'The History of the Interface in Interactive Art,' 1994, available at www.kenfeingold.com/dinkla_history.html.
2 For examples of the *Hole in Space* interactions, see www.youtube.com/watch?v=SyIJJr6Ldg8.
3 Campbell's website is at www.jimcampbell.tv/portfolio/installations/interactive_hallucination.
4 Rokeby's website is at www.davidrokeby.com/vns.html.
5 For more information, see Snibbe's website at www.snibbe.com/projects/interactive/boundaryfunctions.
6 Further details can be found at www.kenfeingold.com/artworks90s.html.
7 See online details of the project at http://acg.media.mit.edu/projects/stream/InteractivePoeticGarden.pdf. The installation can be seen in action at www.youtube.com/watch?v=5onPBBpGed8.
8 Quoted from http://acg.media.mit.edu/projects/stream/InteractivePoeticGarden.pdf.
9 See www.jeffrey-shaw.net/html_main/show_work.php?record_id=83.
10 See www.jeffrey-shaw.net/html_main/show_work.php?record_id=102.
11 A short set of extracts from the Installation can be found at www.youtube.com/watch?v=2_6YzmAJjJo.
12 See www.jeffrey-shaw.net/html_main/frameset-works.php.
13 Quoted from ibid.
14 Maurice Merleau-Ponty, *The Phenomenology of Perception*, p. 320.
15 See www.davidrokeby.com/gon.html (accessed August 18, 2017).
16 Quoted from Rokeby's website, www.davidrokeby.com/gon.html.

17 See the artist's website, www.immersence.com.
18 Quoted from ibid.
19 Ibid.
20 Ibid.
21 Gareth Evans, *Varieties of Reference*, 1982, p. 70.
22 The work can be found online at www.teleportacia.org/war.
23 See the artists' website for *The Apartment* at www.bewitched.com.
24 Ibid.
25 See Kac's website at www.ekac.org/raraavis.html.
26 Ibid.
27 Klima's website is at www.cityarts.com/earth/#Projection.
28 Quoted from www.cityarts.com/earth/#Projection.
29 Cosič's website is at www.ljudmila.org/~vuk.
30 See http://netzspannung.org/cat/servlet/CatServlet?cmd=netzkollektor&subCommand=showEntry&entryId=138784&lang=en.
31 See Snibbe's website at www.snibbe.com/apps#/motionphone-app.
32 See http://secondlife.com.
33 There is also an ambiguous development vis-à-vis the relation between the avatar and commercial context. For after clicking on the button that 'accepts' the copyright restrictions, one is taken to another page where we are told that: 'Bodies built become your personal property, operating in and circulating through public space, free to be downloaded into your private hard drive/communication system at any time.' Quoted from www.bodiesinc.ucla.edu/welcome.html.
34 Quoted from www.bodiesinc.ucla.edu/frames1.html.
35 Quoted from ibid. In this passage, Vesna appears to be adapting material downloaded from the esoteric Makara.us blog.
36 See the artist's website at www.orlan.eu/texts.
37 The project is described online at www.ladomir.net/bio-summary.
38 This is a recurrent theme in every book written by the present author. See, for example, *Defining Art, Creating the Canon: Artistic Value in an Era of Doubt*, 2007, pp. 70–88.

Bibliography

Books

Benjamin, Walter. *Charles Baudelaire: A Lyric Poet in the Era of High Capitalism*, trans. Harry Zohn, Verso, London, 1983.

Benthall, Jonathan. *Science and Technology in Art Today*, Thames and Hudson, London, 1972.

Borsch-Supan, Helmut. *Caspar David Friedrich*, trans. Sarah Twohig, Thames and Hudson, London, 1974.

Cassirer, Ernst. *An Essay on Man*, Yale University Press, New Haven, 1944.

Crary, Jonathan. *Techniques of the Observer: On Vision and Modernity in the Nineteenth-Century*, MIT Press, Cambridge, Mass. and London, 1990.

Crowther, Paul. *Philosophy after Postmodernism*, Routledge, London and New York, 2003.

Crowther, Paul. *Defining Art, Creating the Canon: Artistic Value in an Era of Doubt*, Clarendon Press, Oxford, 2007.

Crowther, Paul. *The Phenomenology of Modern Art: Exploding Deleuze, Illuminating Style*, Continuum, London and New York, 2012.

Crowther, Paul. *How Pictures Complete Us: The Beautiful, the Sublime, and the Divine*, Stanford University Press, Stanford, 2016.

Crowther, Paul. *What Drawing and Painting Really Mean: The Phenomenology of Image and Gesture*, Routledge, London and New York, 2017.

Crowther, Paul and Wunsche, Isabel (eds.) *Meanings of Abstract Art: Between Nature and Theory*, Routledge, London and New York, 2012.

Cubitt, Sean. *Digital Aesthetics*, Sage Publications, London and New York, 2009.

Em, David. *The Art of David Em: 100 Computer Paintings*, Harry Abrams, New York, 1988.

Evans, Gareth. *Varieties of Reference*, Clarendon Press, Oxford, 1982.

Fishwick, Paul (ed.) *Aesthetic Computing*, MIT Press, Cambridge, Mass. and London, 2006.

Gadamer, Hans-Georg. *Philosophical Hermeneutics*, trans. David E. Linge, University of California Press, Berkeley, Los Angeles, and London, 1977.

Grau, Oliver (ed.) *MediaArtHistories*, MIT Press, Cambridge, Mass. and London, 2007.

Hansen, Mark B.N. *New Philosophy for New Media*, MIT Press, Cambridge, Mass. and London, 2004.

Heidegger, Martin. *Being and Time*, trans. John Macquarrie and Edward Robinson, Basil Blackwell, Oxford, 1967.

Hope, Cat and Ryan, John. *Digital Arts: An Introduction to New Media*, Bloomsbury, London and New York, 2014.

Kwastek, Katja. *Aesthetics of Interaction in Digital Art*, MIT Press, London and Cambridge, Mass., 2015.

Leavitt, Ruth (ed.) *Artist and Computer*, Harmony Books, New York, 1976.

Lopes, Dominic McIver. *A Philosophy of Computer Art*, Routledge, London and New York, 2010.

Lovejoy, Margot. *digital currents: art in the electronic age*, Routledge, London and New York, 2007.
Lyotard, J.-F. *The Postmodern Condition: A Report on Knowledge*, trans. Geoff Bennington and Brian Massumi, Manchester University Press, 1984.
McCorduck, Pamela. *AARON'S CODE: Meta-Art, Artificial Intelligence, and the Work of Harold Cohen*, W.H. Freeman & Co., New York, 1990.
Merleau-Ponty, Maurice. *The Phenomenology of Perception*, Routledge-Kegan Paul, London, 1974, p. 320.
Merleau-Ponty, Maurice. *The Merleau-Ponty Aesthetics Reader: Philosophy and Painting*, ed. Galen A. Johnson, Northwestern University Press, Evanston, Ill., 1993.
Paul, Christiane. *Digital Art*, Thames and Hudson, London and New York, 2015.
Popper, Frank. *From Technological to Virtual Art*, MIT Press, Cambridge, Mass. and London, 2007.
Reichardt, Jasia. *Cybernetic Serendipity: The Computer and the Arts*, Studio International Special Edition, London, September 1968.
Sartre, Jean-Paul. *Nausea*, trans. Robert Baldick, Penguin, Harmondsworth, 1971.
Taylor, Grant D. *When the Machine Made Art: The Troubled History of Computer Art*, Bloomsbury, London and New York, 2014.
Todd, Stephen and Latham, William. *Evolutionary Art and Computers*, Academic Press, London and San Diego, 1992.
Wittgenstein, Ludwig. *Philosophical Investigations*, Basil Blackwell, Oxford, 1972.

Articles, and Chapters in Books

Broeckmann, Andreas. 'Image, Process, Performance, Machine: Aspects of an Aesthetics of the Machinic,' included in Oliver Grau (ed.) *MediaArtHistories*, MIT Press, Cambridge, Mass. and London, 2007, pp. 193–205.
Davidson, Donald. 'The Method of Truth in Metaphysics,' included in *Inquiries into Truth and Meaning*, Clarendon Press, Oxford, 1984, pp. 199–214.
Greenberg, Clement. 'Modernist Painting,' included in *The Collected Essays and Criticism. Volume IV: Modernism with a Vengeance*, ed. John O'Brian, University of Chicago Press, London, 1993, pp. 85–94.
Klutsch, Christoph. 'Information Aesthetics and the Stuttgart School,' included in *Mainframe Experimentalism: Early Computing and the Foundation of the Digital Arts*, ed. Hannah B. Higgins and Douglas Kahn, University of California Press, Berkeley, Los Angeles and London, 2012, pp. 65–89.
Nake, Frieder. 'Art in the Time of the Artificial,' *Leonardo*, Vol. 31, No. 3 (1998), pp. 163–164.
Noll, A. Michael. 'Human or Machine: A Subjective Comparison of Piet Mondrian's "Composition with Lines" and a Computer-Generated Picture,' *The Psychological Record*, Vol. 16. No. 1 (January 1966), pp. 1–10.
Noll, A. Michael.'First-Hand: Early Digital Art at Bell Telephone Laboratories, Inc,' *Leonardo*, Vol. 49, No. 1 (2016), pp. 55–65.
Noll. A. Michael. 'The Howard Wise Gallery Show of Computer-Generated Pictures (1965): A 50th-Anniversary Memoir,' *Leonardo*, Vol. 49, No. 3 (2016), pp. 232–239.
Preston, Stuart. 'Art ex Machina,' *The New York Times*, Sunday, April 18, 1965.
Rosen, Margit. 'A Record of Decisions: Envisioning Computer Art,' included in *Charles A. Csuri: Beyond Boundaries, 1963 to the Present*, ed. Janice M. Glowski, Ohio State University College of the Arts Advanced Computing Center for the Arts and Design, 2006, pp. 25–46.

Online Resources

Benayoun, Maurice. *The Tunnel Under the Atlantic*. Short set of extracts from the Installation, www.youtube.com/watch?v=2_6YzmAJjJo (accessed August 30, 2017).

Campbell, Jim. His Interactive hallucination work is at www.jimcampbell.tv/portfolio/installations/interactive_hallucination (accessed August 21, 2017).

Cohen, Harold. Artist's website, www.aaronshome.com/aaron/publications/tate-final.doc (accessed April 23, 2017).

Cohen, Harold. 'Parallel to Perception: Some Notes on the Problem of Machine-Generated Art,' 1973, www.aaronshome.com/aaron/aaron/publications/paralleltoperception.pdf (accessed January 01, 2017).

Cohen, Harold. 'The further exploits of AARON, Painter,' 1995, http://web.stanford.edu/group/SHR/4-2/text/cohen.html (accessed March 5, 2017).

Cohen, Harold. 'Decoupling Art and Affluence,' 2001, http://aaronshome.com/aaron/aaron/publications/index.html (accessed March 28, 2017).

Cohen, Harold. 'A Sorcerer's Apprentice,' Talk at Tate Modern, 2004, www.aaronshome.com/aaron/publications/tate-final.doc (accessed February 01, 2017).

Cohen, Harold. 'Driving the Creative Machine,' Orcas Center, Crossroads Lecture Series, September 2010, p. 5, www.aaronshome.com/aaron/publications/orcastalk2s.pdf (accessed May 5, 2015).

Cosič, Vuk. Artist's website, www.ljudmila.org/~vuk (accessed August 23, 2017).

Cosič, Vuk, *ASCII Unreal*, 1999, www.ljudmila.org/~vuk (accessed August 23, 2017).

Csuri, Charles. Major project on the artist, http://csuriproject.osu.edu/index.php/Detail/objects/757 (accessed April 23, 2017).

Csuri, Charles. Online feature, www.siggraph.org/artdesign/profile/csuri (accessed April 23, 2017).

Davies, Char. Artist's website, www.immersence.com (accessed August 20, 2017).

Dinkla, Söke. 'The History of the Interface in Interactive Art,' 1994, www.kenfeingold.com/dinkla_history.html (accessed August 16, 2017).

Dreher, Thomas. 'History of Computer Art,' http://iasl.uni-muenchen.de/links/GCA-III.1e.html (accessed January 11, 2017).

Em, David. Interview with artist, www.technocultures.org.uk/davideminterview.html (accessed March 31, 2017).

Em, David. Online version of *The Art of David Em: 100 Computer Paintings*, Harry Abrams, New York, 1988, http://digitalartmuseum.org/essays/em01.html (accessed March 31, 2017).

Feingold, Ken. *If/Then*, www.kenfeingold.com/IfThen1.html (accessed September 4, 2017).

Feingold, Ken. *Self Portrait As the Center of the Universe*, www.kenfeingold.com/SelfL2.html (accessed September 4, 2017).

Feingold, Ken. *The Surprising Spiral*, www.kenfeingold.com/artworks90s.html (accessed August 16, 2017).

Feingold, Ken. The talking *Head* sculpture can be seen 'in action' at www.youtube.com/watch?v=EK-7w56jN0E (accessed September 4, 2017).

Finley, Chris. Image of the *Mallardbride* picture is available at www.invaluable.com/auction-lot/chris-finley-mallardbride-2002-137-c-vshweps8dg (accessed January 3, 2018).

Finley, Chris. Feature on artist, www.metroactive.com/papers/sonoma/01.21.99/seca-9903.html (accessed January 2, 2018).

Galloway, Kit, and Rabinowicz, Sherrie. *Hole in Space* project can be seen at www.youtube.com/watch?v=SyIJJr6Ldg8 (accessed August 30, 2017).

Hébert, Jean-Pierre. Artist's website, http://jeanpierreHébert.com/17s.html (accessed January 3, 2018).

Hébert, Jean-Pierre. '*Ulysses*: Sand as Medium,' in *The Mathematica Journal*, Graphics Gallery, Volume 7, Issue 3, 1999; www.mathematica-journal.com/issue/v7i3/graphics (accessed December 28, 2017).

Holzer, Jenny. *Protect Me From What I Want*, https://artaspoliticalvoice.weebly.com/jenny-holzer.html (accessed January 3, 2018).

Johnson, Phillip. Machine Art Exhibition, 1934. See www.moma.org/learn/resources/archives/archives_highlights_10_1991 (accessed March 30, 2016).

Kac, Eduardo. *Rara Avis*, 1996, www.ekac.org/raraavis.html (accessed August 21, 2017).

Klima, John, *Earth*, 2001, www.cityarts.com/earth/#Projection (accessed August 23, 2017).

Lambert, Nick. *A Critical Examination of 'Computer Art'*, http://computer-arts-society.com/static/cas/computerartsthesis/index.html (accessed January 20, 2017).

Latham, William. Online resource concerning *Mutator* project, http://latham-mutator.com (accessed April 23, 2017).

Latham, William. Original *Mutations* animation online at www.youtube.com/watch?v=7sadS5wuOjU (accessed April 23, 2017).

Lazzarini, Robert. Artist's website, www.robertlazzarini.com/motel-door (accessed January 3, 2018).

Lazzarini, Robert. Feature on artist, www.museomagazine.com/ROBERT-LAZZARINI (accessed September 4, 2017).

Leavitt, Ruth (ed.) *Artist and Computer*, www.atariarchives.org/artist/sec16.php (accessed April 11, 2017).

Lialina, Olia. *My boyfriend came back from the war*, www.teleportacia.org/war (accessed August 21, 2017).

Lozano-Hemmer, Raphael. Artist's website, www.lozano-hemmer.com/displaced_emperors.php (accessed December 18, 2017).

Mallary, Robert. Artist's website, www.robertmallary.com/Art/Art.htm (accessed December 25, 2017).

Mantz, Gerhard. *Gerhard Mantz, Berlin 1998 and New York*, 2004, translation by Jay Judge, www.gerhard-mantz.de/wp/text/landscape (accessed April 18, 2017).

Mohr, Manfred. Artist's website, www.emohr.com/ww2_out.html (accessed January 4, 2017).

Molnar, Vera. Artist's entire *oeuvre* is set out in chronologically successive order on her website, www.veramolnar.com/diapo.php (accessed February 6, 2018).

Molnar, Vera. Selection of her work, http://dam.org/artists/phase-one/vera-molnar/artworks-bodies-of-work/works-from-the-1960s-70s (accessed February 6, 2018).

Nake, Frieder. Selection of works, www.vam.ac.uk/content/journals/research-journal/issue-02/computer-art-at-the-v-and-a (accessed January 2, 2017).

Nechvatal, Joseph. 'Theoretical Statement Concerning Computer-Robotic Paintings' accompanying *The Informed Man* in the Documenta VIII exhibition (Amsterdam, 1987), www.nictoglobe.com/new/articles/jn.html (accessed December 20, 2017).

Nechvatal, Joseph. 'Emergence of the New Paradigm: Viractuality.' Talk/demo delivered at École Supérieure d'AudioVisuel, Université de Toulouse le Mirail, November 3, 2010, www.eyewithwings.net/nechvatal/Viractuality/Viractualism.html (accessed December 22, 2017).

Nechvatal, Joseph. Interview with the artist, *Brooklyn Rail*, Art, December 9, 2015, https://brooklynrail.org/2015/12/art/joseph-nechvatal-with-thyrza-nichols-goodeve (accessed December 21, 2017).

Nees, Georg. Some works accessible at www.heikewerner.com/nees_en.html (accessed August 28, 2017).

Nees, Georg. Interview, www.gasathj.com/tiki-read_article.php?articleId=42 (accessed December 29, 2016).

Nees, Georg. Newspaper feature, http://magazin.spiegel.de/EpubDelivery/spiegel/pdf/46272435 (accessed December 29, 2016).

netzspannung. digital art site, http://netzspannung.org/cat/servlet/CatServlet?cmd=netzkollektor&subCommand=showEntry&entryId=138784&lang=en (accessed August 22, 2017).

Noll, A. Michael. Memo of August 28, 1962, *Patterns by 7090: Case 38794–23*, http://noll.uscannenberg.org/Art%20Papers/BTL%201962%20Memo.pdf (accessed January 11, 2017).

Orlan. Artist's website, www.orlan.eu/texts (accessed August 31, 2017).
Palyka, Duane M. Artist's websites, www.pal-katoonz.com/early_art1/early_art1 (accessed April 14, 2017) and www.pal-katoonz.com/early_art2/early_art2 (accessed April 13, 2017).
Peljhan, Marco and Nicolai, Carsten. *Polar*, 2000, www.ladomir.net/bio-summary (accessed September 14, 2017).
Redl, Erwin. Artist's website, www.paramedia.net/installationpage/cornerstudyii.php (accessed August 29, 2017).
Rokeby, David. Artist's website, www.davidrokeby.com/home.html (accessed August 16, 2017).
Schwartz, Lillian. Artist's website, http://lillian.com (accessed September 21, 2017).
Second Life. Organization's website, http://secondlife.com (accessed August 18, 2017).
Shapiro, Bruce. Artist's company website, www.sisyphus-industries.com (accessed December 26, 2017).
Shaw, Jeffery. *The Golden Calf*, featured at www.jeffrey-shaw.net/html_main/frameset-works.php (accessed August 21, 2017).
Shaw, Jeffrey. *The Legible City*, featured at www.jeffrey-shaw.net/html_main/show_work.php?record_id=83 (accessed August 21, 2017).
Shaw, Jeffrey. More recent version of *The Legible City*, featured at www.jeffrey-shaw.net/html_main/show_work.php?record_id=102 (accessed August 14, 2017).
Small, David, and White, Tom. *Stream of Consciousness/Interactive Poetic Garden*, featured at http://acg.media.mit.edu/projects/stream/InteractivePoeticGarden.pdf (accessed August 17, 2017); can be seen in action at www.youtube.com/watch?v=5onPBBpGed8 (accessed January 22, 2018).
Snibbe, Scott. Artist's website, www.snibbe.com/projects/interactive/boundaryfunctions (accessed August 29, 2017).
Snibbe, Scott, *motionphone*, www.snibbe.com/apps#/motionphone-app (accessed August 20, 2017).
Tresset, Patrick. Artist's website, http://patricktresset.com/new (accessed September 17, 2017).
Vesna, Victoria. *BodiesINCorporated*, 1995, www.bodiesinc.ucla.edu/welcome.html (accessed August 31, 2017).
Wattenberg, Martin, Walczak, Marek. *The Apartment*, www.bewitched.com (accessed August 17, 2017).
Werner, Heike. Gallery for Computer Art and New Photography, www.heikewerner.com/nees_en.html (accessed December 29, 2016).
Whitney, John. *Catalog* tape at www.youtube.com/watch?v=TbV7loKp69s (accessed September 4, 2017).
Zajec, Edward. Artist's website, www.edwardzajec.com/tvc4/pil/index.html (accessed April 23, 2017).

Index